ADOLPHE APPIA

Frontispiece   Portrait by René Martin of Adolphe Appia in front of his setting for *Parsifal*, 1922.

ADOLPHE APPIA

Texts on Theatre

Richard C. Beacham

London and New York

First published 1993
by Routledge
11 New Fetter Lane, London EC4P 4EE

Simultaneously published in the USA and Canada
by Routledge Inc.
29 West 35th Street, New York, NY 10001

Reprinted 2002

© 1993 Richard C. Beacham

Routledge is an imprint of the Taylor & Francis Group

Phototypeset in 10 on 12 pt Baskerville by
Intype, London
Printed in Great Britain by
Biddles Short Run Books, King's Lynn

British Library Cataloguing in Publication Data
Beacham, Richard C.
Adolphe Appia: Texts on Theatre
I. Title
792
Library of Congress Cataloging in Publication Data
Also available

ISBN 0–415–06823–1

For that former and future Hellerau

Contents

CONTENTS

Part IV Aesthetic and prophetic writings

List of Figures

Preface

The work of Adolphe Appia is gradually attracting the attention and recognition it deserves. This is particularly welcome in the case of the English-speaking world, where despite acknowledgement of Appia's extraordinary importance by some theatre critics and practitioners earlier in the century, the wider reception and appreciation of his contribution has been hindered by the absence of translations of Appia's primary texts. Many of his ideas were taken up and assimilated – indeed they provided a basis for a great many innovations, attitudes and practices that we now take for granted – but the man himself, including the actual works through which he first advanced those' ideas, remained in the background.

With the publication in translation of Appia's two major books, *The Work of Living Art* (1960), and *Music and the Art of the Theatre* (1962) the situation improved, and did so further when Walther Volbach (who had been instrumental in securing publication of these works) brought out his own pioneering biography in 1968, *Adolphe Appia, Prophet of the Modern Theatre: A Profile*. Volbach intended to publish his translation of a large collection of Appia's essays at the same time, but this was most regrettably thwarted for many years, by factors quite beyond his control. Meanwhile, in 1982, Peter Loeffler published his excellent edition of Appia's short study, *Staging Wagnerian Drama*. In 1987 Cambridge University Press published my critical account, *Adolphe Appia, Theatre Artist*. In 1989 Volbach and I at last succeeded in bringing out his long-delayed English edition of Appia's work. This book, *Adolphe Appia, Essays, Scenarios, and Designs*, includes much which had never before been published in any language. Since 1983, Marie L. Bablet-Hahn has been editing and publishing the monumental, fully annotated French-language edition of *Adolphe Appia, Oeuvres Complètes*, four volumes of which have now appeared, covering Appia's written work to 1928, the year of his death.

The purpose of the present book is to make generally accessible to English readers a wide selection and survey of Appia's work gathered together into a single volume. It covers the entire span of his creative life, and includes both abridgements of many of the most important essays and extensive excerpts from his full-length books.

Appia is notorious for the difficulties he presents translators. His style is highly idiosyncratic, and fluctuates between ecstatic passages of almost mystical evocation – and imprecision – and sections of virtually opaque abstraction. Compounding this is the fact that frequently he is attempting to chart what is an aesthetic *terra incognita* where few have ventured before. We observe him in the very process of formulating the aesthetic basis for a total revolution in theatre practice; one which changed it for ever and is still extraordinarily influential and relevant today. His analysis, and in particular the process by which he fashions and refines ordinary words or phrases into critical concepts or terminology, is rarely clear or straight-forward, and this is further troubled by what he described as a tendency to think in German syntactic structures, while writing in French.

A translator is tempted either towards being too literal and thus leaving his reader mired in ambiguities, or conversely, over-translating; homogenizing Appia's prose into an English version that both obscures his critical process and risks destroying his individual tone and the resonance of his ideas. I have tended to lean (and sometimes perhaps to err) towards a more literal rendering of Appia's writing. I have resisted oversimplifying his prose, by putting it into blandly smooth English which sacrifices the personal voice – including often the note of struggle – so characteristic of the original. In the interests of including as wide a selection as possible of Appia's work, I have abridged, sometimes substantially, most of the essays. I can only urge English readers offended or perplexed by the result to have a look, if possible, at the French edition of the texts to puzzle out Appia's meaning, while savouring the sense of his personality.

I would like to extend my thanks for support and assistance in preparing this book to a number of individuals and institutions. I am grateful to the staff of the Beinecke Rare Book and Manuscript Library at Yale for their cooperation. I also received assistance from the Swiss Theatre Collection, Berne, and wish to thank its director, Dr Martin Dreier, for his continuing support, and in particular for his aid in securing a number of the photographs reproduced here. Portions of the critical commentary have appeared in my study of Appia published by Cambridge University Press, or in the edition of Professor Volbach's translations which I prepared for UMI Research Press, and are used by permission. I would like to thank the British Society of Authors for the invaluable services they provide in advising and supporting authors, particularly in regard to securing fair and reasonable publishing contracts. Finally, I would like to thank Mr Neil Monro-Davies for his assistance both in translating and in preparing the manuscript.

Introduction
Adolphe Appia, 1862–1928

Adolphe Appia has for many years been duly recognized as the most important turn-of-the-century innovator in the use of theatrical lighting, but his ideas and practical investigations went far beyond that to encompass fundamental changes in the use of stage setting, theatrical space, the concept of the role of the director, and ultimately the very definition of theatrical art. Much of his thought, which was extremely advanced for his time, has subsequently been generally accepted and put into practice, while his writings are at last being brought to the attention of a wider audience. Despite this, Appia's contribution has still to receive the general acknowledgement and critical exploration it deserves.

By laying out in a most comprehensive and detailed fashion both the theoretical and practical elements required for the pursuit of a root and branch reform of theatrical art, Appia cleared the path and provided guidance for a host of others to follow. Indeed, as early as the 1930s Lee Simonson was able to claim that 'most of what we call innovation or experiment is a variation of Appia's ideas, deduced from his original premises', while suggesting that theatrical history prior to Appia should simply be termed 'B. A.', so pervasive and lasting were his reforms (Simonson 1932: 352, 359).

These reforms took place throughout a creative life that may usefully be divided into three periods, during each of which Appia fundamentally advanced the art of the theatre. The first of these was from about 1885 to shortly after the turn of the century, during which he closely analysed Wagner's operas, and used them to develop a comprehensive theory of scenic reform. In the second period, from about 1905 to the end of the First World War, Appia devoted his efforts to investigating the implications which an understanding of the human body as it moved in space had for new forms of theatrical art. The final period, lasting from about 1919 until Appia's death in 1928, saw the artist move beyond conventional concepts of theatre altogether to describe entirely new manifestations of aesthetic activity in a series of extraordinarily imaginative and prophetic writings evolving from his concept of 'Living Art'.

1

THE FIRST 'WAGNERIAN' PERIOD

In his youth, Appia was captivated by the works of Richard Wagner, and intrigued by the challenge they held for conventional stagecraft. With few exceptions the stagings that he saw both from Wagner's own hand and by others were disappointing and dispiriting for him. Despite his negative impressions of the productions he saw, the new ideas he gradually developed in reaction to them began to come together into a theory of general reform. Although initially hesitant, his deeply sensitive and imaginative mind began to respond to the affront of the inartistic and crude stagings he witnessed, and began to formulate first the practical and then the theoretical outlines for a more beautiful and expressive style of staging. His own accounts from the period demonstrate how his approach focused directly on the works themselves and their inner integrity and meaning, and not on any received notions about how they ought to be presented in theatrical terms.

Such an approach was itself revolutionary, since Appia abandoned the traditional provision of external historical or fictive locales to illustrate the stories, and sought instead to derive the setting directly from *within* the work itself as it was generated and conveyed by the music. It was only later, when he compared and evaluated the results of such a direct visualization of the work, that he drew back and attempted to outline an overall theory and set of precepts.

In his search for basic principles and a refined art of production, Appia dismissed Wagner's own directions as irrelevant, since only the work itself could provide reliable guidance regarding its own staging. According to Appia,

> for the director the musical score is the only interpreter: whatever Wagner has added to it is irrelevant . . . [the manuscript] contains by definition its theatrical form, i.e. its projection into space, and so any further remarks he adds are superfluous, and even violate the aesthetic truth of an artistic work. Wagner's scenic descriptions in his libretto do not have any organic relationship to his music-poetic text.[1]

Appia thus began by attempting to visualize, purely and simply, the settings suggested to him by the music and requisite stage actions. In doing this he always held firmly in mind the crucial manner in which the performer acted as intermediary between the written composition and its ultimate realization on stage. He sought to determine what the text and score required of the performer in terms of physical movement and location within the scenic arrangement. In conceiving the appropriate setting, Appia took account of another major factor. A Wagnerian opera, in addition to its story, has an emotional and intellectual plot, which gives further meaning to it. This interior drama, which Wagner used to contribute massively to the impact of his works, must also somehow be expressed through the staging. Failing this, the production, while depicting the external circumstances of the action and its environment, would fall far short of conveying the real substance of the work. In Appia's opinion this was precisely the critical limitation of Wagner himself as a producer, and the reason why his stagings failed to fulfil the potential of his operatic compositions.

The reforms that Appia derived from his analysis were based on two major premises. The first of these was that from the Renaissance onwards theatre had developed and maintained a set of conventions that were inherently contradictory, and consequently divided the theatre against itself. By adopting and manipulating the newly discovered rules governing perspective painting, which during the Renaissance came to dominate the visual depiction of dramatic art, the theatre deployed carefully chosen and composed images to an audience which, in order to perceive those pictures to best advantage, had itself been organized along systematic and hierarchical lines. Not only did it lose thereby much of its communal and democratic potential; it was placed in the service not of genuine artistic creation and the active expression and experience of profound emotions, but was confined to imitating surface reality and, in a phrase, to putting on a show.

Theatre had for centuries been subject to the conventions and requirements of scenic illusion – of perspective *painting* – while the drama itself was composed of *actions* occurring in time and space according to a quite different and incompatible set of conventions.

The second major premise informing Appia's work in this period was the perception that theatre could never be an integral and genuine art form unless the conception, fashioning and ultimate realization of the work of art – the production itself – could be guided and controlled by the intentions of the original autonomous artist. Otherwise, the final expression of the work in its staging had no direct connection with its creator.

According to Appia's analysis, the contemporary theatre had two fundamental flaws. The first was the essential incongruity between the appropriate conventions for the enactment of a drama and those required for displaying painted perspective scenery. The second was the gulf that separated the creative artist, the playwright, from the eventual presentation of his work in a theatre. Appia undertook to correct both faults by carefully organizing theatrical production according to a specific hierarchy.

At the top of this hierarchy he placed the composer-dramatist who had conceived and written the music and dramatic libretto. His musical notation dictates the duration and rhythms of the production, while, at the same time, the libretto determines the actions required of the performers. Such actions as the music requires have to take place within a particular space, and this, the setting for the performance, provided the actor with the areas and objects required for his movement and actions. Thus, Appia observed, through the primary medium of the music, the original composer could express his artistic control over all the separate production elements to achieve a mutually subordinated synthesis of them – a work of theatrical art – which, as ultimately realized at the moment of performance, would possess and exhibit an artistic integrity.

It was vitally important that the entire production process be coordinated by a single, highly sensitive artist, whom Appia conceived as a 'designer-director', responsible for carrying out the complex task of applying the hierarchical principle to the particular work that was being produced. The concept of the director was a relatively new one in the theatre, and Appia went further than anyone before him in providing a detailed and concrete description of the principles governing his work.

The most important of these was the recognition that the *mise en scène* was already contained within the score. It was the original music-drama itself that encompassed not only the temporal element, but, by extension, the movement and consequently the physical setting as well, which the director should think of as music projected and taking form in space.

A second principle was that the actor must serve as the intermediary between the music and its spatial expression: the setting. The performer was placed by Appia at the very heart of his revolutionary production theory; the setting was no longer to be thought of as an illustration or background to the drama but as a direct extension of the actor himself, as he in turn was given meaning and motivated by the musical score.

Appia demanded utter simplicity in his settings, in marked contrast to the sumptuous spectacle that characterized contemporary operatic production. The stage should be set 'only so far as is necessary for the comprehension of the poetic text; a mere indication is enough to enlighten us to the nature of the visible environment'.[2] He demanded the abolition of painted scenery, and criticized the ridiculous incongruity between the moving, three-dimensional actor and the static two-dimensional *trompe-l'œil* flats. Absurdly, the scenic illusion was shattered the moment the actual performer intruded on to the stage.

The customarily flat surface of the stage floor should be changed to provide a variety of levels, steps and slopes: there must be variations in height and depth calculated to emphasize the solidity and mass of the actor and the space that supported him. Instead of flats, solid 'practicables' should be used, whose reality was established by their displacement of space. But such solid settings should not be in the service of realistically depicting the *external* appearance of fictional locations; rather they should suggest, as simply as possible, the artistically appropriate locale generated from *within* the drama as conveyed by the actor.

Appia's concept of stage setting as an expressive aesthetic element and his call for solid scenery which would convey the meaning of the drama were revolutionary; his further achievement in describing light as the soul of stage production, and in accurately predicting in detail its future evolution and use, was even more astonishing. He delineated the course that light must follow to become a fully expressive medium in its own right. Light must, like the actor, break free from its subjugation to the demands of painted scenery, which denied and mocked its very existence. Instead it should be placed in the service both of a three-dimensional setting, and of the underlying music itself. In order to do this, Appia identified and used two types of light.

The first was the general illumination and brightness of *diffused* light, which could supply a sort of luminous undercoat upon which later, more suggestive effects could be realized. The second, *formative* (or active) lighting, was composed of more concentrated and mobile radiance, which in the hands of the scenic artist became a highly subtle tool. With it he could emphasize objects or cause them to disappear; like a sculptor, he could build up or diminish; distort, compose, give mass to or dematerialize the physical objects on stage, including the performer himself. This light that selected, identified and moulded what it fell upon provided the means for enhancing both the external setting of the drama and its inner emotion and meaning.

Appia anticipated a number of technical developments which at the time were not in place, yet his description of what was necessary and how it ought to be used was direct and precise. His call for movable spotlights in place of the fixed overhead strip lighting which provided the primary source of illumination in the theatre of his day was particularly important, since the fluid and dynamic formative light at the heart of his reforms depended upon them. By controlling and modulating the intensity, colour, movement and size of the beams projected by these lamps, the scenic artist could obtain a vast range of extraordinarily expressive effects.

Appia's eloquent presentation of his advanced ideas for the use of light completed and crowned his theoretical writings of the 1890s. While formulating them he had also created by way of illustration a set of highly detailed scenarios for a number of Wagner's operas, along with many astonishing designs depicting his descriptions of appropriate stage settings. As these ideas became known, developed and put into effect by theatre practitioners everywhere, they were ultimately to sweep away both the theoretical and technical foundations of post-Renaissance theatre.

THE SECOND PERIOD: EURHYTHMICS

However exemplary Appia's ideas and designs now seem to us, or how superior to prevailing practice in Wagnerian production at Bayreuth, they were firmly rejected and ridiculed by Wagner's widow, Cosima, to whom suggestions of fundamental reform were most unwelcome. Consequently,

although elements of Appia's new approach were gradually adopted elsewhere, they were blocked in the very venue for which they were primarily
intended, and this was a source of deep frustration to Appia. He lacked
both influential supporters and a strongly assertive personality, as well as
the ability to organize and direct the talent and energy of other artists.
He was an inspired but reclusive genius with little talent and less taste
for intense collaboration with others. That, in the end, his far-reaching
renewal of theatrical art was realized through the efforts of others – a host
of pragmatic men of the theatre – attests to both the essential efficacy of
his concepts and to his own unfortunate limitations as a man of action
and practical affairs.

In May 1906 Appia encountered Emile Jaques-Dalcroze and the system
of rhythmic exercises which he devised and taught, eurhythmics. Dalcroze,
who taught harmony at the Geneva Conservatory of Music, had begun by
composing 'gesture songs' which used physical movement to accompany
short pieces of music. Later he developed an entire set of 'musical gymnas-
tic' exercises designed to enhance his pupils' perception of musical nuance,
as well as their awareness of the responsive movement of the body in
space. In effect he taught them to translate musical composition directly
into space through the reactive medium of their own bodies, and his
exercises trained students until this happened virtually automatically.

Appia recognized the relevance of eurhythmics to his own developing
concepts of stage space and the role of the human body, and gradually, over
the next several years during which Dalcroze and he closely collaborated –
experimenting and enlarging their vision of eurhythmics – he began to
realize the full potential of the system for advancing fundamental theatrical
reform. In the spring of 1909 he created about twenty designs which he
termed 'Rhythmic Spaces' and submitted them to Dalcroze, who viewed
them with great excitement. Appia perceived that the way to bring these
settings to life was by contrasting them with the human body. Their
rigidity, sharp lines and angles, and immobility, when confronted by the
softness, subtlety and movement of the body, would take on a kind of
borrowed life.

In that same year, Appia and Dalcroze were offered a decisive opportunity to make practical progress towards their shared goal of basic reform.
On the outskirts of Dresden a small settlement modelled on the English
concept of the 'garden city' had been founded. The project was pursued
as a noble social experiment, with its supporters hoping that within a
harmonious natural surrounding a new utopian community could be established and nurtured; one based on principles of social equality, liberal and
universal education and the revival of unalienated art and labour. The
settlement was called Hellerau.

Dalcroze was invited to establish an institute at Hellerau to provide the
primary site for the practice, further investigation and propagation of

eurhythmics. The directors of the new town thought that such an enterprise would prove of great practical and spiritual benefit to Hellerau's inhabitants, and they offered to set up and construct an institute exactly according to Dalcroze's specifications. He, in turn, suggested that Appia should be directly involved in every aspect, from the beginning.

As plans and construction got under way, Dalcroze constantly sought advice from Appia (who remained for most of the time in Switzerland), particularly in regard to the design of the new building, and the provision within it of 'practicables' – rostra, platforms, stairs, podia and the like – which comprised his designs for rhythmic spaces. In addition, Appia advised about the crucial role of lighting and the influence it should have upon the expressive quality of the musically coordinated exercises that would take place in the new facility. For some time he had envisaged a building which would help to abolish what, increasingly, he considered to be the unacceptable distinction between spectator and performer. For this to take place, he needed an entirely new theatrical architecture, and at Hellerau it was achieved for the first time.

As the central and largest room in the Institute, he designed a great open hall, fifty metres in length, sixteen metres wide, and twelve metres high, which would enclose both performers and audience with no barrier or obstacle between them. The orchestra and its light were also hidden from view. Thus he abolished the proscenium arch and raised stage, using a completely open performance area for the first time since the Renaissance. The hall, which had seating for 560 spectators and space for about 250 performers, was constructed exactly according to his plans.

It was fitted with a totally unprecedented lighting system. In his earlier writings Appia had laid down the theoretical basis for modern stage lighting, yet he had not been able to realize his ideas in practical work, or to extend them through experimentation. Now he collaborated with another participant in the Hellerau undertaking, Alexander von Salzmann, in devising a system for creating diffused light, as well as for special spotlight effects. The entire hall at Hellerau – the area for performance as well as for viewing – was lit by means of thousands of lights, installed behind translucent linen that had been dipped in cedar oil and covered all the walls and ceilings of the building. This method created the diffused light that Appia had demanded years earlier. The space literally glowed.

To obtain the formative or plastic light called for, Appia suggested a system of movable spotlights placed in the ceiling of the hall behind sliding panels. Light could, in effect, represent the music visually in space, complementing the physical embodiment of the music expressed through the eurhythmic gestures and movements of the performing students.

To display the results of the Institute's work, two festivals were held, in the summers of 1912 and 1913. At the first of these a varied programme was offered including a number of school exercises and improvisations, some pantomime dances and rhythmic representations of selections of classical music. The highpoint was a presentation of part of Act II of Gluck's opera, *Orpheus and Eurydice* – the descent of Orpheus into the Underworld. It caused a sensation. Orpheus entered at the highest point of the scenic structure, in a glare of light, and slowly descended a great monumental staircase into ever-greater darkness, confronted and opposed by the Furies. Dressed in dark tights, they were in constant motion, carefully coordinated with the ebb and flow of the music. Arranged along the steps and platforms, their naked arms and legs seemed like snakes, and formed a veritable moving mountain of monstrous forms, before being overcome and subdued by the sound of Orpheus' playing and the poignancy of his pleas. The whole scene was bathed in an otherworldly blue light: the glow of Hades.

The reaction to the music, staging and, above all, to the setting and lighting was overwhelmingly favourable. A number of perceptive critics recognized that the work at Hellerau presented a real and direct alternative to contemporary staging techniques and believed that, almost inadvertently, eurhythmics was opening up quite extraordinary new vistas for the theatre. Greatly encouraged by the success and recognition achieved by the first festival, Appia and Dalcroze decided for the following year to present a full production of the entire Gluck opera. This too was an enormous success. The festival was attended by several thousand people, drawn from throughout Europe and America, and included a great many illustrious theatre artists and critics. Most were highly impressed by what they saw and, as a result, Appia's ideas became much more widely known and appreciated. His use of abstract settings was greatly admired, and soon widely emulated in contemporary stage design. Spectators were struck too by the careful coordination between movement, music and light, which created a unified artistic expression of the opera's meaning. As one observer noted,

> Through all three acts one never had the feeling that one was at a presentation: we had before us real life, translated into music, magnificent music, which became living. It could not be otherwise, since all the performers were possessed by music; it possessed them both physically and emotionally; the music was for them a principle of life like the act of breathing . . . The radiating inner beauty was indescribable. Most impressive of all was the naturalness – one forgot that it was an opera – the most conventional and unbelievable of all arts.
>
> (Wolkonski 1960: 24)

The success of the collaboration at Hellerau between Appia and Dalcroze was prodigious. Appia had been able to realize a portion of his audacious dream of recreating the theatre, putting into practice earlier ideas, and testing new ones. There were plans for a third festival in the summer of 1914, but the threat of war and its eventual outbreak destroyed them. Although the two men were afterwards involved in several joint ventures, Hellerau, to which neither of them ever returned, marked the climax, triumph, and effective end of their work together.

THE THIRD PERIOD: 'LIVING ART'

Appia's earliest writings and his subsequent work with Dalcroze had far-reaching implications for theatrical development during the first decades of this century. The product of his last years – his book *L'Oeuvre d'art vivant (The Work of Living Art)*, and a remarkable series of prophetic and philosophical essays – contained ideas which, although they had little immediate influence, did nevertheless display Appia's extraordinary and continuing ability to infer and predict future developments from contemporary conditions. As in the 1890s so again in the 1920s, Appia looked well beyond his time to evoke and describe new directions in the performing arts.

In a letter to Gordon Craig of November 1918, at the end of the First World War, he outlined the evolution of his thought and plans:

> I've decided to do a series of essays linked one to the other by the same theme. The complete work will probably be called *The Work of Living Art*; that's to say, the *moving art* (human body, light, etc.) as opposed to immobile art (all the rest!) . . . If this is successful I will then publish several of my numerous articles and prefaces similarly gathered into a volume. For this I will do some new drawings, always with a vision of *The Hall*, a kind of cathedral of the future, which reunites in a vast, free and *changeable* space, all the expressions of our social life, and in particular, dramatic art, *with or without spectators* . . . From there we shall arrive, I have a strong and profound conviction, at majestic festivals where an entire people will give their cooperation, and where no one will be allowed to remain passive, and we will express all our joy, our passions, and our pains.
>
> (Beacham 1988: 278)

The book that Appia was working upon was indeed *The Work of Living Art*, which he completed in May 1919 and published late in 1921. The 'numerous articles' are included amongst those that have been excerpted and published in this present volume.

Appia realized that his work, which had begun in an analysis and critique of the state of theatrical art, must end in a fundamental attack on contemporary culture itself, and, crucially, on the role that art was forced to play within it.

People observed art passively: if it moved them at all, it did so *artificially*, having lost most of its pristine power to disturb, excite or invigorate an audience who now might contemplate and collect it but could no longer actively enter into it. It was necessary to return to the wellspring of all art, 'the living experience of our own body',[3] and from there to express and understand both the reality of oneself and, simultaneously, one's communal relationship with the rest of society. Instead of being an isolated 'eternal spectator',[4] one could become whole again, reintegrated 'into living contact with our fellow men'.[5]

In confronting this crisis of art in society, and suggesting a solution, Appia once again places the actor at the very centre of his concept of theatre. But the actor in Appia's more advanced theory is not, as earlier, in the service of the work: he becomes the work itself.

The earlier theory had emphasized the actor's function as the vital link through which the musical score and the dramatic text were realized in space, and through whose movement the scenic elements were in effect 'generated'. Now, even more radically, Appia conceives art forms in which the moving body simultaneously creates the work and, doing so, *is* the work. It was necessary to experiment in creating less 'literary' art forms in the recognition that theatrical art need not have a plot or story to sustain it any more than a symphony requires a title or notional programme to make it expressive and sensible. An art form based on the body moving to music in space was ultimately capable, Appia believed, of extraordinary expressiveness – communicating directly to all present – since all alike have bodies.

In the essays excerpted in this volume he writes enthusiastically and at length about the social implications of this new collaborative art, the benefits it may bring, and the need to begin exploration of the various forms it might take. Thus, at the close of his life Appia still retained that astonishing ability, so evident in his youth, to peer into the future of 'theatrical' art to trace (and sometimes to determine), however limited in practical detail, a proximate outline of things to come.

It was not until 1923 that, at the age of sixty-one, Appia was at last given an opportunity to stage one of Wagner's operas according to the detailed plans he had first drawn up in the 1890s. He was invited by Arturo Toscanini to stage *Tristan and Isolde* at La Scala opera-house, Milan. Back in 1899 Appia had included a masterful scenario for this work as an appendix to his book, *Music and the Art of the Theatre*. That scenario and the designs accompanying it now served, with only slight modifications, as the conceptual and scenic basis for the Milan production.

The radical nature of Appia's vision is indicated by the fact that at this time, a quarter of a century later, his ideas still seemed too advanced for La Scala and its audience readily to assimilate them. The place was a bastion of conservative tradition within an Italian theatrical establishment almost wholly innocent of the reformist ideas now clearly evident (if not yet predominant) in much of the rest of Europe. Consequently Appia had difficulty in getting the personnel there to understand the theoretical basis for the intended production. Moreover, Appia, a perfectionist by nature, found the pragmatic and sometimes haphazard compromise of actual production difficult to endure.

Despite all the problems, and his personal distress, in the end Appia was satisfied that the scenic presentation conformed to his designs and intentions when the production opened in December 1923. It was lavishly praised for the magnificence of its musical interpretation and for Toscanini's superb conducting. But there was little understanding and less sympathy for Appia's settings amongst the opera-going public, although they received a more mixed response from the critics, ranging from one who termed them 'ridiculous, shameful, pretentious, and oppressing to the eye', to another who praised them for their 'poetic use of light, psychological intimacy and sense of mystery'.[6]

Spectators were perplexed by the relative drabness of colour, the absence of elaborately painted scenery, and the austere simplicity of the décor, without understanding that it was the opera's essential transcendent quality, impossible to convey through purely realistic and objective settings, that Appia sought to express through more subtle means.

Despite the situation at La Scala, by the early 1920s Appia's demands for such elements as three-dimensional scenery, the expressive use of light and the evocation of psychology and atmosphere in scenic presentation had been widely introduced, though frequently his influence was unacknowledged. The experience of the First World War brought about fundamental and permanent shifts in artistic sensibility and practice, and such change was particularly evident in the theatre. The old aesthetic of scenic illusion, already widely repudiated, was further discredited as part of a larger and general reaction – even a revulsion – against traditional cultural norms. Obviously, Appia's post-war manifestos concerning 'living art' were directly relevant to this new spirit, but so too was his earlier work; in particular his designs for rhythmic spaces, which were found now to provide a ready practical and, in part, theoretical basis for experiment.

One of Appia's followers, a young director named Oskar Wälterlin, who was stage director of the Municipal Theatre of Basle, noted in this period that although 'in the realm of the theatre, Appia was a prophet' (Wälterlin 1945: 18) he was far 'better known to the connoisseurs and enthusiasts of theatrical reform, than in the theatre itself, or to the theatre-going public' (Wälterlin 1945: 16). Determined to correct this situation, Wälterlin persuaded the management of his theatre to present an entirely new production of Wagner's *Ring*, to be executed according to Appia's conception and to commence in the 1924–5 season. It offered Appia, now in failing health and with only a few years to live, the chance to realize at last a goal which had eluded him throughout his career: to produce Wagner's great cycle according to the principles first painstakingly formulated at the turn of the century and meticulously refined and developed in the course of his life's work.

Appia at once prepared for the production a new set of designs and scenarios for *Rhinegold* and *The Valkyrie*. Although the underlying goal of providing a staging directly expressive of Wagner's work remained the same, and Appia's basic principles were still valid, the means for achieving them needed revising. Under the influence of his experiments with Dalcroze, Appia had long since freed his later settings from the last vestiges of romanticism still evident in those created in the 1890s. He now produced new 'rhythmic designs' for the *Ring*, which incorporated the spatial concepts derived from eurhythmics.

What Appia hoped to achieve through this new approach was to establish unequivocally the actual dimensions of the performance space and the solid elements within it. Traditionally scene design tended to abolish real space, together with its solid components, by substituting for it through perspective technique an extended *imaginary* space which was incompatible with that occupied by the audience on the other side of the proscenium arch. It was this approach that Appia had overturned at Hellerau, and he wished to do the same, as far as possible, using the conventional theatre architecture of the Basle theatre. As a result of his experience and aesthetic analysis of eurhythmics, and his desire for 'living art', Appia was determined to create the closest possible proximity and affinity between performers and spectators and between the realms of the stage and auditorium.

The scenarios that Appia prepared were conditioned by his concept of 'living art' and stress constantly that the characters and the plot of the *Ring* must be viewed not as belonging to and contained by a mythical past but as the agents of a theatrical event, here and now, which the audience must experience directly in all its visual, physical, emotional and intellectual power. Because much of the staging of these operas was widely considered established and orthodox, they provided particularly interesting (if volatile) material through which to test such a concept and to observe its effect upon an audience.

Rhinegold opened in November 1924. The performance went extremely well, and was favourably received both by the audience and by the critics. Most of the attention was focused on Appia's settings and the stage direction. His attempts to rid Wagner's work of its nineteenth-century ballast and of any suggestion that it should be revered as a romantic expression of German mythology was certain to encounter opposition, but little, at first, of such hostility was evident in the audience or the press.

Behind the scenes however, intrigue developed as members of a grossly intolerant and reactionary faction marshalled their forces to combat what they chose to see not merely as a controversial staging, but somehow as perverse and decadent, an affront to the Basle public, and a conspiracy

Figure 1 Appia's design of 1924 for the first scene of *Rhinegold*, as presented at Basle.

against its morality and reputation. When *The Valkyrie* opened in February 1925 before a largely appreciative audience, a group of these dissidents erupted in a chorus of shouts, hisses and boos, which led to a near riot in the theatre. In the days following, the press comment was largely favourable, but there were some virulently abusive articles by a few reactionaries.

Appia was devastated by this vicious attack. In the face of threats to its public subsidy, the theatre management was forced under protest, and with resignations by some of its members, to abandon plans for producing the remainder of the *Ring*. Appia returned dejected to Geneva, intensely disappointed at seeing this last great effort to reform Wagnerian staging end so disastrously.[7]

Nevertheless, the final period of Appia's life was one of astonishing creative work. Within a few years he produced a great many richly suggestive essays as well as numerous designs and scenarios. As these eloquently confirm, he had moved far beyond the revolutionary reforms proposed in his earlier theory into even more prophetic and advanced beliefs about the nature of new, emerging art forms. These radical concepts pulled him decisively away from any kind of traditional theatre.

He pointed this out in a letter written in 1922 to Gordon Craig: 'My vision and all my thought are indeed much advanced. I don't see the theatre anymore, it doesn't inspire me – and if one wishes to comprehend how I have evolved, it can't be conveyed by my drawings. One must wait, therefore, until I've brought new elements.' Without defining the nature of the ideas he was now developing – 'the great joy which I am charged with placing before my fellow men' – he noted that being 'retained in the atmosphere of the theatre – the theatre such as it is – contradicts even my most profound convictions'. He then promised to produce a further volume of writings exploring his new theories in a practical context. 'Until then, I ought to work, work well, and . . . keep quiet, at least in public' (Beacham 1988: 283).

From this and other references, it seems likely that Appia saw his late essays (to be assimilated into a single volume) as the culmination of his creative work: the furthest point attained by his restless imagination. Portions of these essays are found in the latter sections of this book; reading and evaluating them may provide the best and most direct evidence of Appia's importance and foresight. They remain fascinating and at the same time poignant evidence of a genius who, however limited the scope for practical realization of his deeply felt and keenly intelligent ideas, never ceased to innovate, explore, prophesy and inspire. 'In order to kindle the flame of aesthetic truth we have had to extinguish along our path, the deceitful torches of a deceitful artistic culture. Now it is our own fire – that of us all – that will rekindle these torches.'[8]

Part I

The reformation of theatrical production

Introduction

The challenge of staging the works of Richard Wagner provided Appia with his first and most fundamental task, one leading ultimately to the provision of a completely new approach to theatrical art. Preoccupied to the point of obsession with the problem of adequately realizing Wagner's works in the theatre, Appia spent the last decade of the nineteenth century focusing all his creative resources and mental energy on its solution. This achievement was prodigious and, eventually, its effect upon contemporary staging – indeed upon the very concept of the theatre – was revolutionary. Within a period of fewer than ten years, Appia articulated theories and expressed them in designs that swept away the foundations that had supported European theatre practice since the Renaissance. In their place he laid down what became the conceptual and practical basis for theatrical art for many years to come. As Lee Simonson wrote, Appia's theories

> elucidated the basic aesthetic principles of modern stage design, analysed its fundamental technical problems, outlined their solution, and formed a charter of freedom under which scene designers still practice . . . The light in Appia's first drawings, if one compares them to the designs that had preceded his, seem the night and morning of a First Day.
>
> (Simonson 1932: 352, 359)

Appia's passionate critique of traditional stagecraft was soon taken up by others, some of whom conceived similar although less comprehensive ideas independently of him. Before long, the 'new art of the theatre' was being promulgated everywhere, often by people with little direct knowledge of Appia or of his decisive contribution to the movement which they so ardently promoted. But it was Appia alone who in the 1890s, with extraordinary clarity of vision, first provided a complete assessment of the disastrous state of theatrical art, and who, with quite astonishing foresight, first suggested the solutions which in time, and frequently at the hands of others, laid down a new foundation for the modern theatre.

Richard Wagner succeeded in his later operas in creating a new art form – a union of drama and music – which overturned the conventional concept of opera and, in time, that of theatre in general. Having joined within himself the roles of composer and dramatist, he achieved a remarkable creative breakthrough, fashioning a new type of musical drama in which a work's inner values as expressed through the music were conjoined with its outward meaning as articulated through dialogue and plot. The new medium thus achieved could become, as Wagner both practised and prophesied, a uniquely expressive art form.

He recognized, moreover, that if the autonomous artist, the composer-dramatist, were to present his work successfully before an audience, it would be essential for him to master and, ideally, control all the disparate elements of production. Since his operas were simultaneously music and drama, the latter not fixed for performance by a score, their integrity could be maintained only through rigorous attention to all the details of theatrical production.

Yet despite drastic and far-reaching reforms, in the end Wagner himself failed to carry through any genuine revolution in *staging*. To be sure, his purpose-built theatre, the Festspielhaus at Bayreuth, completed in 1876, was highly innovative. Its semicircular amphitheatre, modelled on ancient example, in theory allowed every spectator an equally good and unimpeded view of the performance. From it he banished the customary distinctions of social hierarchy, as well as all the elaborate décor and ornament – anything that could draw attention away from the stage itself. For the first time the auditorium was darkened during performance, and even the orchestra was hidden from view to allow the spectators to observe the world of the opera without distraction.

On stage, however, the situation was different. Wagner spared no expense or effort in equipping his theatre with the most advanced technology of the period, but it was all essentially in the service of the traditional aesthetic of scenic illusion. It is difficult to assess the extent to which Wagner himself was aware or troubled by the incompatibility between his works and their realization on stage. Whether consciously or not, by placing his performers within a relentlessly illusionistic scenic environment where little or nothing was left to the imagination, he ensured that, visually, the settings could never express the inner spiritual world suggested by the music. Although his librettos abound with precise stage directions and scenic descriptions, Wagner was generally less than satisfied with the results and seems to have desired more than he could visualize – something at any rate other than the romantic naturalism which his craftsmen invariably produced. At the end of his life he lamented that 'in this field of musical dramaturgy, alas, all is still so new and hidden in the dust of bad routine' (Roth 1980: 155).

Appia first saw Wagner's own last production, that of *Parsifal* in 1882; and later attended Cosima Wagner's faithful restagings of *Tristan and Isolde* and *The Mastersingers* in 1888. In Dresden he witnessed a production of the *Ring*. He was overwhelmed by the impact of these works as music, while goaded by the unshakeable conviction that their potential as pieces for the theatre, and as the basis for an entirely new form of theatrical art, had been left unexplored and unexploited, and, moreover, had been all but totally obscured under the gross burden of contemporary stage practice. Here, at last, in Wagner, Appia recognized an artist whose titanic genius might redeem theatre and raise it to the level of true art. Here were sublime works whose full power and beauty could only emerge, be revealed and realized, could only *exist* in the theatre itself – but only if a theatre could first be fashioned to contain them.

As Appia recorded later in the autobiographical essay 'Theatrical experiences and personal investigations', he began his work by first trying to understand and explain Wagner's fundamental failure himself to develop an appropriate means of staging his own works; a failure that had resulted in a style of production which, with all its inadequacies, became enshrined as orthodox after his death. With the help of his friend, Houston Stewart Chamberlain (who later married Wagner's daughter, Eva), Appia was able to spend time at Bayreuth, observing and analysing both the productions themselves and the technical intricacies of the Festspielhaus. He acquired a direct and concrete understanding that challenged him at the time to develop his own theory further and later ensured that the theory when it emerged was firmly grounded in sound technical expertise and practical knowledge.

The expressiveness of Wagner's operas resides in the music and the dramatic actions generated by the music and libretto on stage. To attempt at the same time to give that music a completely realistic materialization was not only impossible, but, inevitably, it buried and obscured from the audience the essential qualities of the work. It was this perception that gave rise to the first series of scenic reforms formulated by Appia in the 1890s, which were outlined in the introductory section of this book. His study of Wagner's operas formed the critical core of his work for many years to come, with subsequent investigations, practical experiments and theoretical essays all radiating outward from the mass of these explosive ideas.

Wagner's composition as a work of art was conditioned by an overall unity of conception, and in performance this conception – the meaning of the work – was bodied forth on stage. Any genuinely artistic staging must therefore also exhibit a unity of expression which would be the sum of its parts: each scene, each event on stage, each setting must be carefully balanced and coordinated with the others to contribute its appropriate measure to the overall quality of the production. To do this, Appia formulated his concept of a hierarchy of production through which all the expressive elements – scenic space and objects, light, movement and gestures of the performers, all conditioned by and subject to the demand of the musical score – would be integrated and harmonized.

His first extended essay, written in 1891–2 but never published lifetime, was 'Comments on the staging of the *Ring of the Nibelungs*'

Figure 2 Appia *c.* age twenty.

de mise en scène pour *L'Anneau de Nibelungen'*). In a concise and straight-forward format, Appia discusses, essentially through concrete description, the problems that Wagner's work presents and his own solutions to them, solutions that required comprehensive reform of contemporary stagecraft, although not as yet of its technical resources. His second essay, published as a small book in 1895, was *Staging Wagnerian Drama* (*La Mise en scène du drame wagnérien*). This was a more theoretical rendering of the earlier work, presented now in the context of a totally new analysis of the principles governing the relationship between music, stage actions and setting. Finally, in 1895 Appia began to write his major work, *Music and the Art of the Theatre* (*La Musique et la mise en scène*), which both summarized and revised his two earlier essays, moving beyond Wagner altogether to describe the implications of his theories *generally* for a radical and funda-mental reformation (amounting virtually to a rebirth) of theatrical art. It was published in German in 1899 as *Die Musik und die Inscenierung*.

The writings through which Appia first expressed his observations and ideas reflect the intensity of his passion, and sometimes also the struggle he had in trying to capture logically and coherently – to wrestle into language – perceptions and concepts which first came to him only visually and emotionally. One must bear in mind Appia's own description of the process: how he first contemplated and reacted to Wagner's works by striving imaginatively to give them their appropriate (and somehow inevit-able) theatrical realization, and only later attempted to extrapolate from the results of this process a conceptually unified aesthetic theory. It is not, therefore, surprising that his writing is sometimes convoluted or vague, and occasionally repetitious and overwrought. He is, after all, attempting to use language to map out an altogether unfamiliar mental landscape. But when in retrospect one reviews and responds to the overall pattern of his work, in a sense retracing to its core the process out of which Appia himself first formulated his theory, one is startled finally by the intensity, the genius and the beauty of the original vision. One is also struck palpably by the realization that to review and summarize the concepts generated from within that vision is to compile a concise compendium of the first principles of the modern theatre, for as Lee Simonson described *Music and the Art of the Theatre*, 'the first one hundred and twenty pages are nothing less than a textbook of modern stagecraft' (Simonson 1932: 354).

Theatrical Experiences and Personal Investigations

(1921) [Excerpts]

Volbach, pp. 47–72[1]; Bablet, 4, pp. 36–56

The way in which an author expresses his dramatic intentions must be perceived through the technical aspects of his text. What the performers must say or sing is less important than how they present it to the audience. If the author limits himself to the spoken word, the technical scope is also restricted. If, on the other hand, he deems a musical element to be necessary for his communication, there is virtually total freedom in delivering the words. Between the two extremes – a recitation in which music is subordinated to speech for the sake of purely spoken expression, as opposed to a performance of those passages in which music alone is the revealing element – every nuance is possible, and staging must be adapted to them.

The imagination of the author or the director, although stimulated by the verbal text, should not be the source of scenic conception; that must always and entirely derive from the nature of the poetic-musical text. Music determines modifications in time duration and, through that, in the space . . .

I directed all my efforts in order to liberate the actor. I was very much aware of this principle; only the manner of its application and the results were not yet clear to me, although they were starting to develop.[2]

I therefore approached the *mise en scène* of the *Ring* with the single desire of being true to my own vision . . . After many years of experience, or rather years of noting them in what was necessarily an unorganized fashion, I began to practise an altogether unknown art, for which neither my environment nor my memory could provide any guidance, and for which all the elements had not yet been discovered or analysed. Nevertheless, I was convinced that in following my own vision, I would discover the truth . . .

Deep in my heart and before making any designs, I knew that for me production means the performer. I therefore took the score of [Wagner's opera] *Rhinegold* and analysed the opening scene entirely from this point of view. I will attempt to give the reader some sense of my approach. First of all I try to isolate the episodes of the action to determine their precise

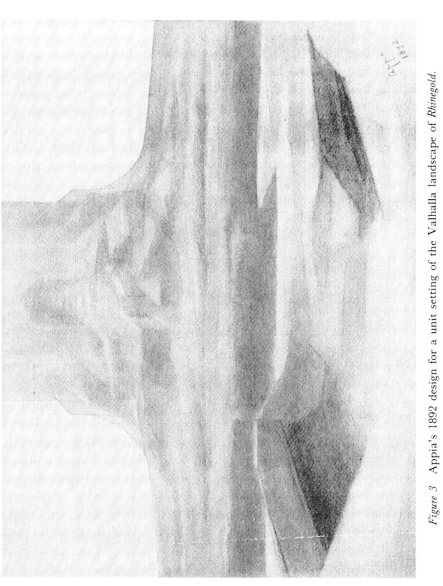

Figure 3 Appia's 1892 design for a unit setting of the Valhalla landscape of *Rhinegold*.

character, bearing in mind the elements that bind them together rather as a mason does with his mortar . . . Another invaluable judgement involves the theatrical significance of the episodes . . . A still more important one is . . . the role each episode plays in the inner drama, i.e. its significance for the universal meaning transcending visible action and casual appearance . . .

With the essential facts in mind, we can then begin to design the setting, while remembering that the second factor, theatrical significance, is determined by what we have provided for the performer . . . Everyone will agree that an interesting flower arrangement requires more flowers than in the end are actually used. It is the same with the *mise en scène*, and therefore I prepare various drawings depicting interchangeable and suggestive locales, rather like a word puzzle when not all the letters provided are necessary to compose a specific word . . . It involves an element of guesswork, surely, and this in turn demands some general sense of form. It requires too a faith in the unconscious which, oddly enough, has never misled me. One might go further and arrange all these tentative settings within a general framework suggested by the place of action without strict regard for the hierarchy [of production elements]. It then becomes an approximate unit setting that can be changed as desired until it finally suits each episode. It is at this point that the mortar – the binding elements – comes into play . . .

Imagine all the elements involved in this work: text, music, external dramatic design (plot), the hidden reality of the inner drama, peculiarities and social status of the characters, their actions and reactions, the manner of their delivery, the areas assigned to them, organic relationships, lighting with all its variations, shades, shadows, colour. All of these to be managed within the range of technical feasibility and all made to converge at a single moment, the time of performance! No single method could accomplish this; the field is too vast and complex to mould into a single frame . . .

The question may now be put whether unity is desirable at all for staging; whether the director cannot use various devices within the same work, even though the score ought to suggest only a single mode for achieving the style that captures the poetic image of the music? Perhaps we ought to put the question differently: i.e., 'What is the nature of unity of production?' In fact this is how the problem should be formulated in order to reveal the principle that determines everything else.

For the poet-musician, unity lies in the dramatic intention that inspired a specific work, and only that work . . . The source of one of Wagner's scores is forever inaccessible to us. Our knowledge of it begins with the technical application of such elements of expression as the score conveys. Because these elements are' subordinate, the unity they display does not originate with them. In the same manner, the unity of the production does not depend on its elements, since they are subordinate as well. But to what? That is the question!

Currently, stage production is on the agenda, and any occasion for undertaking a new experiment is thought good. But too often the drama itself is only a pretext. If the playwright is dead and cannot defend himself, so much the better; if he is still alive, he will collaborate with the director, since, notwithstanding appearances, the scenic designer is so independent that he can experiment with a play's setting without first giving thought to its needs . . . the setting is one thing, the drama another, and the two are brought together like ready-made shoes and a customer's feet . . . In fact, the playwright, and not the director, ought to be free. Like the commander of a victorious army, the director ought to present his arms and subordinate himself to his sovereign. Freedom should be first for the playwright, and then for the stage . . .

In the theatre as elsewhere, we have, alas, established a division of labour. Under proper conditions, the playwright might be his own leading actor, designer and stage director; if he is a composer, he ought to be a singer and a conductor . . . Of course, this asks too much of him! But in the absence of such versatility, he ought at least to perform as many of these functions as he can. A modern production tends more and more to offer him this opportunity – which is already a considerable improvement – as long as he remains in charge. For the unity of a production is dependent not upon the technician, but on the dramatist . . . A Wagnerian score is a medium between the inaccessible origin which we cannot attain and the projection of the original concept into space. Wagner himself did not understand this, and that is the reason for his failure . . . Wagner incorrectly believed that we require explicit instructions from the dramatist. But for the director, the musical score is the only interpreter: whatever Wagner has added to it is irrelevant. On this question, the hierarchy is relentless.

We can now begin to comprehend how important the score is for the scenic artist; he cannot manage without it. The score serves him as inspiration, regulator, guide and balance; it alone has the last word to which we must listen and obediently respond . . . If the director does this, unity is assured . . .

Recommencing our analysis where we left off, we now understand what power it is that enables us to make so many diverse elements come together at a single point, i.e. the production. This power is not within ourselves . . . Wagner was not himself aware of the hierarchic principle which should have shaped the realization of his works on stage without the directions that his imagination caused him to record in the final version of his libretto . . . Imagine a dramatist with an incredible talent for music-poetic expression, using it freely, and simultaneously setting down in great detail every minute detail of staging in his score! His work contains by definition

Figure 4 The 1896 Bayreuth setting for the Valhalla landscape of *Rhinegold*. Cf. Appia's design in Figure 3.

its theatrical form, i.e. its projection into space, and so any further remarks he adds are superfluous, and even violate the aesthetic truth of an artistic work. Wagner's scenic descriptions in his libretto do not have any organic relationship to his music-poetic text . . .

Wagner thought himself independent, but it can hardly be imagined that he was not influenced by his conception of the contemporary stage. Certainly he cracked its mould, but by no means destroyed it. The stage director has to take this into account . . .

On the one hand, the director is confronted by Wagner's traditional conception of staging practice; on the other, by a music-poetic text ostensibly liberated from that tradition and not influenced at all by contemporary staging. This contradiction reveals a fundamental conflict in the dramatist's thinking, and the director can only resolve it by seriously compromising the normal hierarchy of production. The consequence of this compromise is that the staging of a Wagnerian opera will never be derived solely from the score; other factors will have to be taken into account.

In preparing a complete scenario for the *Ring*, I identified the basic principles of Wagnerian production, which I summarized in my small book, *Staging Wagnerian Drama* (Paris, 1895) . . . A year later I started to prepare an entire volume on this subject. It was *Music and the Art of the Theatre* (Munich, 1899). I continued to rely upon the example of Wagner, for at that time his were the only works that could provide a point of departure. But in writing it I gradually grew aware of the extent to which my thinking had separated itself from Wagner's work, in order to deal with the subject in all its complexity and implications.

That book, therefore, can no longer be properly termed Wagnerian. As its title suggests, it provided a theoretical and technical analysis of the relationship that exists, and must be recognized, between music and the stage, i.e. between the sounds that reach our ears and the moving images that are presented to our eyes . . .

It is not necessary to discuss the book here, since gradually it has become widely known and influential on the art of staging. It may be regarded as having been the first impetus towards all contemporary reform, and it contained the elements required to continue that movement and consolidate it. Some designs are included in the book . . . These broke with tradition, extending beyond anything that could be expected by way of reform at the time, and they therefore at least commanded attention. If initially they were adopted only in certain of their details, they were eventually accepted as a whole.

But nobody had the key to understanding the designs! No one even understood that the key, the scenario, was crucial for the settings, which remained insoluble without this key. The result was misunderstanding. The letter of what I said was divorced from the spirit, and my assertion

27

that I based my entire theory of production entirely on the score met with disbelief. These settings, however, contained something that defied analysis, and gave the impression of a finality which, because the source of my inspiration for it was not understood, was attributed to me. I could not explain any better than I had in my book, and had to let this false impression stand. Bayreuth refused to take any notice of my scenario for the *Ring* . . . and also refused to consider *Music and the Art of the Theatre* . . .[3]

Music and the Art of the Theatre[4]

(1899) [Excerpts]

Die Musik und die Inscenierung, 1899
Music and the Art of the Theatre, 1962
La Musique et la mise en scène, 1963
Bablet, 1, pp. 43–207

THE *MISE EN SCÈNE* AND MUSIC[5]

Every work of art must contain a harmonious relationship between feeling and form, an ideal balance between the ideas which the artist desires to express, and the means he has for expressing them . . .

The more types of media required for the realization of any work of art, the more elusive is this harmony. Drama (all works written for actual theatrical production) is the most complex of all arts on account of the large number of media the artist has to use to communicate his ideas.

The poet, painter or sculptor observes the form of his work as it develops and always retains it under his control, since its content is the same as its form, and therefore the object of expression and the means used to communicate it are in a sense the same. But this is not the situation for the dramatist. Not only does he have no control over the final form of his art, that form appears to be relatively independent of his actual dramatic intention. This is because the creation of a drama occurs in two phases. In the first, the dramatist must translate his ideas into a dramatic form; then the written text that results has to be translated to accord with the requirements of staging before an audience. Unfortunately, this second part of the process, the realization of the staging or *mise en scène*, is not under the control of the dramatist.

The method through which a text takes shape in the theatre is of the greatest importance to those who are concerned with the difference between dramatic art and literature; i.e. those for whom a drama is inseparable from its staging.

What then, is this form which is indispensable to the dramatist, but over which he has no control?

What do we mean when we refer to the *mise en scène*?

Until now it has been thought to be the means for realizing any dramatic

29

conception on stage for the eyes of the spectators. But an author's dramatic conception is conveyed to us through a text which contains only that part of the drama intended for our comprehension. Of course, the action is indicated in its continuity and length, but only from a dramatic viewpoint, and with no attempt to indicate the formal process by which such elements are expressed on stage. As a result, staging is subject to a variety of whims and tastes. That is why the same play can be presented in the most diverse styles, depending on particular tastes or periods. It therefore follows that not only is drama (as staged) the most complex of all forms of art, it is also the only one in which one of the most fundamental elements must be deemed a *medium of expression* to be outside the dramatist's control; a situation which seriously curtails the integrity of drama as a form of art, and reduces it to an inferior status . . .

A work of art is not a presentation of some aspect of life to which everyone can contribute from their own experience and ability; it is rather the harmonious integration of various technical means with the sole object of communicating to many people the conception of a single artist[6] . . . A work of art is able to retain its integrity only if all its expressive elements are controlled by its creator . . .

If we mean by the expressive media of a form of art those elements which are directly controlled by the artist, then, by definition, the *mise en scène* as we understand it in the contemporary theatre is not a *means of expression* for the dramatic artist. He may see the production in his mind's eye as he writes, and may even intend that many of his ideas will be brought out through production alone. He may provide a detailed description of how his drama should be staged. He may even direct every production of it during his life; nevertheless his *mise en scène* will not be an artistic expressive medium, and he must know in his soul how arbitrary is his will, and how vain his hope of being obeyed once he is dead; in other words, despite everything, how independent his play remains from the staging which he has laid out in such detail . . .

In order, therefore, for the *mise en scène* to become an integral part of the drama, and in order to enable it to become a medium of artistic expression, *a principle, derived directly from the dramatic work's original conception, and not passing again through the will of the dramatist, must be found to determine the* mise en scène.

What can this principle be?

. . . Our inner life itself provides music with the form in which music then expresses that life. Any contradiction disappears as soon as the form and object of expression are the same.

This assertion would appear to present a formidable problem: how is our inner life precisely to dictate its form to music; or, conversely: how can musical expression manifest itself *clearly* in the form of this inner life? . . .

It has become necessary that the musician approach the dramatic poet whose language on its own no longer satisfies our need for expression: in Beethoven, music approached the drama; Wagner completed the process by joining in himself poet and musician, thereby solving the problem. From now on, the poet can express the inner life of his characters, and the musician can submit himself without fear to the expression of this life, because his own medium is itself inspired by it . . .

In this new realm, music is discovered to be closely linked not just to the word, but also to that part of the drama to which the scenic elements of production give visible form. It ought therefore to be possible to examine the expressive quality of music and consider how it relates to the *mise en scène*.

Seen entirely in visual terms, how can music function?

. . . The poet-musician, by virtue of the music, presents to us not just the external effects of emotions, the outward appearance of dramatic life; but, using these emotions themselves, the dramatic life in its fullest reality, as we can know it only at the most profound level of our being.

MUSIC AND THE *MISE EN SCÈNE*

We have observed that if staging is to be entirely expressive of the intentions of the dramatist, the means for determining it must be found within the text.

The *mise en scène*, as a setting in space which changes in the course of time, presents in essence a question of proportion and sequence. Its governing principles must therefore regulate its spatial proportions and their temporal sequence, each dependent upon the other . . .

The length and sequence of the dramatic text on its own are not sufficient to determine how it should be staged. Music, by contrast, governs both the time duration and the continuity of the drama . . .

Therefore the word-tone poet [the author of a music-drama][7] has in music the guiding principle which, by virtue of having come directly from the artist's original intention, necessarily and inevitably dictates the *mise en scène* without being subjected to the will of the dramatist – and this principle is an integral part of his drama, and partakes of its organic life.

Production thus achieves the status of an expressive medium in the drama of a poet-musician; but we should emphasize that it can only achieve this status in such a drama.

In the word-tone drama, the performer is given both suggestions for his acting and the precise proportions he has to follow. He cannot interject the changes in intensity which he has observed in real life, because the musical expression itself contains the required variations in intensity . . . Just as the performer of the spoken drama has to achieve the versatility required for recreating those aspects which he has learned from his

31

experience of everyday life, so the performer of the word-tone drama has to achieve a similar versatility in order to follow the precise and direct instructions given him by the life encompassed by the score.

We see now how on stage music can be carried into the gestures and actions of the characters.

But how can music be conveyed into the painting, lighting, and the arrangement of backdrops and flats? . . .

In a staging of spoken drama, the presence of the actor is absolutely essential for any communication, and therefore he assumes a disproportionate importance . . . But for the author of a word-tone drama, the actor is not the only nor even the most important interpreter of his intention. He is instead only one medium, neither more nor less important than others, available to the poet . . . [The actor] becomes part of an organic unity and must submit to the rules governing the harmony of this organic entity . . . his facial expressions and gestures are dictated by the music. Moreover, we observe that these are no longer isolated on the stage, because the actor has *become the intermediary* between the music and the inanimate part of the stage production . . .

But, one will ask, how can the actor's gestures and movements on their own determine the arrangement of the setting? . . .

The inanimate elements of production (which comprise everything except the actors) can be reduced to three: lighting, the physical arrangement of the setting on the stage, and scene painting. How are these related to each other?

Painted scenery has to be set up in order to be effectively lit; this spatial arrangement therefore serves as an intermediary between painting and lighting. The lighting is required to make the painted setting visible, otherwise its spatial arrangement is entirely random; nor can lighting ignore the painting in favour of the spatial layout, since its whole purpose is to illuminate the painted canvases and thereby justify their placement in terms of the settings they are meant to represent . . . Lighting and painting on flats are two elements which, far from complementing each other through mutual subordination, in fact are entirely incompatible. The layout of painted flats to represent the setting requires that lighting be entirely at its service in order to make visible the painting; a relationship which is entirely distinct from the active role of lighting and in total conflict with it. Because it is three-dimensional, the spatial arrangement allows light to exercise a small part of its active function, but only at the expense of the two-dimensional painted flats. When we bring the actor on to the stage, the importance of the painting is at once entirely subordinated to the lighting and the spatial layout, since the living form of the actor can have no contact and consequently no direct relationship with what is depicted on the canvas.

Of the three elements of production, painting is unquestionably the one controlled by the narrowest conventions. It cannot on its own display any living or expressive reality, and to the extent that the other elements of the setting play an active role in the production, its power of representation diminishes; that is, to the extent that lighting and the spatial arrangement are integrated with the actor. Lighting and spatial arrangement are therefore more expressive than painting, and lighting, apart from its obvious role of basic illumination, is the most expressive. This is because it is subject to few conventions, is unobtrusive, and is able therefore to communicate external life in its most expressive form . . .

The rules controlling sight and sound, which taken together govern the conventions of staging, make it impossible actually to present the location of the action in a production with the same truth as that characterizing the language of the actors . . .

One might well object that the illusion so admirably achieved by today's scenic artists is very worthy of consideration. But that illusion has no aesthetic value unless it achieves its purpose, which is to create a setting, a living atmosphere on stage; for we all know that the moment the actors enter, the finest setting immediately turns into an ineffective arrangement of painted canvases . . .

By its very nature, the spoken drama has brought about the excessive development of scene painting. Currently, when the need for expression is substantial, the playwright is constrained to substitute decorative suggestion for that which music alone could give him. This results in continuous conflict between the pretensions of the production and the actual content of the dramatic text . . .

If the dramatist abandons the painted hieroglyph [i.e. scenic artifice] in favour of living light, he retreats from the notion that nothing can take the place of painted scenery in his play, when the text does not itself supply a setting; on the other hand, if he encumbers his text with descriptions of the setting, he robs the actors of the dramatic life which evokes the active role of light. It is therefore understandable that he reject a form of staging that seems inimical to the integrity of his work, and that he prefers to rely on painted scenery.

The origin and evolution of opera explain adequately why the visual elements of staging in this genre have developed without any dramatic motivation to exist merely to satisfy the eye. Because such satisfaction derived from a wish for ever-more marvellous spectacles, and because the scenic conventions severely limited three-dimensional realization, it was necessary to depend upon painting. Because living light was not employed, the spectators grew accustomed to imaginatively interpreting the flat painted perspective depicted on vertical canvas; they grew to enjoy having life presented to them by means of signs,[8] the easy manipulation of which allowed great freedom in the selection of subject matter. Thus the actual

Figure 5 The 1876 Bayreuth design by Joseph Hoffmann of the setting for *The Valkyrie*, Act III. Cf. Appia's setting in Figures 6 and 22.

life that only lighting and three-dimensional settings can provide is abandoned to the desire to view enthralling and spectacular things as *indicated*.

The degree to which, in staging, spoken drama and opera have influenced each other is only of historical interest, and I will not therefore dwell upon it, but note simply that this mutual influence still continues because a shared scenic principle binds them together under identical conventions . . .

By noting the three elements comprising an inanimate setting, we sought to suggest that music may be translated not just into the gestures and actions of the actor, but into the entire inanimate setting as well. Through analysing the relationship between these three elements, we demonstrated how inferior painting is as an expressive means in comparison to three-dimensional settings and light. Despite such obvious inferiority, painting still dominates modern stage setting. This odd domination has to be found in the basic nature of spoken drama and opera. It is now necessary for us to determine how the word-tone dramatist, wishing to follow the requirements of the music, must employ these three elements, and from this it will become readily apparent how music is conveyed into the spatial arrangement of the stage.

All the elements of a setting which are not painted but actually constructed and therefore may come into direct contact with the performer are termed 'practical' . . .

The most important thing is that the space be organized not to serve the painted 'signs' but instead to lay out the *fictive* form of the inanimate setting in order to relate as far as possible to the *actual* form of the actor. Only when painted scenery is curtailed and its importance reduced, will the *practical* setting have the necessary freedom. When this has been accomplished the setting will be transported into a more direct relationship with both the actor and the drama itself.

As a consequence of this new relationship, the dramatic text will be able more precisely to determine the role of the actor, and this in turn will allow the actor to determine the spatial arrangement of the setting. This, consequently, will increase the already existing antagonism between the three-dimensional and painted scenery, because by its very nature the latter must always be in conflict with the actor and work to his disadvantage. This conflict between the representative potential of scene painting and the more dynamic forces of the theatre will eventually diminish the importance of painted settings. Lighting, once liberated for the most part from the task of simply illuminating painted flats, will recover its proper independent role, and will begin to serve the actor actively . . .

It is essentially music, because of its fixed duration, that determines the actor's role and so his visible expression is already contained within the earliest conception of the drama, and is beyond the scope of the scenic

Figure 6 Appia's design of 1892 for Act III of *The Valkyrie*. Cf. Figure 5, and the extensive description of the setting given by Appia in his scenario, which is included in the Appendix together with Figure 22 depicting the arrangement and lighting later in the act.

designer, as well as of the actor, and even to some degree of the dramatist himself . . .

To summarize: a dramatic conception which requires musical expression in order to manifest itself must arise from the hidden world of our inner life, because this life cannot be *expressed* except through music, and music can express only that life. The poet-musician encompasses this vision in his *music*. Through language, he gives it specific dramatic form and composes the poetic-musical text, the *score*. This text imposes on the *actor* his role, which is already living and defined for him to assume. The proportions of this role determine the form of the actual arrangement of *three-dimensional* elements (the point of contact between the living actor and the inanimate settings); the degree and nature of these elements determine the *spatial arrangement* of the setting, which in turn controls the *lighting* and *painted flats.*

This hierarchy is composed organically: the soul of the drama (music) provides it with life, and by its pulsations determines every movement of the whole organism in their proportion and sequence. If any link of this chain is broken or missing, the expressive power of the music is interrupted and can extend no further . . . Since the actor is the only intermediary between the score and the form in which it is represented, the production can never dispense with him for revealing its own life . . .

PRACTICAL APPLICATION

The elements constituting the word-tone drama comprise two distinct groups: the sounds as they are transmitted by the voices of the actors and the instruments of the orchestra; and the visual aspects of the staging. The existence of the former outside the drama is quite different from the integrated ideal existence imposed on them by the poet-musician. By contrast, the living mobile form of the human body and the constantly changing aspects of objects in space, light and colour are things we see in an integrated form every day . . . Although music may bring these into a new aesthetic unity, it takes from their independent life only what is required to transpose itself into space: it does not give them life, it merely determines the extent to which they are used . . .

The technical study of approaches to staging is thus divided into two parts: (1) the actor, the living form of the human body; (2) the inanimate setting, both inert and mobile elements . . .

Except for fundamental study of voice and diction, it is training in gymnastics which will enable the actor to respond to the demands of the poetic-musical text . . .[9]

On the one hand there is the as yet unrealized drama concealed within the poetic-musical score; on the other, the actor in full possession of his training and personal resources, together with the director who controls

37

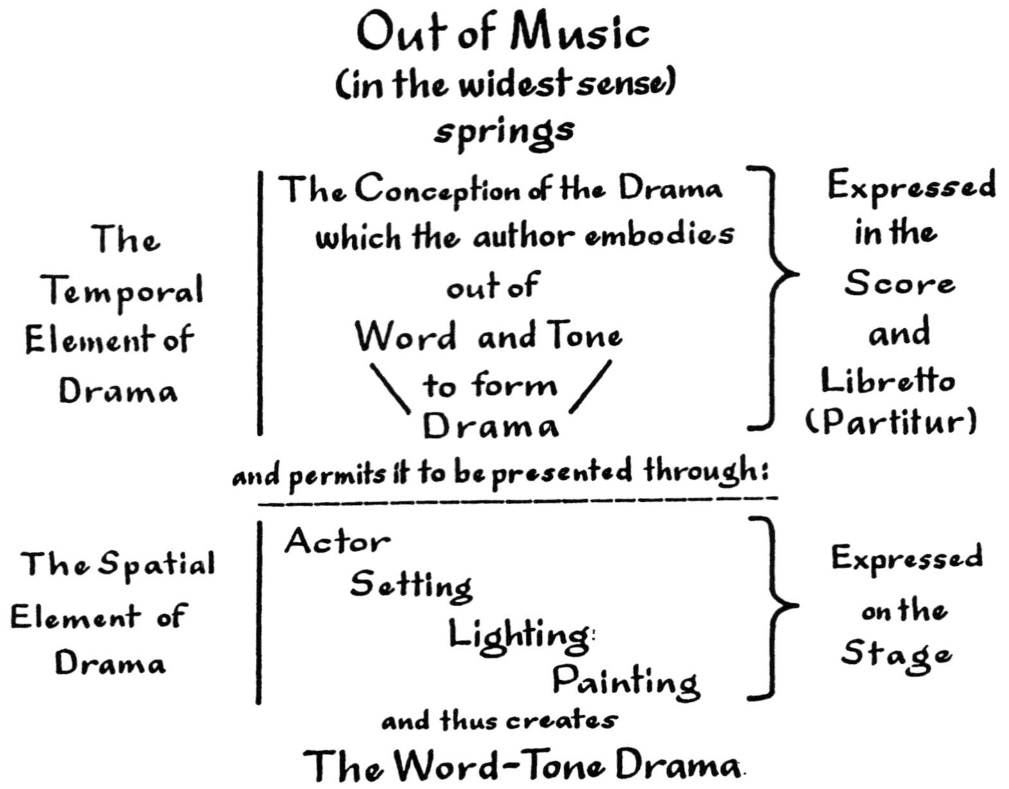

Out of Music
(in the widest sense)
springs

The Conception of the Drama
which the author embodies

out of

Word and Tone

to form / Drama

Expressed in the Score and Libretto (Partitur)

The Temporal Element of Drama

and permits it to be presented through:

Actor
Setting
Lighting:
Painting

and thus creates

The Word-Tone Drama.

Expressed on the Stage

The Spatial Element of Drama

Figure 7 An English translation of Appia's schematic representation of the hierarchy of production, which he included on page 23 of the original edition of *Music and the Art of the Theatre*.

all the other inanimate scenic elements of production. But bringing these all together does not itself produce a staging . . .

It is therefore vital that the score contain a transcription of the requirements of the poetic-musical text in a language accessible to all. The essential part of this will concern the actor, and just as the poetic-musical notation of his role is conveyed through the conventional signs of music and language, so an equivalent method for the visual expression must be found . . . It may be possible to provide them with a form that implicitly – but unambiguously – conveys the essential effect of the actor's role within an inanimate setting. A system of hieroglyphics seems appropriate to this purpose. . . .[10]

In order to establish the production hierarchy demanded by the music, I have used the generally accepted dramaturgical terms, which are at best only approximate. These are associated with existing scenic practice – concepts which inevitably will impose themselves on the reader's imagination – and thus distort, if not indeed destroy, those very ideas which I so much wish to convey. I must therefore first discard the most deeply rooted prejudice of our theatre, one so powerful that it is steadfastly supported – or seems to be – by all the current principles of stage production. I refer to that requirement which demands the search for *scenic illusion* . . .

Any production which did not deliberately seek this illusion would not be accepted by the average audience . . . As a consequence, our current theatrical conventions have been evolved not so much to meet the dramatic requirements of the text – or to supply the means to realize these requirements successfully on stage – as to satisfy the taste of the average audience . . .

Visual deception has no place in art; the illusion which a work of art produces is not to deceive us about the nature of emotions or objects in relation to reality, but rather to draw us so ably into another's vision that it seems to be our own. This demands a certain degree of refinement in us; otherwise our need for illusion is displaced and the crass appearance of reality becomes for us the goal of art . . .

We have seen how the increasing desire for seductive sensation in staging led to the development of painting and décor very much to the detriment of the lighting . . . Such illusion, which is always greatly valued, is achieved only by the sacrifice of life in the setting, and our eyes are so inept in this regard that the illusion seems dangerously weakened if the action of the performers or of the illumination destroys the deception created by the décor. So long as this deception is maintained, we ignore entirely the most awkward and unrealistic acting and lighting . . .

In the drama of the poet-musician, if one expressive element were overemphasized it would come into conflict at once with the others; a supreme will controls everything, and modulates moment by moment the changing relationships between the elements of production. With extraordinary subtlety, and with no regard for scenic illusion, it controls every aspect of production including even the text itself. The staging of a drama is itself *a means of expression*; scenic illusion may be employed as any other tangible instrument of production, but it should by no means dictate its form or be its sole purpose . . .

Music joins the audience together as a single entity; it is not concerned with its needs or tastes; it reigns over them in its rhythmic life, and its force meets a need which is otherwise impossible to satisfy: for men to escape from themselves in order to rediscover themselves. Where is man's true image more wondrously reflected than in musical expression? . . .

Music transforms the original conception [of the poet-musician] and allows it to enter his text in its purest form. Then when the work is produced, it retains nothing imposed on it by arbitrary conventions.

The actor

It might be argued that such harmony cannot be attained because even if we dispensed with the illusion demanded of the inanimate aspects of production, such illusion would remain in the physical presence of the actor on stage . . .

The illusion created by the setting and the dramatic illusion created by the actor, which previously were irreconcilable and mutually destructive, have each made the necessary sacrifices for a shared existence and in the process gained unsuspected power. What the actor loses of his independence is gained by the stage designer; and the setting, by abandoning its illusionistic quality, provides the actor with an atmosphere that encompasses him and allows him to be supremely expressive . . .

In the imagination, music alone is able to create a milieu in which the living body takes on artistic significance. In the absence of music, the body can still by language and gesture serve as intermediary between the dramatist and his audience. But it can do so not as a formal part of that expression but only as a medium through which it passes. Yet when music is combined with words, then as a result of the setting up of new relationships we *see* that the living body discards its arbitrary veil of individuality and becomes an instrument consecrated to universal human expression. It is not yet the incarnation of that expression, but it has become a *visible* part of it[11] . . .

In the dance the body creates an imaginary milieu for itself, and for this it must sacrifice to the temporal value of music the rational elements of its existence – in return it achieves a living expression of its *form*. What music is to our feelings, dance is to the body: an imaginary form which does not require rational understanding for its expression. Dance approaches mime just as pure music approaches drama: it seeks, using its original form, and at the same time in spite of it, to appeal to the intellect.[12] In order for this to happen, music must allow the emotions to take on definite form in language, by means of the poetic-musical text, and dance must allow the body to make its life intelligible.

In surrendering himself to the poet-musician, the actor not only sacrifices the creation of his own role, but also that *natural* emotion contained by the role, which divorced from the music, would be evoked by him. The poet-musician communicates emotion to the actor *by means of the extra-ordinary forms imposed on him:* it is only by means of plastic forms developed separately from passionate expression that the dance can attain its all-powerful force as it joins with symphonic music to create the word-tone drama.[13]

Lyric song and *dance*: these are the two teachers of the actor in the word-tone drama. The former allows him to develop his vocal expression within an imaginary span of time and his voice to rise above the music; the latter allows him great rhythmic subtlety without calling upon his own emotional life. Through these two media he attains the greatest possible 'depersonaliz-ation', with his body obeying spontaneously the most complex rhythmic patterns, and his voice submitting to musical passages quite alien to his inner life. He is thus able to bring himself into a direct rapport with his expressive collaborators – the three-dimensional setting, lighting and paint-ing – and share their common life. These three elements ought also to be able to offer the actor the highest standard of perfection; but they are inanimate, and the artists and technicians who are responsible for putting them on stage are no more qualified to determine the tasks of the actor than is he in controlling their input: they are all merely elements awaiting a superior will to employ them.

The person whom we call 'director', instead of guiding the production according to long-established and fixed conventions as is currently the case, will assume with the word-tone drama the role of a despotic school-master as he presides over the elementary preparation of the staging. He artificially enforces the synthesis of the representative elements by animat-ing the more flexible of these at the expense of the actor, whose indepen-dence must be utterly destroyed. His methods will naturally be completely arbitrary; he must play *imaginatively* with the scenic materials while avoid-ing the creation of mere scenic illusion. Therefore only an *artist* of the highest calibre can accomplish such a mission. He will study the play of his own imagination in order to strip it as far as possible of convention and above all, of current fashion. The vital task of his direction will always be to convince the production personnel that only their mutual subordination can produce a result worthy of their efforts. His influence must be magnetic, rather like that of a genial conductor . . .

Once the actor feels a close dependence upon his inanimate collabor-ators, and has sacrificed himself to rhythmic and emotional depersonaliz-

MUSICAL EXPRESSION

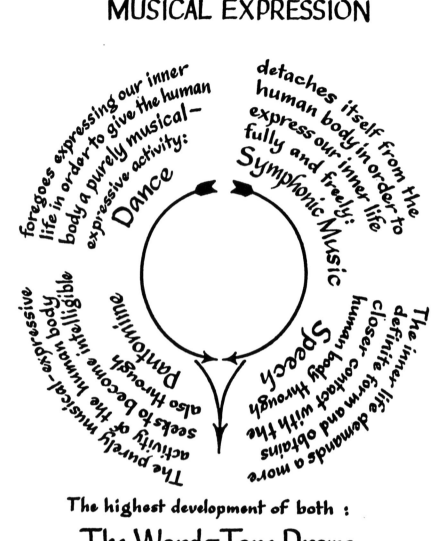

foregoes expressing our inner life in order to give the human body a purely musical — expressive activity: Dance

detaches itself from the human body in order to express our inner life fully and freely: Symphonic Music

The inner life demands and obtains a more closer contact with the human body through Speech

The purely musical or the human-expressive activity of the human body seeks to become intelligible also through Pantomime

The highest development of both :

The Word-Tone Drama.

Figure 8 An English translation of Appia's schematic representation of the elements of the word-tone drama, which he included on page 38 of the original edition of *Music and the Art of the Theatre*.

ation by renouncing for ever – fully conscious of the reasons – his pre-eminent importance, then and only then can he approach the word-tone drama . . .[14]

It is the will of the poet-musician that evokes life for the actor, and acts as interpreter between him and the inanimate setting . . . Is such an alto-gether *formal* education possible at present, and are its elements yet within our power? Alas, even the existence of the poet-musician is as problematic as that of his interpreters and his audience. The elements of the supreme work of art are at hand: sounds, words, form, light and colour; but how shall we kindle the life which sparks the dramatist to expression, the actor to subservience, and the spectator to contemplation? . . .[15]

Just as the dramatist in employing music dispenses with the variety and development of objective external motifs by preferring to express the inner essence of a more limited number of phenomena, so in the production of his drama must he renounce a large portion of its intelligible objectification in favour of its overall expressive power.

If, for example, the drama demands for its setting an artisan's studio, the gallery of a Moorish palace, or the edge of a pine forest – or any other type of defined setting – merely assembling a mass of objects relating to the particular craft of the artisan, or some Moorish designs, or the botanical details of pine trees, will not create an expressive setting corresponding to that of the music. Music does not express crafts, or styles of architecture or varieties of plant life as such; they all belong to that part of the drama which is addressed to understanding: they are rather a category of 'representative phenomena' which should be presented to us only to the extent necessary to make the dramatic text intelligible. A simple indication is sufficient to locate the setting in the external world, and, this accomplished, the setting need only express what *within the place chosen by the dramatist* corresponds to the inner essence revealed to us by the music.

And what can give to the visible world we perceive every day that wondrous unity which enables us to live through seeing, if not *Light*? Without this unity we could only dimly perceive the external appearance of things, but never their expressiveness; for if things are to be expressive they must have form, and form without light is evident only to our sense of touch. By *light*, of course, I mean not simply 'visibility' but the activity of light . . .

We shall see later that lighting, the principal element of expression in a setting, truly provides a subtlety which painting, the bearer of external representation, can never achieve . . .

The spatial arrangement

Our stages currently are built and organized according to the practice of a decorative mode almost entirely devoted to the illusion produced by painting. Undoubtedly a theatre where concern for such illusion will not dictate the arrangement of scenery will be altogether different. What essential changes will the new system of scenic settings effect in the construction of the stage? . . .

The poet-musician who notes at the beginning of an act 'the scene represents, etc.' does this to help the reader; *but if such indications are not contained within the poetic-musical text they are by no means admissible on stage.*

And this is the crucial difference between the word-tone drama and all other stage settings . . .

Every word-tone drama determines its own staging, so that the expressive hierarchy established by the music is the only *a priori* idea of importance to be had concerning the poetic-musical expression . . .

In order to give to the decorative materials the necessary subtlety, the layout and construction of the stage must allow each of the expressive media its appropriate development. The current arrangement must be rejected to the extent that it inhibits the evolution of spatial settings and lighting . . . A stage for a word-tone drama cannot be designed for only one type of production, as is the case in contemporary theatres: matching the structure and the production can only exist as an ideal . . .

In our theatres the stage and its appendages together form an entity quite distinct from that space intended to accommodate the public . . . the uninitiated experience an unpleasant shock when, leaving the auditorium, one crosses the almost mathematically precise line dividing that part of the theatre from the artificial and provisional elements in the realm opposite . . . The novice will always be a bit disappointed when he observes the clumsy and massive walls enclosing the magic world that had so charmed him. . . .[16] What it represents is not the world beyond the auditorium, because that world is entirely imaginary . . .

The appearance of the ancient theatre was just as clearly intelligible as was their whole way of life. To the Greek eye, clear and pure of vision, the complex encumbrance of our contemporary theatre would seem repugnant and meaningless. The Greek theatre was either a flat circular space, or an amphitheatre defined by a horizontal line . . . The ancient stage was not like ours, which is an opening into a small space where the product of immense individual effort is displayed to an audience. Ancient drama was an *act*, not a spectacle . . . There, as in everything, a sense of harmony served the Greeks in a wonderful fashion. We lack this sense and cannot achieve it; our stage therefore is an *opening* into the unknown and unlimited; we shall not achieve expression in whatever imaginary realm our modern soul longs to enter merely by giving to the technical apparatus of the scenery a tangible form and a place in the physical form of the building . . .

The spatial significance of our theatre is curtailed by the frame of the proscenium arch. The Greek perceived a unity between the spectacle and its boundary; less fortunately, we have located the spectacle on the other side of the boundary because, not being artists, we separate ourselves off from the work of art.

Consequently the drama of the imagination (an unlimited space) has no relationship to the roofed amphitheatre into which we crowd, except for the proscenium arch; everything else is fictive, temporary, and has no other existence beyond the production.

For a production dictated by conventions which derive as much from dramatic form as from the public, it is an advantage to limit the technical expression of these conventions by a permanent stage construction . . . It follows, then, that the construction of our theatres, with nothing to express, is not entirely inappropriate.

We have noted that the production of the word-tone drama cannot rely on any convention whatsoever . . . And the poet-musician himself must maintain complete objective freedom in his conception. As the basis for his production there is a medium – music – whose development cannot be restrained by any convention. He ought not to, and cannot, base his work on habits formed before its existence. Each of his dramas determines not only its own *production*, but the theatre as well. . . .[17]

Everyone has noted that a stage setting works simultaneously in three ways as we view it: (1) the ground level of the setting, that portion sitting on the floor of the stage or upon platforms which raise its level; (2) the central, vertical section; (3) the borders and backcloths that close off the height and depth of the stage and mask the lights.

The base of the stage picture is always the most critical portion in contemporary stage setting, because, in spite of the name, it is not conceived as being set on anything . . . With few exceptions, settings formed of painted flats appear to have been cut off across their base, then placed on an entirely flat surface . . .

Gazing upwards, we receive quite a shock: for now this laborious but imperfect setting is suddenly activated and becomes very impressive – the 'illusion' is at its greatest, and certain details which seemed of no importance when observed against the stage floor now acquire considerable significance for the overall effect. The backdrop, which earlier was merely a painted canvas necessary to define the boundaries for the location of the scenery, now blends harmoniously with the downstage wings and extends their perspective; painted and real light join in one beautiful area of brightness. The eye is entirely satisfied.

Yet, looking yet higher, our pleasure diminishes: by its nature a particular setting either does not justify the use of the necessary borders, or provides an inadequate reason for cutting off the setting at the top . . .

If we now quickly survey the whole stage picture, the conflicting sensations it provides are not rectified by the pleasing effect at the centre. After a little reflection, we soon regard the whole thing as merely a reproduction contrived according to inevitable conventions; and the illusion it attempts to give us is, in the end, something that we in the audience must construct using our own imagination. What might be termed the aesthetic activity of the spectator is misdirected by this process, for we cannot take part in a work of art by replacing its physical representation with the abstraction of our own thought. The setting thus forces the drama into a form greatly inferior to its literary reality. Consequently the whole scenic apparatus and the layout of the auditorium strikes us as being an unpleasant practical joke . . .

Unfortunately the area used by the actor is not at the centre of the setting . . . he is forced to conduct his dramatic activity in that part of the setting where scenic illusion is at a minimum. The physical reality of this or that flat or drop is exposed by the entrance of the actor . . . Obviously, the better the flat is painted with regard to the illusion, the less the actor . . . will blend with it, since none of his moves will fit in with the place and objects depicted on the scenery . . .

The actor therefore is directly subservient to the inanimate setting. The place for the action is realized in one manner, the action itself in another; the two modes come into contact, but are utterly disparate. The inanimate setting is like a coloured engraving, and the actor merely the caption at the bottom of the page . . .

The spatial arrangement as it is today cannot provide the actor with a space in harmony with the setting depicted on the painted flats, and since the entire construction of our theatres is determined by such scenery, the setting for the word-tone drama cannot function at present in such circumstances, because for it the setting must somehow emanate from the ground on which the actor stands, and not the actor from the setting. Everything that is not in contact with the actor is nevertheless still subject to the requirements imposed by his presence and immediate surroundings, and cannot be expressive except through him.

The setting of the word-tone drama should present the spectator with nothing which does not belong to the space evoked by the poetic-musical text . . . This new concept does not desire illusion, which is likely to be destroyed by inappropriate intrusions, and it does not require explicit representation which tends to impose a single meaning on every object regardless of what it is. It demands, rather, *expression* and the fact that such expression can only be achieved by renouncing both illusion and explicit representation lends it a limitless freedom. Therefore the mechanics of production will entail in *visual terms* only that expression or signification which the music provides . . .

Imagine, for example, that it were necessary to *express* within a closed room the multi-coloured, limpid and variable atmosphere of a forest landscape, which as such would be impracticable; the desire would remain unrealized, like a dramatic scene for orchestra alone. But if we place a character within that setting, and for five minutes allow the music to

suggest a mood, or some activity – no matter what – or merely allc
music to flow over his body, the atmosphere will suddenly acquire lii
setting will become *expressive,* and the walls of the room *because they c
part of this expression, will cease to exist.* The same holds for all those eleᵤᵤₑₙₜₛ
of the setting which are necessarily permanent . . . they will cease to
exist . . .

It remains for us to move from purely theoretical descriptions of the
inanimate elements of production, to discuss their practical application.
These elements may be considered in two categories: the 'terrain' set aside
for the actor, and the complex lighting apparatus . . .

The arrangement of three-dimensional structures is currently determined
by the flat surface of the actual stage, and by the surface of the painted
canvases, which are also flat, but perpendicular . . . all are constructed at
right angles to the floor . . .

One can appreciate immediately the difficulties presented by the painted
scenery the moment the actor moves amongst it; above all we note that
his performance is completely thwarted by the extraordinary apparatus
encompassing him. In an outdoor setting, if he wants to sit on the ground,
a spot must be carefully set aside for him against the painted flats, and
the solid piece masked and covered with a bit of painted canvas . . . His
hands dangle in the air; if he wants to put them on anything other than
a solid set piece, the precise location must be determined in advance . . .
If the scene is a long one, and the actor's presence on stage is important,
the set piece will be placed separately apart from the painted flats, creating
an altogether absurd impression . . .

'Architectural' settings are easier to arrange; nevertheless in the interest
of creating a sumptuous picture with painted flats representing all manner
of interesting things, the actor's performance and expressiveness must be
liberally sacrificed by minimizing those parts of the setting he can approach
and touch . . .

In another setting the scene painter will exhaust every resource of perspective technique and colour to represent a beautiful contrast of light and
shade . . . the actor as he steps in front of these painted flats destroys their
effect, because he is lit by the same artificial light to the same extent in
a supposedly murky spot as in one bathed in [painted] light . . .

It is quite futile to multiply such examples; everyone who attends our
theatres . . . knows very well what I mean: whatever the various circumstances, the technical procedure is everywhere the same. Yet one cannot
stress enough the fact that *our scenic practice disregards the expressive effect of
the actor in favour of the illusion produced by painted canvas,* with the result that
both are equally impossible.

Sacrifice, which is possibly the most essential principle of a work of art,
is entirely ignored in this area. In attempting to have everything, we have,
from a strictly aesthetic viewpoint, nothing at all.

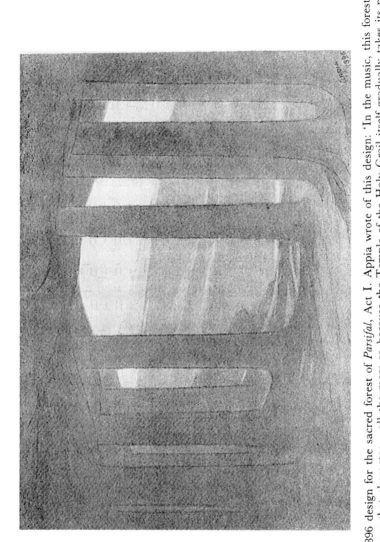

Figure 9 Appia's 1896 design for the sacred forest of *Parsifal*, Act I. Appia wrote of this design: 'In the music, this forest represents a *Temple*. It must have that character – all the more so because the Temple of the Holy Grail itself gradually takes its place at the end of the act. Accordingly, the lines and the general arrangement of the trees will fit in with this architectural arrangement. Then, when this forest-temple is slowly and solemnly withdrawn from our view, to lead us as in a dream to the divine Temple, during the unreal and tragic splendour of the music, the trunks will little by little lose their roots and be based on flat stones; the vegetation will disappear; the natural light of day will give way to the supernatural light of the Temple, and the stone columns will gradually and smoothly replace the great shafts of the forest: thus we will pass from one Temple to another' (Appia 1960: 90)

The terrain intended for the *actor* in the word-tone drama is determined *above any other consideration* by the actor's physical presence. One should understand here that by *terrain* I do not mean merely the part of the stage walked upon by the actor, but rather everything composing the setting that relates to the physical form of the performer and his actions.

Once the terrain no longer seeks to evoke scenic illusion, it can be designed and built with the single-minded intention of fully expressing the attitude which the characters' actions evoke. But it is only the lighting that can lend expressive meaning to this attitude, and so it may be fully taken into account in constructing the terrain . . . whose role cannot be isolated from that of lighting . . . In building it, therefore, the question will be not whether the lighting will allow a particular construction, but whether such a construction together *with* the assistance of lighting will allow the actor to be sufficiently expressive – or, in other words, whether his attitude will be given the emphasis prescribed by the music . . .

When a scene painter undertakes to transform a particular picture into a stage setting, he instinctively tries to reduce to the point of absurdity all the solid forms in favour of artificial ones. For him, the only real difference between the picture in its frame and the same picture on stage is that the latter has to provide a place for those inconvenient things called actors . . . His problem is to supply this necessary place while disrupting the picture as little as possible. The designer does this by breaking his picture into bits to be displayed in the space facing the audience; the actor will then attempt to manoeuvre amongst these slices of painting, while performing the basic requirements of his role satisfactorily. The backdrop is the only part of the setting that does not entail a miserable compromise, since only it can display a complete painting to the audience without doing violence to the actual space which ultimately forms the setting . . . the rest of the set as a whole is nothing but an arrangement – often undoubtedly an ingenious one – of bits of painted canvas each partly overlapping the other . . .

Despite the importance of the actor's terrain and the lighting, and the extent to which these two principles limit the overall composition of the setting, it is obvious that the empty space of the stage must still be filled with various solid objects that cannot be sacrificed. Trees, rocks, buildings, interior walls, etc. must all be presented while conforming to the arrangement determined by the active role of lighting; although in many cases their scale will allow them to be constructed in solid form, in others this may be impossible or undesirable . . . Nevertheless no compromise is possible between the positive three-dimensional representation of objects and painting on vertical flats . . .

Light requires an object in order to retain its expressiveness; it must light something, and encounter obstacles. Such objects cannot be artificial, because real light does not have an artificial existence. In lighting a painted flat, it is only as a *flat* that the light strikes it, and not as the objects that are depicted upon it. But the expressive form of the production subordinates the conventional nature of the flats to the living presence of the actor. If certain decorative elements can only be presented on the stage by painted flats, and are dramatically necessary, the free activity of the lighting is called into question. But often such elements are so closely related to the lighting that some or all of them can be dispensed with, so long as the lighting creates in their place the effect they would have produced. If, for example, a scene takes place in the depths of a forest, the varied terrain and different set pieces demand the activity of light; the practical demands of the actor's role are met, but the forest itself has not yet been expressed, i.e. the tree trunks and foliage. The choice then is either to sacrifice a portion of the expressive potential of the ground and the lighting in order to suggest the presence of trees on the broken-up flats, or else to express only those parts of the trees that can be reconciled with the solidity of the ground, and to *direct the lighting to do the rest through its particular quality* . . .

The latter alternative allows for the maximum scenic expressiveness: a few solid trunks blend into the borders, from which coloured illumination, filtered and allowed to play in various ways, projects on to the stage lighting characteristic of a forest, leaving to the spectator's imagination the presence of objects they do not actually need to see. A minimum of flats serves as a sign, without reducing the activity of the lighting, and thereby both the characters and the solid portions of the settings are immersed in an *atmosphere* appropriate to them . . .[18]

If regarded as a truly expressive medium, theatrical production forbids all that is not part of its expression or part of that minimal intelligible representation permitted to the setting . . .

Expression in the theatre precludes not only the use of visible devices but also, and above all, any attempt to represent actuality in the overall production . . . The current quest for scenic illusion means that each setting must be given a precise appearance, and this is all the more so when it is obtained almost entirely through painted flats and backcloths with lighting allowed only the most restricted function, it being felt desirable that the flats be seen . . .

There is no reason to modify the form of this setting in the course of its use. The different times of the day are indicated by conventional colour and intensity of lighting, and of course, the better painted the setting, the less effective these variations of light will be, since they cannot correspond to the painting . . .

In the word-tone drama the changing relationship between the spoken text and the musical score, between the exclusively inner expression and that which is externalized, between passages of different length and intensity, different sonorities – all this when applied to a single unified action

50

constitutes a bold defiance of what is termed 'realism'. In order to be expressive, the production resulting from such a work must abandon the search for 'illusion', since common sense suggests the attempt is useless.

The task is to represent a place not *as it would be seen by someone transported to it*, but only as it is expressed by the poetic-musical text, with changes in that text so determining changes in the presentation that they are mutually dependent . . . *The place of action is not in itself changeable, but rather the way in which the dramatist wishes us to view it* . . .

The *mise en scène* of the word-tone drama is thus 'ideal' in the sense that its material reality is subject to aesthetic concerns superior to its intelligible form, and this ideal quality is all-powerful since it imposes itself on the audience by perfectly direct means without any reflection on their part . . .

The final spatial arrangement of a scene will be a highly sensitive composition requiring very subtle materials; experiment will reveal how to perfect this. Probably until such perfection is attained in composition, one will have to use fairly crude methods with various designs drawn up to be executed in whatever material each may require. To these designs will be added a lighting plot and notes about the painting, with the whole joined finally with the score as an integral part of it . . .

To summarize: current production technique neglects the effectiveness of the actor in favour of scenic illusion produced by painted flats. The hierarchy which the music sets up does not authorize this state of affairs, since it is the actor who determines everything in the setting that relates in any way to his body and movements. But this is possible only if we renounce what we call scenic illusion. Since stage settings need no longer obey this illusion, they can now serve the superior commands of the poetic-musical text, and provide as required a *material* subtlety corresponding to that of the score . . . Lighting provides a link between the solid settings and the painted flats, and such lighting consists in artificially producing through its illumination the effects conveyed by various objects when they intercept light . . .

The lighting

Light is to production what music is to the score: the expressive element as opposed to external signs; and as in the case of music, light can express only that which belongs to 'the inner essence' of all vision . . . The two elements have an analogous existence. Each of them needs some external object if their activity is to be put into effect: the poet, in the case of music, and the actor (by means of the spatial layout) for lighting. Both elements possess extraordinary subtlety . . .

But, beyond that, there is a mysterious affinity between music and light; as aptly expressed by H. S. Chamberlain, 'Apollo was not only the god of song, but also of light.'[19] And we sense the profound union of the two elements when some fortunate circumstance allows us to experience them simultaneously . . .

If poetic-musical expression and visual expression, functioning in isolation, vary in their effectiveness according to the sensibility of each individual in the audience, their union, organically determined by the music, creates an independent *life* superior to each individual's limitations. For this life is based on 'the inner essence of the phenomenon',[20] and when, on that foundation, *the total expression embraces all our faculties*, personal limitations will be transcended.

The sovereign power of light cannot be proven to one who has not experienced it, and it is even more difficult to discuss its technical use . . . The life of light is altogether too simple to be reduced further. It is only indirectly, in correcting its abuse in our modern settings, that we can arrive by a process of induction at its normal function . . . in fact, these very abuses and their diverse consequences to a great extent encouraged this present study. Here I shall reduce the aspects of light to a few basic concepts which determine its use in the dramatic work, and refrain until a bit later from suggesting its potential in relation to the other elements of production . . .

On a stage whose layout and dimensions have, as it were, no existence except for the particular form lent them by any given drama, the lighting obviously will not be subject to any permanent arrangement. Yet, however impossible to determine *a priori* its use, or to isolate light's function from the simultaneous input of the other production elements, it is possible to establish a fundamental division of its uses, derived from the relationship existing between daylight and artificial light.

Daylight suffuses the whole atmosphere without obscuring our awareness of its direction. But the direction of light cannot be determined except by shadows; it is the quality of shadows which expresses for us the quality of light. Shadows are formed by means of the same light that suffuses the atmosphere. This all-powerful effect cannot be achieved in the same way artificially; the brightness of a lighted fire in a dark space will never create what we term *chiaroscuro*, in other words, the more or less distinct shadow cast in a space which is already lit. In practice this task must be divided, with one part of the lighting responsible for spreading general illumination and the other for casting shadows by means of precisely directed beams, which communicate the character of the lighting. We shall term the one 'diffused light', and the other 'active light'.

In our settings, lighting is handled simultaneously in four different forms:

1 the fixed border lights which illumine the painted flats, and are supplemented in the wings and on the stage floor by similar movable strip lights;

2 what are called 'footlights' – that particular monstrosity of our theatres – used to light both the setting and the actors from in front and below;
3 completely movable spotlights capable of focusing a precise beam, or various projections;
4 lighting by transparency, that is, using light to reveal certain transparent effects on painted flats by lighting from behind.

To harmonize all of these is obviously so complicated that it becomes altogether impossible, as our current productions demonstrate. There are too many contradictory elements ever to achieve real harmony; thus have we renounced and ruthlessly enfeebled this most powerful of all scenic elements. How, after all, can we reconcile a light intended to illumine vertical flats, but which also falls on other adjacent objects, with another light intended for those objects, which nevertheless also strikes the flats?

Under such circumstances how absurd to discuss the quality of shadows! Yet there is no solid object of any kind, whether animate or not, that can do without them. If there is no shadow, there is no light, for light is not merely 'visibility' . . . light is distinguished from 'visibility' by its express-iveness. And if there is no expression, there is no light, as in the case of our stage settings: there is 'visibility' but no light, and for this reason the setting can become expressive only in the absence of the actor, since the artificial light depicted on the flats corresponds to the equally artificial shadows which have also been painted. But the actor is a solid object which cannot be lit by imaginary light: to have light in a painted setting, one or the other must be banished. If we dispense with the actor, the drama is destroyed and replaced by a display of paintings; it is therefore the paintings which must be sacrificed . . .

As far as is possible to judge . . . those lights which are least mobile and easy to manipulate and which spread their light most evenly, i.e. the border, movable strip lights and to a very limited extent the footlights, should be used to produce the *diffuse light*. Undoubtedly their placement and use will be quite different for a setting which is no longer governed by a line of painted parallel flats, but the basis for their construction will not change a great deal. The more mobile and easily handled instruments will produce the *active light*, and will require very careful research to perfect their operation. The installations of relatively fixed diffuse light will be complemented by screens of various transparency, designed to limit too pronounced a brightness falling on objects which are close to them, or on the actors as they step into this lighting. An essential role of the mobile and flexible instruments producing active light will be concerned with various methods for curtailing that light, and if the electrical layout of the light can be approximately determined prior to its use in production, the means for obstructing the light – although invisible – is *part of the actual setting*, and must always be determined at the same time and in harmony with the spatial layout of the stage. In discussing this, I have already noted how important the partial obstruction of active light is for preserving the expressive integrity of the settings. The lighting of transparent flats is only concerned with the painting, and does not influence active light, except that it must allow it free play by illuminating these paintings without lighting the rest of the setting.

The interplay of these two types of lighting is a question of proportion, and there is no absolute technical demarcation separating them.

Diffuse light and active light exist simultaneously only in terms of different degrees of intensity. Diffuse light on its own merely allows for 'visibility' . . . Active light expresses night (moon or torchlight) or the supernatural. The difference of intensity between the two types of light should not be less than required by the presence of shadows. Apart from this, however, their combinations are infinitely variable. However, any imbalance which prevents us from perceiving the diffuse light would result in exclusively active light . . .

To avoid shadows would weaken the effect of active light; diffuse light ought to illuminate all parts of the setting, as well as the actor. Once visibility has been achieved on stage and shadows have been adequately suppressed, active light can be brought into play. With the exception of a few rare instances when one or the other form of light must operate on its own, it is quite clear that we must begin with 'visibility'. The intensity of the diffuse light will then be modified by the active light . . .

We will see that colour, in being externalized and no longer dependent upon the painted flats, will become so closely integrated with lighting that it is difficult to distinguish one from the other. For the sake of clarity, I will reserve this for the section on *painting*, and continue with the order of hierarchy which begins with the actor.

But, you might ask, is the division between active and diffuse light not a gesture towards the realism which earlier was so systematically refuted? Will not the harmony of production be destroyed by the realistic use of lighting in a setting that otherwise is entirely fictive, and peopled by characters whose language, gestures and movements do not in any way correspond to everyday reality?

The literal and fixed representation of familiar forms does not replicate the only mode of existence in which we know them; we can readily imagine them in the most varied combinations, and picture them in movement or even altering their size and nature before our eyes. Music, by contrast, is the most convincing demonstration possible of the ideal flexibility of time in regard to our inner life. But what other form of existence could we imagine for light, except the contrasting intensities produced by shadows, and how can shadows be conceived apart from being produced by an object struck by a ray of light? . . . By its very presence light expresses to us the 'inner essence' of all vision by exhausting any other way we might conceive it. When form is independent of *light* it expresses this 'inner essence' only through its partaking in the manifestation of a production's organic life, either by becoming a part of the overall effect, or by enabling active light to function by providing an object for it.

The ideal quality of time, represented by music through the form of the actor, is extended by light into space to create an equivalent ideal expression there. It is obvious that light's manifestations, which are always absolute, cannot be judged on the same level as the servile and limited imitation of some single aspect of other physical forms.

The realism of lighting, therefore, is not the same as the realism of forms arranged in space, since these are set up in imitation of a particular phenomenon, while light is based on the existence of an *idea*.

This extraordinary quality of lighting explains why the activity of this element . . . cannot be treated in isolation, but only in the context of the other specific materials which are employed in production.

Painting

The more or less faithful depiction of reality on a two-dimensional surface banishes all expressiveness and life. Actual light, when it holds sway, restores that life and at the same time abolishes the principles which control the use of colour. In order for meaning and expressiveness to return to colour they must be subject to a new principle, and since lighting has extinguished their spark of life, it is most likely that lighting will restore it. Painting must somehow externalize itself and renounce its own artificial life. What existence will it find to compensate for this sacrifice? . . .

Obviously when any branch of art is controlled by conventions that are alien to it and is at the same time cut off from its primary and legitimate function, it must lose all its intrinsic value. It can hardly be denied that this is the case with scene painting, since the conventions of stage settings have nothing in common with those governing painting *per se*, and the purpose of such painting deprives the painter of the human element . . .

The independent life of painting may be defined thus: to express on a flat surface with coloured materials as much as possible of the private vision of the artist . . . An artist under such conditions cannot tolerate the intrusion of any intermediary, apart from his own will, between the tools of his craft and the vision that he needs to communicate . . .

When painting retains its independence on the stage, however, it loses the capacity to obey a personal will, since the drama is a barrier between it and the dramatist. Indeed, it is now the poet who is the *artist* (the scene painter is merely his instrument), although the complex arrangement of the setting cannot be deemed to emanate directly from the poet's will, since the dramatic action cannot prescribe its form without music.

On the other hand, everything belonging to the poet-musician's vision, which must be externalized to take on tangible form before our eyes, is brought to the stage *by the music*. It is through the music that the poet-musician finds his vision: music must therefore control every aspect of the staging if that vision is to be given visible form . . .

In this one perceives that the concept of painting is fundamentally broadened when employed in the word-tone drama . . .

The mobility which characterizes stage settings requires that lighting take on many of the functions which colour, on its own, provided to the painter. *The poet-musician creates his picture with light*; it is no longer static colour that depicts the light, but light which takes from colour anything that opposes its mobility . . .

Light may convey colour simply by its own content, or by means of coloured lenses through which it shines, or by projected images, ranging from the most subtle gradation of tones to quite precise effects. A shutter placed in front of the light source can focus a beam on various parts of the stage, while leaving others in darkness, and on this basis a great variety of effects can be achieved from the most simple to various combinations of shapes and projections. The lighting, already mobile on account of the actors, in whose activity it takes part, becomes more so if the lighting instrument is itself moved, or the projections are moved in front of a fixed source, or if the lens in front of the beam is manipulated. The combinations of colours, shapes and movements, varied with one another and with the setting itself, provide endless possibilities. They constitute the palette of the poet-musician.

Both active and diffuse light must fall on some object to enable it to fulfil its function, and although light does not alter the form of these objects, it makes their presence felt and thereby renders them expressive. When coloured, the light changes the tonality of the objects it strikes; when projecting a combination of colours, it creates an image or milieu for those objects which did not exist prior to the projection . . . Such projections alter the very nature of the objects they fall upon (for the spectator), and these objects in turn, through their own form, change the character of the projected images . . .

Whatever colour is not absorbed by the lighting remains an element of the animate or inanimate object to which it belongs, and constitutes that role played by painting (in the narrow and usual sense of the word) in the new type of stage setting. Since this type of painting will no longer necessarily be confined to vertical flats, we return to the spatial arrangement and to the actor himself . . .

The extraordinary dimensions of the poetic-musical text, since they extend into space, do not necessarily create patterns we recognize from everyday experience. The physical form of the actor is the only actual point of contact between reality and the stage setting . . .

It is not the degree of realism that governs the execution of the solid portions of the setting – although at times imitation of actuality may be useful or beautiful – but, disregarding illusion, whether the settings partake of the overall expressiveness called for by the music . . .

Obviously, the painted flats will not be covered with forms and colours that contradict the freedom from realism embodied in the solid elements of the setting . . . painting, no longer required to present realistic or imaginary forms on flats, can instead play in space the harmonizing role of *simplifier* . . .

The poetic-musical text may tend at points of introspection to emphasize the characters, and in doing so will diminish the importance of the other elements of the production hierarchy, and reduce the scenic expressiveness by giving the setting a purely rational and external significance – at times the significance of the actor may to some degree be independent of the development of the other expressive factors. However, because the lighting, by virtue of its flexibility, produces most of the variations in the visual expression, it is also responsible for underscoring the partial and relative independence of the actor.

It is therefore how the actor is lit which determines the degree of importance which his form attains.

In studying the influence of lighting upon the actor's form we return to its purely decorative effect, and must determine how his body can harmonize with the simplifying role of painting.

In our modern settings lighting has no *active* role; its sole purpose is to *render visible* the painted scenery. The actor partakes of this general illumination and in addition is provided with footlights to ensure he is lit from all sides. The lighting intended for the painted flats might be able in some degree to preserve a semblance of activity in regard to the actor, if this were not entirely nullified by the footlights, destroying what little scenic expressiveness had been lent him by virtue of the spatial arrangement.

The paralysing influence of the footlights extends to all the solid objects in the setting, in other words to everything in direct contact with the actor, while also completely separating him from the fictive depictions of the painted flats . . .

The play of facial expression is a *living* thing, which has value only by harmonizing with the essential character of the overall face. Footlights distort the facial expressions because they wash out the contours which are essential to convey character. Features deprived of their true value assume an artificial one . . . the features are divorced from their essential character . . .

Great actors attempting to correct this devise clever makeup to suit their particular style of acting. Sometimes the results are remarkable, but what futile efforts these are, when a different lighting principle – active not just in regard to the overall settings but based on *expressive features* (which naturally would result in greater expressiveness of the whole body) – could be a hundred times more effective in conveying the actor's facial expressions, bodily stances, gestures and movements without encumbering the actor . . .

The stage lighting only serves to make 'visible' the actions of the performer without enhancing their value, and the setting has no relationship to the actor except as a bare minimum of solid pieces with which he can easily become familiar in advance.[21] He has therefore no real regard for the setting, just as it has none for him . . .

Such a state of affairs is not at all abnormal in a dramatic form in which the actor is the only intermediary between the playwright and the audience . . .

Because all the elements of production should work together, as in the example of the staging of the word-tone drama, the particular influence of the footlights, just noted, must be decisively rejected. Their use not only negates the whole *function* of lighting but also, by limiting the scenic expressiveness, distorts the meaning of the production . . .

In any work of art the principle of *sacrifice* rests upon the fairly limited range of our senses. In this regard one could say that the artist adapts nature so that we can appreciate it. But the artist must already have the innate ability to reduce and concentrate the elements that nature provides, for this is what constitutes artistic genius . . . In the case of the word-tone drama, where the sacrifice is perhaps greater than with any other art form, the expressive intensity is at its greatest because the dramatist must renounce a whole range of effects normally used in theatrical practice . . . In fact, when the dramatist employs music he must renounce everything alien to musical expression, while music provides the accurate and continuous expression of the poet's inclination to reduce and concentrate his vision; indeed, the freedom and immense power of musical expression in the word-tone drama depends upon the extent to which the *poet* can achieve such concentration . . . In order to evoke 'the inner essence of the phenomenon' the poet-musician declines to express its insignificant externalities; the production he presents is derived from the major factor of his sacrifice, the music: he thereby realizes for us the concentration imposed on him by the music or, in other words, the *simplification of nature* in favour of the intensification of his expression.

Ideas on a Reform of Our *Mise en Scène*

(1902)

La Revue des revues 1 (9) June 1904: 342–9
Directing the Play, ed. T. Cole and H. K. Chinoy (1953)
Volbach, pp. 101–7; Bablet, 2, pp. 347–52

Dramatic art has been in a process of evolution for several years. Naturalism on the one hand and Wagnerianism on the other have violently displaced earlier boundaries. Certain things which, twenty years ago, were not considered 'theatre' (according to that absurdly hallowed expression) are now almost commonplace. This has caused some confusion: we hardly know now what style suits a particular play; and our taste for foreign productions will not guide us.

On their own, however, such circumstances would not be so bad if the scenery we employ were adapted for each new experiment. Unfortunately, this is not the case. In theory, the author with his text (or score) and the actors may be in full agreement; but on stage in the glare of the lights, the new idea must be forced into the frame, and our directors cut without pity anything that does not fit.

Many assert that it cannot be otherwise, that staging conventions are rigid, etc. etc. I, for one, believe the opposite, and in the following pages I have attempted to set out the basic elements of a *mise en scène* which instead of paralysing and immobilizing dramatic art, not only obediently follows it but also provides the author and his interpreters with an inexhaustible source of suggestions.

Our current stage setting is entirely the slave of painting (scenic painting), which pretends to produce for us an illusion of reality. But this illusion is itself an illusion, because the presence of the actor contradicts it. In fact, the principle of illusion produced by paintings on vertical flats, and the illusion produced by the three-dimensional and living body of the actor, are entirely contradictory. Developing the effects of these two illusions in *isolation*, as is done on our stages, cannot achieve an integrated and artistic production.

Let us examine current staging practice in the light of these two approaches.

It is impossible to place real trees, real houses and the like on our stages, nor would it be very desirable. We suppose that all we can do is to *imitate* reality as faithfully as possible. But the creation of three-dimensional objects is difficult, often impossible, and in any case quite expensive. One might suppose that this would force us to reduce the number of objects to be shown; our stage directors think otherwise: they believe the stage must present everything that seems appropriate, and so anything that can't be created in solid form must be painted . . .

The essential principle of painting, however, is to reduce everything to a flat surface. How then can it fill a space – the stage – which has three dimensions? Without resolving this problem, they cut up the paintings and spread them around on the floor of the stage. The lowest section of the setting is not painted; if the scene depicts a landscape, for example, the upper section will be a green canopy, to the right and left will be trees, upstage an horizon and sky, and the floor, bare boards . . .

Therefore the floor is not actually part of the picture; yet this is the very place where the actor moves! Our directors have forgotten the actor; *Hamlet* without Hamlet, again! Will they not sacrifice a bit of the dead painting in favour of the living and moving body? Never! They would rather renounce the theatre! . . .

We began with painting; now let us see what direction the problem will take if we start with the actor, the solid and mobile human body, viewed entirely with regard to its effect on stage, just as we did with the scenery.

An object appears solid to our eyes only because light strikes it, and obviously its solidity cannot be emphasized artistically except by the artistic use of light. So much for the form. The movement of the human body requires obstacles through which to express itself; all artists understand that the beauty of bodily movements depends upon various points of resistance provided by the floor and other objects. The movement of the actor can therefore only be realized aesthetically in the context of an appropriate arrangement of the floor and objects.

The two fundamental conditions for an artistic rendering of the human body on stage therefore would be light that enhances its three-dimensional quality, and a solidly constructed setting that enhances its postures and movements. We are far removed from painting!

Dominated by painting, stage setting sacrifices the actor and, indeed, as we have seen, a good deal of its own pictorial potential, since the painting has been broken up contrary to the basic concept of such art, and the stage floor is unable to contribute to the illusion created by the flats. What would happen if we subordinated the setting to the actor?

Above all, we would give light its freedom! In fact, dominated by painting, light is completely absorbed by the setting: the things depicted on the flats must be *seen*; light illumines painted light and shadows . . . and from such lighting, alas, the actor takes whatever he can! Under such conditions, there can be no question of true lighting, nor, consequently, of any three-dimensional effect at all! Lighting is an element in its own right, whose effects are limitless. Set free it becomes for us what the palette is to the painter; every colour combination can be created from it; using simple or complex, fixed or mobile projections, partial obstructions, various degrees of transparency, etc. etc., we can achieve infinitely varied effects. Light enables us in effect to give material form to colours and objects which painting fixes on flats, and to bring them alive in space. The actor need no longer walk *in front* of painted lights and shadows, but instead is merged into an atmosphere *which is intended for him* . . .

We are now at the crux of the matter: the three-dimensional quality of the setting necessary for the beauty of the actor's postures and movement. In the past painting has dominated our settings by representing everything that could not be rendered in solid form, for the sole purpose of producing an illusion of reality.

Are the images thereby assembled on the flats indispensable? Not at all: not a single play requires one-hundredth of them; because, do not forget, these images are not alive, they are merely *indicated* on flats as a sort of hieroglyphics; they merely *signify* the things they wish to represent, and this is underscored by their inability to make real, organic contact with the actor. The three-dimensionality demanded by the actor aims at a totally different effect, since the human body does not seek to produce an illusion of reality – *it is itself reality!* What it requires from the setting is simply enhancement of this reality; and of course this in turn entirely alters the purpose of the setting: in the one case it is the realistic depiction of *objects* that is sought, in the other, the greatest possible degree of reality for the human body.

Since these two principles are technically incompatible, one or the other must be chosen. Will it be a collection of lifeless images and a decorative abundance of flats, or the performance of a human being in its physical and moving expression?

If we hesitate, which hardly seems possible, let us ask ourselves what it is we look for in the theatre. We can view beautiful pictures elsewhere, and fortunately not cut up into pieces; photography allows us to travel around the world in our easy-chair; literature inspires us with the most charming scenes, and very few people are so benighted that they cannot appreciate from time to time the grand spectacle of nature. No! We go to the theatre to take part in a dramatic *action*. It is the presence of characters on stage which motivate this action; without them none exists. The actor therefore is the essential element of the production; it is he whom we come to *see*, he to whom we look for that emotion we seek. It is therefore essential to base the production on the presence of the actor and, to do this, to banish everything in conflict with his presence.

The technical problem is thereby quite clearly stated . . .

Our stagings derive from two distinct sources: opera and spoken drama. With few exceptions up to now, operatic singers have been viewed as elegant singing machines, while the painted scenery provided the major visual element: hence its prodigious development. It is different in the spoken drama: here the actor takes first place out of necessity, since without him there can be no play. And if the director sometimes feels he should borrow a bit of luxury from the opera, he does so carefully and without losing sight of the actor . . . Nevertheless, the principle of scenic illusion is the same in spoken drama and in opera, and it is this illusion, of course, which is most seriously impaired. Thus playwrights understand very well the two or three combinations in contemporary staging which can create a touch of illusion despite the actor's presence, and they never venture beyond them.

In recent years, however, things have changed somewhat. In the works of Wagner, opera approaches the spoken drama, which in turn seeks (except for extreme realism) to transcend its earlier limits in order to approach music drama. Yet, oddly enough, we find that our staging practice does not meet the needs of either of them! The absurd display which opera makes of painting has nothing at all to do with Wagner's score (although Wagnerian directors at Bayreuth, like others, do not, it seems, yet suspect this), and the monotonous settings of the spoken drama no longer satisfy the subtle imagination of most playwrights. Everybody senses the need for reform, but the force of inertia still pulls us along in the same rut.

Theories are useful in such a situation, but they do not take us far; we must directly attack scenic practice and gradually transform it.

Perhaps the simplest method would be to take one of our plays that has *already been staged* and demonstrate how production based on the principles outlined above could be achieved . . . A dramatic work should be selected whose requirements are obviously incompatible with our current methods: a play by Maeterlinck,[22] or some other work of that type, or indeed a work by Wagner. The latter would be preferable since music, in precisely defining duration and the intensity of expression, is a valuable guide; moreover, the sacrifice of illusion in this case would be less striking than in a spoken drama . . . The question of light will concern us first of all; we shall experience the tyranny of painting on vertical flats, and come to understand, not just theoretically but in a most tangible way, the immense harm still done to the actor and, through him, to the playwright . . .

We can take, for example, the second act of *Siegfried*. How are we to represent a forest on the stage? First of all let us clarify this issue: is it a *forest* with characters, or *characters* in a forest? We are in the theatre to participate in a dramatic action; an action takes place in this forest which obviously cannot be expressed by painting. This is our point of departure: this or that person does one thing and another, and says such and such in a forest. In order to create our settings, we need not visualize a forest, but we must represent in great detail the entire range of events that occur in this forest. Complete understanding of the score is therefore essential, and totally transforms the type of vision that can inspire the director. His eyes will remain fixed on the *characters*; he will think of the forest as a particular atmosphere encompassing the actors, an atmosphere which can only be achieved *in relation* to the living and moving beings on whom, therefore, he must concentrate. So the setting will never be envisaged as an arrangement of lifeless paintings, but will always be alive. The production thereby becomes the composition of a picture in time: instead of starting with a painting commissioned by one nonentity for another, and then retaining for the actor the whole assemblage of shabby devices with which we are familiar, we begin with the actor. It is his performance which we wish to underscore artistically; we are prepared to sacrifice everything for that. It shall always be Siegfried here and Siegfried there: the tree for Siegfried and the path for Siegfried.

I repeat, we shall no longer attempt to give the illusion of a *forest* but instead the illusion of a *man* in the atmosphere of a forest; man is the reality and the rest is of no importance. Whatever this man touches must be intended for him, everything else must help to create the atmosphere required by him, and if leaving Siegfried for a moment we lift our gaze from him, the scenic picture need not convey to us any further illusion; it serves only Siegfried. And when the forest, stirred gently by a breeze, attracts Siegfried's attention, we, the spectators, *will observe Siegfried* bathed in lights and moving shadows, and no longer moving among bits of cut-up canvas operated by ropes.

Scenic illusion is the living presence of the actor.

The setting for this act as presented to us on all the stages of the world quite fails to meet our conditions! We shall have to simplify it a good deal, refrain from lighting painted flats as is currently demanded, almost completely rearrange the stage floor, and above all we must provide an electrical apparatus for the lighting, installed on a grand scale and controlled with great subtlety. The footlights – those astonishing monstrosities – will hardly ever be used . . .

An undertaking of this sort cannot fail to show us the way forward for transforming our rigid and conventional staging into an *artistic* medium, living, subtle, and suitable for realizing any dramatic vision. We may even be surprised that we have neglected so important a branch of art for such a long time and have abandoned it, as not meriting our direct attention, to those who are not artists. Our aesthetic judgement is still completely anaesthetized in regard to theatrical production; someone who would never tolerate in his own home an object which was not in good taste finds it perfectly acceptable to buy an expensive seat in an ugly hall, constructed

Figure 10 Appia's rhythmic space design of 1909, 'The Forest Glade'. He wrote of it, 'The light is filtered, as necessary or desirable, through hidden cut-outs of cardboard, and the shadows that fall on the characters can thus become mobile' (Appia 1960: 116). Cf. Appia's description of the setting for *Siegfried*, Act II: 'We shall no longer attempt to give the illusion of a *forest* but instead the illusion of a *man* in the atmosphere of a forest; man is the reality and the rest is of no importance.'

illogically, and to witness for hours a spectacle so debased that by comparison coloured postcards sold by a street pedlar are refined works of art.

The elements of stage design are based, like those of other arts, on forms, light and colour; because these three elements are entirely within our control, we can use them artistically in the theatre as elsewhere. Up until now production has had to achieve the greatest possible degree of illusion, and this principle (hardly an aesthetic one) has paralysed us. I have attempted to demonstrate in these pages that scenic art should be based on the one reality worthy of the theatre: the human body; and we have noted the first and most basic consequences of this reform.

The subject is difficult and complex primarily because of the misunderstandings that surround it and the ingrained viewing habits of modern spectators. In order to persuade people, the idea must be far more extensively developed: it would be necessary to talk about an entirely new duty which rests upon the actor, about the influence that scenic and artistic material inevitably exercise upon the dramatic author, the stylistic power of music in production, the necessary modifications in the architecture of the stage and auditorium, etc. etc. It is impossible for me to accomplish this here, but perhaps the reader will find in my aesthetic aspiration something that anticipates his own and, if so, he can easily continue this work himself.

Part II

Writings on eurhythmics

Introduction

In his essay, 'Theatrical experiences and personal investigations' Appia describes the overwhelming importance that his first encounter with Dalcroze's system of musical gymnastics, eurhythmics, had for all his subsequent work. It enabled him to extend the application of his theories for reform beyond Wagner's operas into other works of music-drama, and later to suggest entirely new forms of theatrical art. In his earlier writings Appia had proposed that stage movement should be dictated by the music, although he had not yet determined any formal means whereby this musically motivated movement was to be controlled and measured in space.

He recognized at once the relevance of eurhythmics to his work, and wrote to Dalcroze to introduce himself and announce that 'the externalization of music . . . is an idea that I have desired for many years . . . Nothing can save music from sumptuous decadence except externalization . . . On the other hand, the life of the body tends towards anarchy and therefore towards grossness. It is music that can liberate it by imposing its discipline upon it' (Stadler 1965: 417–18). Dalcroze recalled many years later this first contact with Appia, 'a long letter in which . . . in the very clearest fashion he identified the future course of my efforts' (Stadler 1964: 662).

Appia's first written expression of faith in what was to become a veritable aesthetic religion for him was published in August 1906, only a few months after his initiation. 'Return to music' outlined very briefly the nature of eurhythmics, and invited readers to participate in a two-week summer course. Appia himself took part and later described the experience in his essay of 1911, 'The origin and beginnings of eurhythmics'.

In April 1908 Appia published an article, 'Comments on the theatre', which although not included here, should be mentioned chiefly for its comprehensive reiteration of his critical analysis of the state of theatrical art (in particular his dismissal of current scenic practice), together with a review of his ideas for the future. Written after Appia's first experience and initial espousal of eurhythmics, but before he engaged in substantial practical work with Dalcroze, it shows the influence the subject was already exercising on his thinking, through the emphasis he places on the relationship between music and human rhythm. His insistence that 'the new scenic order will be based on the presence of the human body, of the plastic and moving body', to which everything will be subordinated, foreshadows his great and innovative work. He also presents his analysis of the differing

69

role of 'sign' and 'expression' in dramatic art, a subject that would figure prominently in his later theory.

Appia quickly perceived that the implications of eurhythmics were not limited to musical sensitivity, or consequent bodily movement, but that they extended to scenic design as well. He insisted that henceforth scenic artists should 'design with your legs, not with your eyes' (Van Wyck 1925: 18). The result was the series of about twenty 'Rhythmic Spaces' which he prepared and submitted to Dalcroze in the spring of 1909. At the same time he wrote the article 'Style and solidarity', which was published in September. In this he began to develop ideas he had touched upon earlier, and which would dominate his later theory: the need to overcome the passivity of the spectators by directly involving them in the work of art. Through rhythm, the body could be actively engaged in music and enter what Appia (in one of his earliest uses of the term) designated 'Living Art'.

In the same article he referred in passing to the potential of public festivals for reaffirming 'solidarity' through a sense of reciprocity between a community and its collective expression in art. In the autumn, when the invitation was extended to Dalcroze and Appia to establish an institute at the Garden City of Hellerau, the way was open to realize such ideas in their fullest form. Eurhythmics was to become the defining and motivating spirit of the Hellerau experiment. By March 1910 finance had been secured, and Dalcroze could exhort Appia, 'Take heart, my dear collaborator . . . for our efforts and plans are almost realized' (Stadler 1965: 429).

Dalcroze resisted thinking of eurhythmics as either a technical method or a spectacle. It was meant to enable the student to react to and express whatever music he applied it to, without lapsing into the purely abstract or improvised creation of pleasing visual effects. Only gradually, under Appia's influence, did he come to recognize and accept that what had begun as training in musical sensitivity had vast implications for theatrical reform, an area which initially had held little interest for Dalcroze. He also hoped and expected that its practitioners would move beyond a totally mechanical relationship to the music to use music so that its expression through the body became a deeply personal and liberating experience.

However, as he made clear in 'Eurhythmics and the theatre', an article written in April 1911, Appia nurtured more expansive hopes. In that month the cornerstone of the Institute was laid. This building – which later observers have claimed marked the beginning of the modern theatre – was to embody many of Appia's most advanced ideas and would, in turn, provide the vital testing ground for still others. As he noted in his article, 'Eurhythmics has taken a positive step towards a complete reform of our scenic and dramatic conception.' Slowly the development and gener-ation of a new form of art became the guiding principle and chief goal of the Hellerau Institute. In the same article Appia announced plans for a series of summer festivals which would 'certainly constitute the most significant, the most decisive step on the road to the victory of *living art*'.

A little later, in July of that same summer, after returning from Hellerau, Appia wrote a second article, 'The origin and beginnings of eurhythmics'. In it he described the evolution of the system, and of the process of 'synthesis' through which Dalcroze and he had developed and progressed. It expressed the highest admiration for what Appia characterized as Dalcroze's 'educational genius', and hardly hinted at the role he himself had played in its enlightenment. In fact, Appia became the motivating, somewhat mysterious, but always benevolent genius of Hellerau. Reticent, sometimes remote, and rarely seen, he determined and guided its development.

During that summer of 1911, as the Institute was being constructed, Appia was, typically, analysing, reviewing and developing his theories, while Dalcroze, just as characteristically, was actively engaged with his students on an exhibition tour. On this tour he attended a production of Gluck's *Orpheus and Eurydice* which disgusted him with its heavy and traditional staging. It occurred to him to offer the second act of that opera as part of the Institute's presentations at the first festival. Initially he only wished to demonstrate eurhythmics' usefulness in achieving a purer and simpler staging, while essentially adhering to the traditional tenets and conventions of the illusionistic theatre. But the designs which Appia laid before him were startling, and so unprecedented that they quite precluded the possibility of any remotely orthodox production. They dictated an altogether different approach.

Dalcroze worked on the choreography for *Orpheus* from the first day of classes in the autumn of 1911. He was extremely disconcerted, however, to discover how different practising in the recently completed hall was from work in more traditional venues; his initial plans and exercises were invariably altered when the students tried to perform them in the new building. This made him even more dependent on Appia's confident advice and encouragement. Throughout the year, they continued to refine their ideas and plans.

The evolution of Appia's ideas during this period is evident in the article 'Eurhythmics and light', written in 1912 prior to the first festival that summer but never published in his lifetime. The extraordinary system of flexible lighting, which he had devised at the Institute, was to be used to achieve two of his major objectives: to emphasize the living and expressive quality of the human body in rhythmic movement in space; and to break down the barriers which, traditionally, had governed and restricted the spectators' perception of the work of art in performance. At the same time, because of its great flexibility and control, the lighting system allowed what Appia termed 'luminous sound' to be employed. Light, music and movement could be carefully coordinated and integrated to create subtle

71

and expressive effects which previously had been virtually unimagined, much less achieved.

Appia recognized that light provided an invaluable medium for linking music, movement and stage setting in 'a perfect fusion', thereby creating uniquely expressive works of art. His attention to the detail of such expression extended to every aspect of production, one of which he delineated at this time in the essay, 'Concerning the costume for eurhythmics' (1912). He realized that costume not only had direct practical implications for the effect of the lighting and for signifying the nature of the aesthetic activity (pedagogical exercise, fictive representation, shared communal event, etc.), but that it acted forcefully upon the psychology of the participants as well. Indeed, it could help to unite both performers and spectators in a single act of artistic expression.

In an age when ordinary clothing was quite modest and restrictive and had the effect of de-emphasizing the physical (not to mention the sexual) nature of the body, both the wearing in public and the viewing of scant, form-fitting tights (with bare legs and feet!), were profoundly disorienting. The reaction might frequently be shock or disapproval, but it could also lead to a strong sense of both physical and psychological liberation. Part of the extraordinary appeal of eurhythmics to its adherents (many of whom embraced it as a veritable secular religion, a 'cult without gods') is undoubtedly due to such factors. Appia's analysis shows him to be entirely aware of this phenomenon, and of its aesthetic potential.

In the same essay Appia looks forward confidently to future festivals at Hellerau and the promise there of further marvellous achievements. But, despite the astonishing reception of the 1913 festival, plans had to be dropped for 1914, and with the outbreak of the war the association of both Appia and Dalcroze with Hellerau ceased. Instead, in July 1914, the two men were involved in a patriotic festival in Geneva, the Fête de Juin. For this they employed some 200 pupils of eurhythmics along with the same number of supernumeraries for the presentation of tableaux, performing a very elaborate, intricately organized production: a synthesis of the arts of music, dance, drama and singing. The students functioned rather as a Greek chorus, a great crowd whose words and gestures commented upon and interpreted the dramatic action, and whose movements were themselves a powerful element of artistic expression.

Unfortunately, despite the profound success of the Geneva production, Appia and Dalcroze did not work together frequently afterwards. In 1915 Dalcroze opened a new institute for eurhythmics in Geneva and continued to present the type of exercises and performances seen at Hellerau. Appia from time to time participated in the work there. In June 1920 they presented a new staging of the pantomine *Echo and Narcissus*, first performed at Hellerau and now, its settings adapted to the Institute, with considerable acclaim in Geneva. A production of *A Midsummer Night's Dream*, for which

Appia provided some very novel designs during the same period as he prepared settings and a scenario for *Hamlet*, was planned for the winter of 1921–2, but failed to take place.

Gradually, however, Dalcroze reverted to his former attitude, to emphasize the pedagogical aspects of his work as musical training, and largely abandoned any further work of significance aimed at extending and expanding its relevance to theatrical presentation or dance. For his part, Appia, building upon the ideas suggested by and explored through eurhythmics, moved ever more deeply into theoretical investigations, which further estranged him from Dalcroze. He resigned from the Geneva Institute in 1923. Nevertheless, eurhythmics remained for him an indispensable element, both for effective production of orthodox theatre (he used it in his 1924–5 Basle productions of the *Ring* and *Prometheus*) and for new forms of 'living art'. In dedicating *The Work of Living Art* to Dalcroze, he characterized eurhythmics as his 'aesthetic homeland'.

Theatrical Experiences and Personal Investigations
(1921) [Excerpts]

Volbach, pp. 47–72; Bablet, 4, pp. 36–56

In 1906 . . . I attended a demonstration by Jaques-Dalcroze of eurhythmics, which was then at its beginning. In *Music and the Art of the Theatre* I had already called for a 'musical gymnastics' as essential for the singing performer, but I of course had no idea of how to set about developing these. Dalcroze revealed them to me, and from that point on I could clearly see the route my progress would follow. The discovery of the basic principle of the *mise en scène* was only the starting point; eurhythmics determined my further progress.

One summer in Geneva I experimented myself with eurhythmics . . . Up to now only the musical movement of the body had been revealed to me, but not yet its resonance in space . . . I persuaded Dalcroze to provide stairs and some rostra.

Dalcroze invited me in the spring of 1909 to view a production he had carefully organized using his own music, costumes, coloured light, etc. I left the performance feeling depressed, and . . . seizing paper and pencils I designed feverishly, each day, two or three *space designs* intended for rhythmic movement. When I had about twenty I submitted them to Dalcroze with a note explaining that his pupils were constantly moving on a flat surface . . . My designs caused great enthusiasm . . . This is how the style of space appropriate for the rhythmic movement of the body was first formulated . . .

I shall call this *corporeal space*, which becomes *living space* once the body animates it . . . Whereas earlier, in the case of Wagner, I had based my designs on the performer, now lacking a score, I thought I could begin with space itself, but I failed miserably. Finally I understood! If I lacked a score, I at least had the living body . . . This conclusion liberated me . . . Wherever the pencil touched the paper it evoked the naked body, the naked limbs. The active role of light developed naturally from a spatial arrangement which demanded it, and everything thereby took on the *appearance of expectancy*: the nature of the space made the presence of the body indispensable . . .

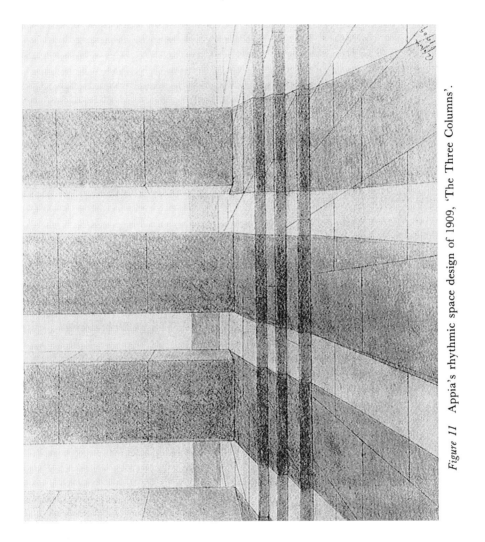

Figure 11   Appia's rhythmic space design of 1909, 'The Three Columns'.

Without changing my basic orientation, eurhythmics freed me from too rigid a tradition, and in particular from the decorative romanticism of Wagner. In order to convince Dalcroze of how important it was to vary rhythmic exercises from their earlier limitation to the flat floor alone, I composed a number of spatial designs. They fulfilled their purpose. By means of these designs I gradually achieved a purity of style which was composed for the most part of lines and solid forms. The resistance they provide to the movement of the body complements its expressive quality and creates a three-dimensional effect . . .

From my childhood, the living human body dominated my imagination and determined my career. It was the motivating force behind my reform of Wagnerian staging; it led me towards the human body as a form of art, which was revealed to me by the Dalcroze method . . .

The first time I attended a eurhythmics session my impressions were complex and surprising. At first I found myself moved to tears, recalling how long I had waited. But soon I was aware of a new force entirely unknown to me! I was no longer in the audience; I was on the stage with the performers! . . .

The Dalcroze exercises that I viewed were suitable as a demonstration, but they should have been arranged differently for a performance, not restricted to a formula that clearly was of no interest to anyone except the actual performers themselves . . . Suddenly the stage curtain seemed absurd and barbarous to me; one after the other, my traditional notions tumbled and I imagined myself in a limitless space with the students. I did not yet realize, however, that my revelation was not complete. A further important step had yet to be taken – that from a vividly imagined intuition to the living experience of one's own body . . .

My personal experience with eurhythmics completed my evolution, precisely determined it once and for all, and decided my future.

Return to Music

(1906)

Journal de Genève 20 August 1906
Volbach, pp. 127–9; Bablet, 3, pp. 32–4

Are we not often uncomfortable when we consider our passive attitude towards works of art?

To what has our degree of collaboration been reduced? Good will . . . sometimes; at best we contribute a few bits of education and culture. In short, we approach works of art, of whatever sort, like tasters; it is there, we are here, each quite separate, and we make the situation even worse by our inclination towards minimum exertion. Thus culture, having provided us with the means to comprehend art at our convenience, appears to keep it at a distance from us, outside of us. And in fact our education encourages this situation by presenting the elements of knowledge as something entirely external to us.

There may, however, be a reaction taking place. Contemporary teaching methods, seeking to find the basis of knowledge within the child itself, have begun to assist him in assimilating such things as can only really be communicated to him from outside.

In some schools which aim at a healthy balance of mental and physical hygiene the instruction has made considerable progress in this direction. Contemporary development in the plastic arts has to some degree achieved communion between the artist and those who appreciate art. Music, by contrast, remains what we have made of it: an object of speculation, ever more detached from inspiration, a contrivance quite separate from us, outside of us, capable of being conveyed only as knowledge. Consequently, we view music as a virtuosity, a combination of elements independent of our personal, physical and moral life; in short, a phenomenon that is entirely intellectual in spite of all its specific appeal to the senses.

The teaching of music remains, therefore, external.

Undoubtedly we have discovered that music finds in the movement of the body a uniquely precise and attractive expression. Wagner desired, without accomplishing it, a visual expression in his dramatic presentation appropriate to that of the music; at our popular festivals we sometimes do this very eloquently; those transfixed by music are able occasionally to express it in visual terms; Miss [Isadora] Duncan[1] has enchanted us with her interesting if not fully realized art, etc. Nevertheless, music remains currently and for us Occidentals an intellectual contrivance inculcated in those who then believe they have mastered it. For example, instead of learning the origin of rhythm, we are taught only the conventional signs of various rhythms . . .

Music, meanwhile, goes its own way, developing to an extraordinary degree its own means and techniques which (despite their completely intellectual origin), do not greatly engage our minds, but instead futilely affect our nerves and often evoke a life of decidedly disordered sensations. The very art that we claim to exalt the most, which we appear to preserve with the greatest care and with which we so recklessly imbue our existence, is ultimately an art which we have lost track of, and must rediscover and renovate.

A musician and teacher, a scrupulous researcher, has become convinced of this deficiency. His conviction does not arise from any personal and speculative impression; rather it has impressed itself on him, gradually, but irresistibly, in the course of his teaching, until he has felt forced to acknowledge that 'music is within man'. He adds that 'the role of the mind is to control and classify, to harmonize and balance the natural responses from which we have become estranged'. His desire is 'to restore to the body its eurhythmics';[2] 'to make music vibrate within it'; he dreams of 'making music an integral part of the organism'; of 'playing this marvellous keyboard, the muscular and nervous system, in order to express in three-dimensional form a definite thought in space as it is [through music] in time . . .'

Instruction in music must therefore begin, before all else, with the search for music in the person of the student himself, by 'awakening in him an awareness of the relationship between body and mind'. Knowledge of the conventional signs required for musical notation should take second place, and the correct execution of these signs on any particular instrument remains optional . . .

But how can such instruction be achieved? What methods can enable us to recover 'these natural functions from which we have become separated'?

This is what M. Jaques-Dalcroze intends to demonstrate for us in a very complete course specifically designed for teachers . . .

Obviously, this course is the result of strenuous labour . . . Only a deep sense of responsibility towards his fellow men could sustain such selfless effort when other routes readily lead to success. This reform, like any other, if it is to be understood, demands our passionate desire to prepare at any price for the future, that which the present cannot provide us.

To attempt to re-establish the relationship between music and our body, and thereby to rediscover that ancient eurhythmics – so long forgotten that it seems an almost fantastic novelty today – is indeed a daring undertaking. It requires magnificent audacity to conceive it. It is up to us now to abandon our indolence and dilettantism, to discard our preconceived ideas and our accumulated prejudices, and follow courageously the way to a rebirth which is infinitely desirable. The immediate results are already surprising. There is every reason to hope that the future will gradually return music to us!

Style and Solidarity

(1909)

Le Rythme 1 (6), Sept. 1909: 49–52
Der Rhythmus 1 (6), Sept. 1909: 49–53
Volbach, pp. 131–4; Bablet, 3, pp. 70–6

In antiquity the word style is known to have indicated the stiletto which was used to write on wax tablets. The great significance which we today ascribe to the word therefore has its origin in the phenomenon of writing.

When we take up a pen and pass it in a methodical fashion over the paper to set down our thoughts, we feel thereby *responsible* for the resulting lines. We consider the slightest error in the writing as a form of deceit, for this mute language arises from our most secret intentions; it is an image of ourselves . . .

Along with the handwriting itself, we also apply the word *style* to the arrangement of our ideas and their expression in written form. We rightly say that one recognizes the individual by his writing: 'style is the man' . . . we reveal ourselves in the ideas we intend for others. Anyone, for example, with some sense of the art of letter writing knows precisely the extent to which a letter is a true expression of himself – quite apart from its actual content – and the psychological importance which may be ascribed to the correspondence.

Style is the man! Let us broaden the meaning of the word still further and apply it to all the arts, with, however, the distinction that we may speak of *belonging* to a style, and *having* a style. By the former term we designate a classification: it is obvious that those who created an architectural form or a type of painting could not give these a name, any more than a warrior could say he departed for the Hundred Years War. To work in this or that style means to imitate it. The latter expression – to have a style – designates a personal and living quality and is directly connected with that which we feel about a style of handwriting or writing itself: it is a quality for which the artist is *responsible*.

Nevertheless, at this point a new element appears: the audience. When the artist displays his works to the gaze of all, he must ask himself if his dream, the subject of his work, deserves the expression he has given it.

80

He feels responsible for what he is, and consequently, for what he has given of himself.

Does this feeling concern only the artist? Are we merely his audience, taking no part in the actual subject of his dream?

What respectful person is able today to feel happy and content amongst the columns of the Parthenon, in St Mark's Cathedral, or in any Egyptian temple? Do we not enter the Louvre, or the [Munich] Pinakothek, shyly? And do we not think it strange when we depart in silence from our seats after listening for two hours to the Ninth Symphony? Finally, do we not in all these places avoid looking at ourselves in the mirror that our modern conscience so ably provides for us?

Yes, indeed! We have a feeling of *responsibility* towards the work of art, and this compels us to lie. We know perfectly well that art must be lived, and not simply contemplated, and we view dilettantism with contempt . . . because in this regard we despise ourselves.

There exists, therefore, a *solidarity* between the artist and us; prudently we arrange the paintings and statues in our museums and the musical selections in our programmes; otherwise, what might we do with them?

It is also prudent to darken our auditoria and always attempt as much as possible to separate the work from the audience, and art from ourselves.

In doing this, however, we forget the fact that the artist creates – or ought to create – his efforts from out of our life! We rob the artist of his subjects and force him into artificial creation. It is we who commit the aesthetic crime, and then accuse the artist of distancing himself from us and no longer *offering* us intelligible works.

But what in the name of justice do we *offer* him that entitles us to be so demanding?

We view art like the manufacture of luxury goods: someone displays them to us, we select from them – just as in a pastry shop – those that suit our taste, and we have forced some artists to become pastrycooks. Those works which do not suit our palate we leave in the shop window and know only by their appearance. We classify, evaluate and reject without having experienced for so much as a moment a work that thus remains foreign to us. But how can we ever respond to a work if we do not feel from the outset that we have ourselves provided the model for it? Do not our tears of aesthetic enjoyment flow *only when* we recognize ourselves in the work of art: who else would shed them otherwise?

We are all responsible for style in our arts. If music debauches itself, then we are to blame; and if the painters have prepared for their works a fictional society, and thereby alienated themselves from life and even from that quality which they most ardently pursue – from style – then the failure lies in us. We must vigilantly nurture in ourselves a sense of this overwhelming responsibility . . . We must preserve the sense of shame and confusion which assaults us when we confront ancient works generated by a homogeneous society, indeed before all that past which seems to sneer at us. We should enter Notre Dame not for pleasure but to be made uncomfortable . . .

Through such repeated discomfort, instilled in us body and soul, and through the passionate desire to liberate ourselves from it, we shall again find and take up the forgotten weapons necessary to conquer the *public* within ourselves.

In the art of the theatre a movement is already evident in this direction. Our eyes have opened and been aroused by the spectacles offered to us. We are shocked by the speculative exploitation of our inertia and at the low social status into which we have carelessly consigned our theatre. It sickens us that we have given over the most powerful elements of theatrical production into whatever servile hands are available, when in fact the forms, colours, light and their thousands of marvellous combinations belong to us!

Our festivals, particularly in Switzerland, have taught us that art must spring forth from *all* of our hearts, and must be presented by *all* our bodies. How often, too, we have wished that these festivals might no longer be offered as mere spectacles![3] The dignity of our dramatic impulse is awakening, and none too soon! *Living* fiction is the triumphal arch that leads to all the other arts; for through it we bear witness to our aesthetic conscience and our feelings of close solidarity.

It alone can return to us once more some sense of dignity in regard to a work of art, and can guide us towards the acquisition of *style*.

That transfiguring art which unites our organism through rhythm with the undeniable expression of our soul seems to have lost its way. But it is not it which has become confused, but rather its shadow. On the contrary, music is quite close to us. Let us not resist it; we have surrendered to it the burning expression of our inner life, let us yield too to its new pleas, and deliver to it unreservedly the rhythm of our bodies, which it wishes to transform and immerse in an aesthetic space of shadows and light, of forms and colours, organized and brought to life by its creative breath.

In embarking on the path of *living* art, who does not feel the law of aesthetic solidarity burning in the depths of his soul, while his dilettantic lassitude vanishes once and for all? Yes, art is indeed a great collective text! One cannot counterfeit it with impunity; and when the pen which must form great living characters trembles in our hand, a voice calls out to us, 'Beware! Style reveals the man!' Let us beware, indeed, of falsifying the text, and of the advice of calligraphers who have hitherto duped us.

Let us *trust* our hand; the lines are clumsy at first. What does it matter? They are ours and *they will have style because we shall be responsible for them, and art will live in us!*

The Origin and Beginnings of Eurhythmics

(1911)

Les Feuillets 11, Nov. 1911: 393–403
Der Rhythmus, Ein Jahrbuch 1, Sept. (?) 1911: 20–31
Volbach, pp. 141–7; Bablet, 3, pp. 140–5

The origin of a work of any type is found in the personality of its author and not in external circumstances; these may play some small part in impeding or encouraging the success and promulgation of the work, but they cannot initiate it.

The essential quality of eurhythmics can be seen to lie in the fact that from its beginnings it has gathered the elements of its *discipline* not from without, but from within, just as a shrub draws its sap from the nourishing soil through which it spreads its roots. In looking for the cause of this phenomenon within the personality of Jaques-Dalcroze, we shall undoubtedly attain a firmer and more profound understanding of his great work and its origin.

Two distinct qualities led him in his search for an *organic* unity between music and the human body. These correspond precisely with his two major traits: on the one hand, his *educational genius*, and on the other what I shall term his *genius for synthesis* . . .

One of the most remarkable traits of Dalcroze's educational genius is that the Master is unable to regard his pupils *en masse*. They are to him a group of quite separate individuals, and instinctively he treats them as such. As a result he develops a keen sense of observation; an observation which is uniquely creative. If we add to this, almost by way of corollary, that he is absolutely incapable of crystallizing or systematizing anything, desiring a free field of vision at all times in order to recreate *with his pupils* an ever-renewed life, then we shall have a better understanding of the beginnings of eurhythmics, which from the first were so simple that they almost defied definition . . .

By genius for synthesis I mean the driving need to combine all the expressive elements of an integrated artistic life. Dalcroze possesses the *gift for life* to a rare degree; one might say that individual elements, of whatever sort, have no value for him except as they take part in the concert of life . . .

Thus, on the one hand, were his observations of individual students during his lessons – and particularly those in *solfeggio*[4] – which provided him with an inexhaustible source of ideas; on the other were his attempts at synthesis, such as his children's songs which were partly mimed and dramatized . . . The two traits of observation and synthesis joined to supply Dalcroze with the evidence and experience required for his first experiments with bodily rhythmics.

In his educational role, he asked his students during the *solfeggio* lessons to beat time, because he sensed the advantage of a movement that would somehow provide direct physical contact with the music. In the majority of them such gestures engendered a feeling of harmony and even of beauty, and did not remain merely a technical aid. As a teacher-artist, Dalcroze observed that this discipline caused his pupils' bodies to lose some of their passivity, as if these were taking part in the gestures of the hands and thereby allowing the musical rhythm to permeate them.

From the other point of view, that of synthesis, he observed in the course of the children's performance of songs the very special pleasure the child took in combining the songs with appropriate movement, and the beneficial effect of this movement on the body, quite apart from the enjoyment the child always takes in any kind of make-believe . . . He noted that the gestures and attitudes accompanied the music quite well, but only in a simple juxtaposition; no matter how precisely these actions were done, the movement and music were not organically and inseparably fused to create a single mode of expression . . . he realized that to achieve such organic fusion he would first of all have to get the will to act in harmony with the delayed reactions of the body, through rigorous rhythmic training . . .

The situation was actually becoming dangerous. Certain callisthenic displays had led them into experiments in pure plasticity and external beauty, and to the imitation of works of art; his extraordinary talent, along with the youthful enthusiasm of his pupils, carried them relentlessly towards the superficial pleasing of eyes and ears, without the discipline necessary to control and direct such pleasure . . .

The development of what we now know as eurhythmics arose from Dalcroze's understanding of his pupils as individuals. He would never have achieved the prudence and sense of aesthetic respect which now ensure the future of his art had he not been able to perceive in each of his pupils the purely human feeling, and they in turn would not have extended to him the unswerving loyalty so necessary to a man of genius had they not felt their teacher's concern and affection for each of them as an individual. This entirely personal *interchange* enabled the genius of Dalcroze to find its way and achieve victory.

. . . The *solfeggio* exercises, which had demonstrated the problem, now provided the key to resolve it.

The Master and his students – henceforth inseparable – wondered if while beating time with their arms, it might somehow be possible to mark the rhythm with the legs and feet . . . They attempted this, and called it 'faire les pas'.

It was the beginning of eurhythmics . . .

Gradually a sort of basic alphabet was established; attempts were made to develop physical exercises which would provide the equivalent for the body of the musical elements of *solfeggio* for the voice . . .

In the autumn of 1904 Dalcroze rented a small hall close to the Geneva Conservatory [where he worked]. There the heroic labour, the slow and difficult conquest of the unknown[5] continued in the free time available after formal instruction. While Geneva ignored, or attempted to ignore, the great work germinating within its walls, a few young girls, the pupils of Dalcroze, and their parents began quietly and without being aware of it to prepare, through the example of their confidence and loyalty, the brilliant future of Hellerau.

In May 1905 the results of this training allowed a public demonstration to be given on the 'steps' at Soleure during the annual festival of Swiss musicians. The substantial success and the reaction of teachers and musicians encouraged Dalcroze to submit a detailed report to the governing board of the Geneva Conservatory with the request that a regular course [in eurhythmics] be introduced. The board remained entirely unmoved and categorically refused this request. In order to enlighten the public, in September of the same year Dalcroze gave a long lecture, without, however, any demonstrations with his pupils. As always, he was heard with pleasure, but did his audience understand him?

Finally, his desire to commence a regular course induced him to rent an appropriate hall. And in this hall the great year of discovery began!

The artist of genius sees the completed work of art before him as if it were an enigma. He questions it; sometimes it responds. When this work is a finished whole, such as a painting, a statue, a symphony or a poem, then the answer is clearer. When the work is not presented to the public in so definite a form, but, on the contrary, must evolve slowly and gradually in the course of time, and even though finished when it begins can never be really completed because it is *living*; in such a circumstance the enigma is overwhelming . . .

This was the situation of Jaques-Dalcroze and his students at the point when they began their regular course in eurhythmics.

That winter an incident took place that had a fortunate effect on Dalcroze's work. An artist often suffers from being unable to define and organize the ideas that crowd and clamour in his mind. He needs a terminology . . . Monsieur Edouard Claparède, the professor of psycho-physiology at the University of Geneva, who was keenly interested in what he had seen and understood of eurhythmics, had a number of discussions with Dalcroze. In these he provided him with an invaluable terminology and enabled him to ground his educational and aesthetic experiments on scientific facts . . . From this point on he developed what – although certainly not a systematic approach – was a deliberate and rational method of instruction and observation.

In the spring of 1906 an extended demonstration of eurhythmics and plasticity, together with lectures, was presented in a municipal hall.[6] The audience was full of curiosity, but had no understanding of the significance of the event. Often the Master had to leave the piano to go to the front of the stage and entreat the spectators not to think of the demonstration as an act of theatre . . . he had to remind them that it was a new educational experiment; an attempt to transfer musical rhythm into the body. It was a successful presentation, but produced no practical result.

During the summer of the same year the memorable first regular course took place, in which Dalcroze over the period of a fortnight undertook to present the results of his investigations. All the participants expected that the course would be a series of lectures illustrated with student exercises, and thus edified, they would return home thoroughly informed about eurhythmics. How mistaken they were! After five minutes the Master let us know that everyone had to descend into the arena to undergo the great experience for themselves! Everyone refused. Was intelligence not enough; did the whole body have to take part!? Did one have to expose oneself to this ridiculous test? The moment was both comic and serious. Indeed it was serious; for eurhythmics it meant 'to be or not to be'. It was *necessary* that from then on everyone should understand that eurhythmics is a *personal experience* and not a method. At all costs, it must be so. Oh, the power of a personality! After a quarter of an hour, ladies and gentlemen of every age and nationality, dressed in street clothes, were moving about attentive and dutiful to the Master's commands! . . . Of course, to those not in the know, they presented the most incomprehensible spectacle.

Similar courses were given during the summers of 1907, 1908 and 1909. They were ever more fully attended and more sophisticated, and ever more remarkable since each winter further study had enriched the experience of the teacher and enhanced the form of instruction. At the end of the 1909 course the first examination for teachers' certification took place . . .

Meanwhile Dalcroze organized lecture tours and demonstrations, using some of his best students. How is one to describe the amount of work, exertion and initiative; how can one measure the indomitable perseverance and courage displayed by this fearless man during these five years!? In Geneva, where in fact he was amongst friends, his work met with mere indifference, if not outright rejection; or even more depressing, with the empty and transient enthusiasm of a few aesthetes. It was only in Germany that his work found a response and serious attention . . .

In the spring of 1910, after a triumphal demonstration at Dresden, Herr

Schmidt, founder of the Garden City of Hellerau near Dresden and of the factory there of the *Werkstätte*, invited Dalcroze to organize and direct the musical life of this small town as it was being brought into being.[7] Dalcroze requested a little time to consider, and returned to Geneva.

Shortly thereafter Dr Wolf Dohrn, the founder of the *Werkbund*, who was also interested in the establishment of Hellerau, came to Geneva together with his brother Harold.[8] He came to offer to construct for Dalcroze a model institute on a hill at Hellerau, and to provide along with this impressive establishment everything necessary for the development and expansion of his work. Along with students from many countries who would flock to this centre of life, the Master would have the opportunity to teach the children and young people of that little garden city and to find, as it were, virgin soil better suited for receiving his instruction than that already spoilt by the practices of our ordinary schools. Thus Dr Dohrn, with affection and respect, held out his powerful hand to an artist of genius who up until then had for years had to rely only on himself as he battled against impossible odds. And this hand offered a tireless worker a most valuable reward: the means to continue his work, but now with successful results.

How could he refuse such an offer? After some discussion necessary for the security of the venture, Dalcroze accepted and departed for Dresden.[9]

This retrospective review of the origin and beginnings of eurhythmics demonstrates once again that if a work is to *live*, it has to develop in harmony with the principles governing its life. Its flourishing cannot be forced; only patient and persistent nurturing can enable it to spread its roots in the soil, while assuring that the tree grows and blossoms openly in the sun.

We have witnessed the struggle and anxiety which is inherent in creative work. But we have omitted one factor . . . With his beautiful gift for radiating Life, Jaques-Dalcroze possesses something further: he has the sacred talent of arousing happiness! His pupils know this very well; even during their darkest days – and there were many – the flame of joy ignited by their Master led and enlightened them. Their life will be forever illumined by that flame.

One who has breathed deeply the air of the Dalcroze Institute, who has felt this unique atmosphere vibrate with fraternal solidarity, mutual support and a shared effort towards an eagerly pursued ideal, and one who can now envisage the Master standing before the serene facade of the new building, surrounded by his pupils and by the happy assembly of the children of Hellerau – these people of diverse age, nationality, and social background, yet joined by the same thought – such a person who can conceive all this can only exclaim:

By thy magic is united
What stern Custom parted wide,
All mankind are brothers plighted
Where thy gentle wings abide.[10]

Figure 12 The Hellerau Institute, 1912. The man on the left talking with the two women is Jaques-Dalcroze. Note the yin–yang symbol in the pediment of the building.

Eurhythmics and the Theatre

(1911)

Der Rhythmus, Ein Jahrbuch 1, Sept. (?) 1911: 57–64
Les Feuillets 14, Feb. 1912: 49–56
L'année 1913, 3: 498–503
Volbach, pp. 135–9; Bablet, 3, pp. 146–52

The aesthetic discipline which eurhythmics lends to the body undoubtedly will greatly influence the theatre, and it is interesting to examine what the nature of this influence will be.

As theatre, one means both the auditorium and the stage, the spectator as well as the performer. Let us begin with the stage, and because music presides over eurhythmics, let us determine what type of music the performer currently uses to express himself bodily on the stage.

In our lyric drama, at its best, the singer is rightly seen as the representative of the action; he sings the words, accompanying them with appropriate mime. Nevertheless, the dramatic action remains embedded in the score; despite his singing and gestures, the performer cannot fully embody it. He wavers painfully between the music which expresses a purely inner conflict, and therefore cannot suggest any motif by which it can be given plastic form, and that music which, by contrast, forcefully demands that it be projected externally. But this latter type of music, because its origin is symphonic just like that of the inner music, is no more capable than it of producing patterns and rhythms that can be expressed physically. Undoubtedly there are exceptions, although these are more apparent than real; and of course sensitive directing might greatly improve on the results. Nevertheless, what is produced remains merely a juxtaposition of music and the performer. No *organic* union is possible, because in the end, modern dramatic music is only a specific and extreme development of an art form which has long since lost any contact with the living body. This is the cause of the invariable falseness of our contemporary musical theatre.

We must not, therefore, blindly attempt to apply to the extraordinary but decadent art of music those principles which belong to an arising form of art, for which eurhythmics is preparing the way. One would have to ask what use training in eurhythmics could have for our singers, who have so little opportunity to use it on the stage.

90

Obviously by inculcating rhythm naturally in singers, and thereby revealing to them the pure aesthetic harmony of their organism, this discipline will exercise beneficial influence on their musicianship and on the sincerity and aptness of their acting – which will demonstrate a moderation that approaches style. But this is a general result . . . having more to do with education than art. We can only touch on it here, since our subject is rhythm and the body.

Although the actor in the spoken drama may not find any equivalent of the art to which eurhythmics has introduced him, he will discover one shared and essential element: *Space!* The discipline of eurhythmics will make him particularly sensitive to the dimensions of space, which correspond to the infinite variations of sound. He will instinctively attempt to bring these to life on stage, and will be bewildered at the injustice done to him, three-dimensional and living, amongst dead paintings on vertical canvases. He will, moreover, realize that in the musical drama no organic connection between himself and the setting is possible. Another juxtaposition! He is trapped within two contradictions: one arises from music, which he cannot interpret physically but must nevertheless present visibly on stage; the other relates to the scenic environment, which has no contact or rapport with the solid and moving body, and must therefore obstruct his rhythmic movement in space. The singer, who thereby realizes the painful role assigned to him, may insist upon his rights, and *fully aware of the cause*, assist in the dramatic and scenic reform in which, almost involuntarily, we are already engaged. By supplying the aesthetic education or, more accurately, the education of the performer, eurhythmics will enable him to do so. This will be of tremendous value.

Of all those present on stage, the most real, though unseen, is the author, the poet-musician. If he has experienced eurhythmics and felt deep inside himself that spark of joy and beauty which is kindled by true physical realization of music, then he will, just as the singer, become aware of the discordant juxtaposition in our musical drama, and therefore in his own work. From then on he will on the one hand hear his music, while on the other he witnesses its action on stage; no longer can he confuse the two. The rhythmic sense of his body will reawaken within him a harmony that he has seldom experienced, and never before been able to create on stage. An implicit understanding will quickly be set up between the author and his interpreter, the performer. Each *will have doubts* about his work. But doubt is always where one begins to search for truth. How can they discover this truth, this harmony?

The author will not deceive himself for long: contemporary elements of dramatic expression (score, singer, staging) have all developed without any coordination between them; the result is anarchy. Anyone who uses them in their current condition cannot make any progress at all towards their harmonious integration. *We must change direction!* What is required is conversion in the true sense of the word. Music, having developed along its path for so long a time, cannot now be brought into contact with the living body of the singer by arbitrary adjustments; nor can this be accomplished using the lifeless substance of our stages by means of an equally arbitrary imposition of style. Conversion in this case means henceforth taking the human body resolutely as the point of departure both for music and stage setting – and this dictates a change in our very conception of the drama, including all the changes that must follow. Conversion always requires sacrifices, and in this case they may be very great. To start with, it demands total objectivity and complete submission. The musician must turn back and boldly acknowledge the body which he has neglected for centuries. Of course, the living body will assist him by making itself an ever more willing and responsive instrument, ever more conscious of its latent harmony. The contact has been lost; *eurhythmics will try to discover it once more*. That is its principal significance for the theatre.

We have yet to examine the influence of eurhythmics on the spectator. This may, together with the preceding steps, lead us to a new conception of the theatre.

We are entirely justified in assuming that, before long, rhythmic discipline will be incorporated into the curriculum of our schools, and also be sufficiently disseminated among adults for a significant number of the audience to understand it, and some may even have taken part in it. What will be their inner attitude towards the performance?

Up to now, only quiet attention has been required of the audience. To encourage this, comfortable seats have been provided in semi-darkness, to encourage a state of total passivity – evidently the proper attitude for spectators. In other words, here, as elsewhere, we have attempted to separate ourselves from the work of art; we have become eternal spectators!

Eurhythmics will overturn this passivity! Musical rhythm will enter all of us, to say: *you yourself* are the work of art. And, indeed, we will feel it then, and never more be able to forget it.

The Brahman said to every 'living creature', 'it is yourself' (*Tat twam asi*).[11] Sensing 'ourselves' henceforth in every work of art, we shall ask: what has it made of *me*? We will have altered our attitude; instead of accepting passively, we shall participate actively and win the right to revolt against every wrong done to us. Returning to our true concern, the theatre, it is clear that our productions constantly offend this sense of active participation. As just noted, those who perceive this violence will quite naturally start to revolt against it. They will begin to doubt, just as the author and performer did and, like them, they will look for the truth *elsewhere*.

Surely I do not exaggerate! The awakening of art within ourselves, in our own organism and our flesh, is the death knell of a great part of our contemporary art, particularly the scenic art. But what then will replace

92

this scenic art, which we value so highly and consider so important that we seem unable to give it up?

The spectator too must undergo that change in direction, the conversion which the author and those who interpret him can accomplish. He, too, must start with his own body out of which the living art must radiate, expanding into space and bringing it to life. It is this body that dictates the arrangement of settings and lighting; it is this same body that creates the work of art!

The transition will be gradual and will require at each step a firm belief in the truth that now is scarcely glimpsed. The festivals at Hellerau will certainly provide the most important and decisive step along the path to the victory of *living* art. Each year they will homogeneously integrate the various exercises of the Institute, from the most basic to the most complex, into impressive dramatic experiments. They will be a festival for the participants! And the audience that is invited to attend them will feel profoundly that these pupils of every age group and station in life have assembled there to *represent the audience*, to provide, like the ancient chorus encircling the flame of the altar, the audience's immediate and wondrous spokesmen for living art.[12]

After so many centuries in isolation, filled now with gratitude, the spectator can exclaim, 'Yes, it is myself!'

Our theatre will have been conquered for him.

We can thus observe that eurhythmics and the theatre as it is now are two opposed concepts. By restoring the human body to its place of honour, and by banishing everything that does not emanate from it, eurhythmics has already taken an important step towards a comprehensive reform of our scenic and dramatic art.

Our theatres, however, will continue in existence for a long time yet, and we can foresee that eurhythmics will both continue to exercise a valuable influence on the actor – stylistically enhancing his performance – and, moreover, will particularly influence scenic practice. Instead of presenting an arrangement of dead paintings on flats, the setting increasingly will approximate the solidity of the human body in order to enhance its three-dimensional effect in space. The consequence will be significant simplification and a marked reduction in those objects depicted only by painting. Light, no longer forced to illuminate the painted flats, can radiate, carrying form into space, filling it with living colour and the limitless variations of an ever-changing atmosphere. No longer will it serve exclusively the scenic artist, but now . . . the dramatist! The scenic illusion which at great cost to the actor currently is attempted through painted settings, we shall finally achieve in harmony with the author, greatly to the benefit of the actor. It is impossible to go into further detail here about the results of such a reform. It may nevertheless be understood that in delivering staging from the yoke of lifeless painting and the illusion it was supposed

93

to produce, in having thereby given it the utmost subtlety and the greatest freedom, we have also liberated the *imagination of the dramatist*. The influence of this scenic reform on dramatic practice itself cannot be even remotely estimated.

Eurhythmics, for its part, will retain its fundamental scenic principle; that is, it will not allow anything in its midst that does not emanate directly from the rhythm expressed through the human body. In its natural development, eurhythmics will generate for itself a setting that emanates inevitably from the solid form of the human body and its movements, idealized through music.

Omnipotent light, conditioned by music, will then join in creating the setting – light that gives us plasticity, that imbues space with highlights and moving shadows, that flows in placid beams, or breaks out in colourful, vibrant flashes. The human bodies, bathed in this vital atmosphere, will recognize it and salute *Music in Space*.

For 'Apollo was not only the god of music; he was also the god of light!'[13]

Eurhythmics and Light

(1912)

Le Rythme 34, Dec. 1932: 15–17
Volbach, pp. 149–51; Bablet, 3, pp. 166–8

We anticipate from the Hellerau festivals not definite and therefore premature solutions to certain aesthetic problems, but a clear and precise indication of the direction we should take if we are to progress year by year towards such a solution. Then no doubt further problems will arise!

As with everything else concerning the Jaques-Dalcroze Institute, these matters are related to teaching. So I may be allowed to present here a brief sketch of the Institute's principles, and some thoughts about one of its essential elements: the role to be played by light within a school dominated by musical rhythm.

It is rare that one's senses are equally developed. Within the same individual a sort of equilibrium is attained in regard to the sum of his powers: if one sense strengthens, another grows weaker, but it is evident that their overall power, which determines a personality, remains the same. It follows that we can only influence our senses in their *reciprocal* relations: the variations in sensory response are unlimited and they distinguish one person from another far more than we tend to assume.

With regard to education, what will we find to be the most useful approach if we want to attempt to regulate the activity of our senses? In our schools where the student is taught what people before him have thought and discovered, the problem is simple: we address ourselves only to the intellectual and rational faculty of the personality. But how should we proceed if we require access *directly* to the student's senses themselves in order to harmonize their relative value? It is particularly here that the differences in personality will be felt; for there can be no intermediary between instruction and the senses . . . In the first instance the individual must discover his own senses; he must become *aware* of the reciprocity of his senses; only then can he attempt to bring them into harmonious play.

By appealing to our two noblest senses, those of hearing and sight, we can best awaken this awareness, which will then be reflected throughout the sensory system, exposing its deficiencies and any lack of equilibrium.

At the present time it is precisely eurhythmics that is the proper method for this training; through it, the personality validates its body and soul and no dissimulation is possible. In a contemporary rural boarding school, for example, the student finds he can easily assert himself except in what might be termed the aesthetic will of his body. His sense of life is entirely aroused, but without ever penetrating to the actual source of sensory equilibrium, and this leaves his personality with no reliable touchstone to teach him how to obtain that equilibrium. Now because we can only assess the equilibrium of our senses through those same senses, it is only a temporary *modification* of what they normally feel that can enable them to become aware of what their normal proportions are. Music provides the ideal means for this since, existing through a continuous variation in time values, it has an instructive power of the first order. Eurhythmics was born out of this power, and it is not necessary to repeat here how it affects our entire organism through the art of modifying time values. But our work of self-discovery must not stop at this point; our second major sense, that of sight, seems only indirectly to be connected to music. The means must be found to reach this sense *directly*, and just as with music, by varying the usual proportions.

It is at this point that light must come into the process! In what form? Daylight does not lie within our control. Although we can dim it (using curtains, coloured glass, etc.) we cannot control daylight *itself* and alter its proportions as we like. We have to resort to artificial light created by ourselves, i.e. stage lighting. As far as our eyes are concerned, this light is to basic daylight what, for our ears, the art of sounds is to shouting. It will be the *aesthetic regulator* of brightness – capable of modifying its intensity.

We therefore possess two stylizing elements which can complement one another for the purpose of the aesthetic instruction of our senses. For, as we know, there is an intimate relationship between music and light. The ancients, perceiving this, recognized Apollo as the god of both these integrated elements. This relationship will allow us to employ music and light *simultaneously* as a single art that will potently affect our personality.

But although we are quite familiar with the art of sounds, our *aesthetic* understanding with regard to light is still rather basic; so we must study light with the aid, and under the control, of music. This entirely new study, whose future importance cannot be overestimated, undoubtedly holds great surprises for us! We shall learn first of all that merely 'to render visible' is not light in this sense at all, and on the contrary, to be form-giving or plastic, light must exist in an atmosphere, a luminous atmosphere. Therefore a harmonious and endlessly changeable balance between illumination and creative or plastic light will engender . . . *luminous sound*, the precise coordination of luminous vibrations in space to those of the music.[14] Through its systematic investigation and study of light, the Jaques-Dalcroze Institute will engender in each student a new sense that might be

Figure 13 The 1912 setting at Hellerau for *Orpheus and Eurydice*, Act II, 'The Descent into the Under-world'. Orpheus gradually descended the staircase, bringing the light with him as he was opposed by, then gradually subdued, the Furies.

termed the *musico-luminous sense*, which will allow him to seek a harmonious equilibrium between auditory and visual sensations, and to discover in this equilibrium a new source of inspiration.

This research will demand considerable time! It is not necessarily a question of discovering something of beauty. Just as eurhythmic exercises achieve beauty only as it arises as their natural, organic, and somehow intrinsic result, so too the beauty of light, inseparably associated with music, can only be a by-product, or risk remaining merely a decadent game. Gradually we must learn that to see and to hear can be one and the same thing, and must understand intuitively that the whole art form itself must henceforth be founded on this essential experience.[15]

But music alone can guide us along this new path, for only it possesses the power of evocation.

Therefore, like the slaves in *A Thousand and One Nights*, we must respond by 'listening and subservience', dutifully assisted if possible by candid and submissive eyes.

After the Hellerau festivals present the product of such study they can provide the public with instructive suggestions about how to satisfy its desire for harmony and beauty. Each year, further progress will bear witness to scrupulous and persistent work which cannot fail again and again to open up new vistas of future development to the spectators.

Concerning the Costume for Eurhythmics

(1912)

Der Rhythmus, Ein Jahrbuch 2 (1), 1912: 56–64
Volbach, pp. 153–8; Bablet, 3, pp. 154–61

Warmly dedicated to the pupils of the Dalcroze Institute in Hellerau

'As naked as possible,' the artists say.

'Why, and on what grounds?'

Some people suggest a subtle dress, to reveal the contour of the body, while it cloaks it in expressive and light folds. Others demand colour; still others would like a sense of freedom and imagination.

'And why all this, and on what grounds?'

My neighbour at the rear of the auditorium whispered to me during a class at the Institute: 'Those awful black tights! Do you not see how they *cut through the line?*'

'I do see, but you sir, do not, since you merely observe and that is the wrong attitude here.'

'Why?'

'So you really believe that these men and women, boys and girls have disrobed in this way just to please . . . your eyes?!'

Eurhythmics is recognized as the art that arouses in us a sense of bodily musical rhythm and thus permits us, through the gradual realization of that rhythm within space, to become fully aware of its beauty and to enjoy its beneficial power. The experience, however, develops outward from within. If an earnest pupil stepped before a mirror to perform a rhythmic exercise, he would perceive immediately that he had made a most serious error: having taken the wrong direction in attempting to modify from the outside what he ought to approach from within. The mirror takes his image and, in reflecting, falsifies it. No relation is possible between the student's experience during free exercises in space, as he follows his inner rhythm alone, and that image dutifully reflected in the mirror. Here your eyes, sir, play the part of the mirror. As incorrigible spectators, they seize upon the external form of Jaques-Dalcroze's students and reflect a falsified image. Undoubtedly some of the students must be uncomfortably aware

Figure 14 The great hall at Hellerau. Students perform a eurhythmic demonstration within its open rectangular space, from which the traditional proscenium arch and conventional settings have been banished. The radiance emanates from thousands of lights, placed behind the cloths covering the walls and ceilings.

of this, for more things occur here between the auditorium and the stage than are dreamt of in your spectator's philosophy.

A student comes to the Hellerau Institute not to study the aesthetic life of the *body*, but to awaken this same life in his own body.

The visitor distorts his own judgement if, when attending a class, he does not attempt above all else to perceive this marvellous awakening – which every personality expresses differently and with innumerable nuances – this awakening that no other discipline can provide. And if he does not bow his head, deeply moved by such an effort, his sensual curiosity disturbs the class, and far from being drawn nearer to Dalcroze's work, he drifts further away. Of course, in order to approach such work, one must take some steps for oneself . . . and take them quietly and respectfully, encouraged by an irresistible and purely human sympathy for the Master *and his pupils.*[16]

Besides, sir, the tights you dismiss so lightly were not invented in a single stroke and imposed from the beginning on eurhythmics students. There is a story behind it, and here it is in all its simplicity.

Ten years ago at the beginning of eurhythmics in Geneva, Dalcroze's students – young girls – performed their exercises in the ordinary clothes they wore to school. Then sandals were substituted because 'strong beats' could not be performed in our ridiculous modern footwear. Then a skirt was designed which was slightly shortened and sufficiently wide to give the legs the required freedom of movement, and a sort of blouse was added, which left the neck and arms relatively uncovered. This skirt was soon found to be inconvenient, and puffed breeches [culottes] fastened beneath the knee, and thick woollen pullovers were introduced. The friction of the cloth between the knees suggested a new type of breeches, all in one piece but fitted more loosely. At this point a few courageous students took off their stockings, but kept their sandals! A bit later, the breeches were snugly fitted, leaving the knees uncovered and permitting yet more freedom of movement. Finally, some removed their sandals: this was the final decisive step to total freedom! Soon all students had bare legs and feet; and a little later, with the inauguration of the Institute at Dresden, the black tights in one piece were adopted, which provided the minimum of clothes, both for men and women. Black was chosen to avoid any expression of the usual diversity of individual taste and, on the contrary, to give this simple costume the impersonal, I might say austere, quality necessary for the exercise.

A woman wrote recently to Jaques-Dalcroze on this subject: 'The short period when one is free of all those distracting clothes, when one can move one's limbs to the heart's desire, unhindered by the black tights, when one becomes aware of strength and space, of line and movement according to the laws of Nature, this period gives me a feeling of being at one with the

Universe, of expressing life not in accord with human laws, but with divine commandment.'

Perhaps the 'spectators' may find in these few words a judgement against which there can be no appeal.

This gradual and noble liberation from ancient habits suggests on the part of both parents and pupils a confidence and passionate concern for a grand cause. It guarantees in itself a serious contribution to the study of eurhythmics.

Remove your clothes, sir, and bravely donning these wicked tights – which will break up the line of your body, alas – undertake the notorious experiment. By the end of three or four lessons the garment will cease to exist for you; it becomes merely a necessary precaution for aesthetic decency, and to allow freedom of movement; nothing more. Then, after an exercise that has absorbed your vitality, after you have struggled against and overcome the resistance of your organism and have finally leapt joyously free visibly to express the intended rhythm – then turn your eyes to the spectators' gallery, where you will meet the gaze of your former self, a poor visitor whom you will pity as you do all those at whom, this very moment, you are gazing.

By discarding your clothes in order to assume the black school tights you have similarly abandoned the miserable shell of a spectator, to which you will never return.

So much for the black tights.

The study of bodily rhythm makes one acutely sensitive to the dimensions of Space. The study of Space will therefore form part of the Institute's curriculum. Space must include simple and flat surfaces, as well as obstacles designed to make the body aware of its balance and subtlety – the infinite possibilities of its expressive power – such as different kinds of stairs, platforms, ramps, wall, pillars, etc. But with so active a role, in order to manifest itself clearly to the body, Space requires the appropriate light, and the body, engaging with that light, in order to receive and make the most of its potential, requires all the resources of three-dimensional space. Obviously black absorbs light and does not reflect it. It is therefore inappropriate for the study of light, and the tone of the school tights must be somewhat modified for this purpose. Grey, if chosen with great care, seems just right: it retains the neutrality necessary for a serious study of the body, and becomes quite expressive in combination with a beam of luminous light. The school tights had therefore to be of two tones: black for basic rhythmic exercises without special lighting effects, and grey for study with such effects; work which will always be more or less unusual.[17]

A subject of secondary importance in the study of rhythm will be what might be termed 'the study of folds'. In fact, the student who has mastered his spatial expression of music will undoubtedly feel the need to obtain a more complete understanding of this plasticity by combining it with another element: the cloth that covers his form and follows his movement in a softened rhythm. And he requires this understanding not for the sake of the eye, but in order to sense the effect of this union and the new richness it can lend his *inner* rhythm. A simple white or grey tunic perfectly cut and arranged – since the value of the study depends on the shape of this tunic – will be sufficient. This is the third costume of the school. It is worn over the black or grey tights and may be quickly removed when, in the course of a lesson, the nature of the assignment is changed. Thus the same exercise might be conducted alternately, first without the tunic (that is, without folds) and then with the tunic (with folds). This can be a source of valuable information both for student and teacher; it is certain to inspire further expressive nuances.

There remains the Dance, naturally derived from eurhythmics, but which Dalcroze keeps quite separate in his instruction.

The Dance, in whatever form it may be conceived, contains an element of freedom and of fantasy which, in fact, sets it apart and may even cause it somewhat to resemble a dramatic performance. At the school, the question of costume depends, as in other things, on the feeling of the students. If the students feel more comfortable in performing their tasks in the school tights, they may certainly wear them; if, on the other hand, at a public demonstration for example, they themselves feel the need for a lighter garment for communicating more ably their enjoyment to the spectator, this would be appropriate. The question therefore is simple, so long as dance and eurhythmics are not confused; but if they are, then experience alone can guide us, and it becomes a matter of taste, *because it will always be eurhythmics that sets the tone.*

The question of costume for eurhythmics is actually for the Hellerau Institute a simple one. It rests on the following points: how should the students dress to receive the greatest benefit from the instruction they receive, and in addition, how should they dress to facilitate the Institute's study of the lighting which is intended for them? The students have every right to keep for their work the clothing which their own experience has proved most comfortable and proper. Moreover, nothing in the world should force them to wear at a public demonstration a costume which their pure and highly reliable instinct, refined through their study, would reject.

You may, however, object, asking if this so highly esteemed art of the Jaques-Dalcroze Institute is not really a load of egoism? Everyone comes there to cultivate and perfect through rhythm his own personality; visitors, although politely received, are not encouraged; and everything, it seems, must take place behind closed doors. But wait! All of us crave the same blessing; all of us would like to take our modest share! In our era, when

103

the sight of the body in motion, free and harmonious, is completely denied to us – just when this alone might revive and renew our art, our literature, and our overall conception of life – the sole refuge, the only sanctuary where this sight might inspire us anew – must it remain closed to us?

The objection is entirely legitimate: we must all share in this invaluable blessing. Is, however, the question properly stated? Would it not be better to ask ourselves what we should do, and how, in order to accept what the Hellerau Institute can give us? This accords precisely with the very question posed by the Institute itself at this moment: how can we communicate to the public that which in our hearts we long to give? For if the public is not prepared, neither is the Institute, involved in its strenuous educational activity. The task is to establish the link that will relate its activity to the activity and quite different habitual inclination of the public.

For that there is only one option: on the one hand to affirm categorically and definitely the educational character of this great undertaking – this must be the role of the Institute. On the other, to approach the Institute and what it offers with the intention of seeking the educational benefit which it alone can provide – this must be the role of the public.

And let the public not be mistaken; its role is extremely beautiful! Sympathy, unselfish and respectful, joined with a sincere desire to understand and to know, this is the *indispensable* complement of every aesthetic activity. The Institute too has need of this sympathy.

If, therefore, at the beginning of this article, the curious visitor felt – on good grounds – that he was mistreated, we can affirm that, by contrast, an audience informed in advance and more eager to understand and penetrate into the admirable work of Dalcroze than to contemplate pretty sights will always be welcomed with open arms. The festivals are intended to accomplish this union. After a year of dedicated work, the students feel the need to demonstrate for themselves in some fashion the ultimate result of their work in an official school festival. But they also need, not admiration, but sympathy. They keenly desire to be able to communicate something of their own pleasure to others; they know very well that they cannot do this unless the invited audience attempts *to understand* them: what they have received they wish to give; just so!

The great instructional task of the Institute must therefore be expanded to embrace the public, so that it may become an educator. It cannot show simply the present to the audience, nor should it. Suffused with what will be, the Institute must offer, in a living and necessarily imperfect symbol of the present, *the Future!* In this sense the Hellerau festivals will prove great pathfinders, directing our attention year by year towards a higher and more desirable goal: they will be *Life* itself, no longer its representation; they will be living, not merely representative; their influence . . . will be immeasurable, for life defies all measures.

And the public will come here to be revived with this invigorating breeze and to express officially its sympathy and gratitude. A fraternal body will thereby be firmly established.

Perhaps you may ask what such matters have to do with the question of costume? It is indeed odd that a wholly concrete question should assume such great importance.

Nevertheless, one must acknowledge and loudly affirm it!

It will not be solely through the composition of its programme that the Institute proves its educational character to the public, but also by maintaining this same quality in the performance it offers. The audience must sacrifice many of its desires, and so too must the Institute, at the risk of grave objections.

Do not, moreover, be afraid of the austerity of a body so costumed; so much marvellous beauty, so many exciting developments have already taken place here that the Future, far from being obscured by such austerity, on the contrary reveals itself therein, and only therein, as quite radiant.[18]

Part III

Essays on the art of the theatre

Introduction

The essays included in this and the following section were written during the last decade of Appia's life. They were probably meant to form the greater part of a volume that Appia himself intended to publish, but never did. In a letter to Craig at the end of the war in November 1918, Appia announced his forthcoming book, *The Work of Living Art*, and also mentioned plans for a volume of essays and prefaces. Several years later he referred to it again, as a volume 'where the reader will find practical ideas and social practice' (Beacham 1988: 286). In 1926 he wrote a 'Preface to the edition of my essays in one volume', in which he referred to 'the New Presence' as providing the 'touchstone' for these essays. Their common theme was to be the awareness of 'Living Art' and the consequences this would have on diverse forms of aesthetic expression: '[The New Presence] implies the giving of oneself and thereby demands an attitude . . . it will ignore the barriers with which, unfortunately, we surround our personality, for it demonstrates the common humanity in each of our gestures, our emotions, and our thoughts' (Appia 1989: 171).

The works selected for Part III, the first section devoted to these late essays, are of a more practical sort; Part IV includes those of a more speculative and prophetic nature. 'Actor, space, light, painting' (a later title; the original had none) was written for a conference in 1919, and is Appia's first extant post-war essay, apart from a brief preface written a year earlier for a projected English version of *Musik und die Inscenierung*. It represents his return to productive work after a period of relative inactivity. During the war Appia was frequently unwell, and did little apart from occasional collaboration with Dalcroze at his Geneva Institute. He was prone to periods of deep depression and mental fatigue.

After the armistice in November 1918 his spirits greatly improved, and in a letter to Craig at the end of that month, he noted that now, aged fifty-seven, he was anxious to embark on important new work, undoubtedly including the essays excerpted here.

This short essay is a succinct exposition of Appia's hierarchy of scenic presentation, as formulated much earlier, and also gives emphasis to the insights developed through his work with Dalcroze: the role of the human body as a means of expression, and the need to overcome the passivity of the audience. It introduces a subject that will loom large in his future essays: 'the cathedral of the future', a changeable space where a variety of aesthetic activity could occur 'with or without spectators'. Appia explored the idea at length in *The Work of Living Art*. He conceived of a theatre in which the traditional architecture, the activities taking place and the relationship between the audience and performance would all be radically transformed. New expressions of scenic art would be presented in buildings capable of providing the venue for a variety of as yet unimagined aesthetic events. It is interesting to note that four years later, Gordon Craig, to whom Appia had confided these ideas, predicted that 'the theatre must be a *hollow* space with roof and floor only: within this space must be erected for each new type of play a new temporary stage and auditorium' (Bablet 1971: 21). Both men shared a similar conception of the theatre of the future.

The following year Appia wrote a short piece, 'Art is an attitude', which repeated both his prediction that new forms of art would emerge, inspired by the human body, and his desire to abolish the barriers between spectator and performer. It was first published in 1928 as a preface to the important and influential book, *Twentieth Century Stage Decoration*, by Walter Fuerst and Samuel Hume.

Appia's suggestion in this essay that new artistic expression would consist of 'moving, more or less dramatic symbols, agreed upon by all' was an idea he explored in greater depth in several subsequent essays, including 'Living art or dead nature', one of his most widely published pieces.[1] It was written in 1921 for the catalogue of an exhibition on modern scene design held in Amsterdam the following year. It attracted a good deal of attention for its argument rejecting traditional settings and static dramaturgy in favour of more expressive and vibrant formats emanating from the dynamic presence of the living actor. Its discussion of 'rhythmic spaces' and theatrical architecture based on this concept undoubtedly drew upon his experiences at Hellerau; the analysis of the 'Hall' is particularly suggestive.

Similar ideas were explored more thoroughly in a piece written later the same year, 'Theatrical production and its prospects for the future', which was Appia's most widely published essay. In addition to renewing his call for the reform of theatrical production using careful coordination of a hierarchy of expressive elements, it also addressed the question of spoken drama, a subject barely touched upon in his earlier writings. The actor in spoken drama was usually participating in works that imitated reality, whether directly or in a stylized fashion, through what Appia termed *indication*. The actor's words and gestures, together with the scenic environment, were all aspects of this indicative mode, which he contrasted with pure *expression*, of which music was the primary source. In the absence of music much of the expressive quality of theatrical works was sacrificed, as well as the suggestion of an appropriate 'rhythmic space' generated by the actor as he moved under the control of the music.[2]

Appia believed that existing dramatic works could in part be redeemed by introducing music into them so that, though unable to exercise its primary expressive function, music might nevertheless serve to support and round out the action, ennobling the drama by forging, if only in passing, that unity between itself and poetry which Appia considered the basis for true dramatic art. Similarly, the art of acting should be refined by engaging the performer in rigorous training in musically coordinated movement; in fact, in eurhythmics. The body itself would become an instrument of artistic expression instead of mimetic impersonation.

Finally, Appia believed that dramatic works could be endowed with a measure of control and integrity by using their staging to reflect and respond to an altered awareness and expectation on the part of the audience itself. An audience conditioned by realism expected theatre to provide the direct reproduction not only of details of manners and behaviour as conveyed through the action, but also of a drama's notional historic and geographic locales, as represented by the scenery. The 'idealistic' vision, however, only requires those elements which intensify and convey most readily the work's expressive qualities. This approach, a prerequisite for what came to be called production 'concepts', was based on the potential that art has to raise the consciousness of the audience and release the imagination from the random demands and events of ordinary life. Appia believed that, through a theatrical art freed from the burden of simulating the petty details that encumber and obscure the deeper values of life, audiences could in turn awaken and intensify their own capacity for self-awareness and the experience of profound emotion.

Thus, by carefully investigating the meaning which a given work could have for its audience, and using staging to refine and express that meaning, one might create dramatic works that – even in the absence of music – could aspire to the controlled, coordinated and unified condition that Appia insisted must be the basis for any autonomous theatrical art.[3] He went still further, to assert that once the audience came to regard the theatrical piece as an expression in effect of its own self, in which it was directly and actively involved; once the actor's training in music allowed him to use his body not as an instrument for imitation but as capable of direct expression, then the basis would have been provided for entirely new forms of art.

Such ideas would, indeed, engender new forms of theatrical expression in the future, including much of modern dance and 'performance art'. To provide the venue for such new work – and the experimentation leading to it – new forms of theatre architecture would be required, and it was to this subject that Appia turned in July 1922, in the essay 'Monumentality'. In it he emphasized that what he termed 'people's theatre' should stimulate an audience to learn and participate through the informal and sociable nature of the building itself.[4] Even its exterior walls should be constructed to allow performance to move out of doors when appropriate. The stage must be capable of merging with the other portions of the building into a single architectural unit, and, if desired, the lateral walls of the auditorium should be removable to allow it to combine with the lobby and other public areas, encouraging aesthetic and social activities to merge. This informality would in turn benefit the performance itself; the spatial arrangement could help overcome the passivity of the spectators by giving them the impression that their own bodies are helping to create and define the space.

The proliferation in recent years of performing arts complexes, multimedia studios, workshop and laboratory theatres and arts centres may legitimately be considered a distant but organic outgrowth and continuation of Appia's work. So too is much of the work of later practitioners who sought to expand the concept of theatrical art, in part through the reform of the space and conditions governing performance.[5] Jacques Copeau, Antonin Artaud, Jerzy Grotowski, Richard Schechner, Joseph Chaikin and Julian Beck, together with the groups they founded and their followers, all found that the new varieties of theatrical art of the sort called for in Appia's essays dictated the spatial reforms that he saw as inevitable. Analysis of the practice and underlying theory of each of such artists instantly reveals an affinity with Appia, as well as the prescience of his ideas, however obscure the line of conscious influence or direct indebtedness may be.

The final essay in this section, and one of the last that Appia wrote, is 'The art of the living theatre'. Here he returns to the concept that much of the expressive quality of theatrical production is subjective; the audience itself helps to create the *mise en scène* through the active engagement of its own imagination and emotion. If such 'living' collaboration between audience and artists were to occur, it was vital to enlarge and open up the public's imagination and to make it receptive to new possibilities in popular art. Appia was concerned that the restrictive social conditions of the twentieth century and the growing pressure of technology were a serious challenge to human sensitivity and must be vigorously opposed. The burden on the individual – now increasingly passive, demoralized and exhausted, as well as painfully isolated from his fellow man – threatened to destroy the vitality of art and weaken society at the moment when the regeneration of both was critically important.

Direct participation must come to replace the morbid collecting and curating of individual impressions; the audience's compulsive desire to gaze upon images of itself was inimical to 'living art'. What was necessary were new types of activity which could integrate life, making connections between different modes of experience and different individuals: multiple art forms that could forge links from the individual's body and emotions to the larger body and concerns of the community. The achievement of such links could be accomplished only through a change in awareness and attitude on the part of the public, who must understand that new art forms represented not merely 'technical development on the part of the stage director, but an inner and very profound evolution expected of the spectator himself'. It was this subject that provided the essential theme of the visionary essays comprising the final section of this volume.

Actor, Space, Light, Painting[6]

(1919)

Journal de Genève, 23–4 January 1954
Théâtre populaire 5, Jan.–Feb. 1954: 37–42
Volbach, pp. 183–5; Bablet, 3, pp. 335–8

The art of stage production is the art of projecting into Space what the original author was only able to project in Time. The temporal element is implicit within any text, with or without music... The first factor in staging is the interpreter: the actor himself. The actor carries the action. Without him there can be no action and hence no drama... The body is alive, mobile and plastic; it exists in three dimensions. Space and the objects used by the body must most carefully take this fact into account. The overall arrangement of the setting comes just after the actor in importance; it is through it that the actor makes contact with and assumes reality within the scenic space.

Thus we already have two essential elements: the actor and the spatial arrangement of the setting, which must conform to his plastic form and his three-dimensionality.

What else is there?

Light!

Light, just like the actor, must become active; and in order to grant to it the status of a medium of dramatic expression it must be placed in the service of... the actor who is above it in the production hierarchy, and in the service of the dramatic and plastic expression of the actor.

... Light has an almost miraculous flexibility... it can create shadows, make them living, and spread the harmony of their vibrations in space just as music does. In light we possess a most powerful means of expression through space, if this space is placed in the service of the actor.

So here we have our normal established hierarchy:

the *actor* presenting the drama;
space in three dimensions, in the service of the actor's plastic form;
light giving life to each.

But – as you have inferred, there is a but – what about painting? What do we understand about painting in terms of scenic art?

A collection of painted backcloths and flats arranged vertically on the stage, more or less parallel to one another, and extending upstage. These are covered with painted light, painted shadow, painted forms, objects and architecture; all of it, of course, on a flat surface since that is the nature of painting . . .

Our staging practice has reversed the hierarchical order: on the pretext of providing us with elements which are difficult or impossible to realize in solid form, it has developed painted décor to an absurd degree, and disgracefully subordinated the living body of the actor to it. Thus light illuminates the backcloths (which have to be seen), without a care for the actor, who endures the ultimate humiliation of moving between painted flats, standing on a horizontal floor.

All modern attempts at scenic reform touch upon this essential problem; namely, on how to give to light its fullest power, and through it, integral plastic value to the actor and the scenic space.

Our stage directors have, for a long time, sacrificed the physical and living presence of the actor to the dead illusion of painting. Under such a tyranny, it is obvious that the human body could never develop in any normal way its means of expression. This marvellous instrument, instead of sounding in freedom, exists only under severe constraints.

Everyone knows today that the return to the human body as an expressive element of the first rank is an idea that captures the mind, stimulates the imagination, and opens the way for experiments which may be diverse and no doubt of unequal value, but are all directed towards the same reform . . . Yet our contemporary productions have forced us into such a despicably passive state that we conceal it carefully in the darkness of the house. But now, with the current attempt by the human body to rediscover itself, our feeling almost leads to the beginning of fraternal collaboration; we wish that we were ourselves the body that we observe: the social instinct awakens within us, though in the past we coldly suppressed it, and the division separating the stage and the auditorium becomes simply a distressing barbarism arising from our selfishness.

We have arrived at the crucial point for dramatic reform . . . which must be boldly announced: the dramatic author will never liberate his vision so long as he believes it yoked by necessity to a barrier separating the action from the spectator . . . The inevitable conclusion is that the usual arrangement of our theatres must evolve gradually towards a more liberal conception of dramatic art . . .

We shall arrive, eventually, at what will simply be called the *House*: a sort of cathedral of the future, which in a vast, open and changeable space will welcome the most varied expressions of our social and artistic life, and will be the ideal place for dramatic art to flourish, *with or without spectators*.[7]

Art is an Attitude[8]

(1920)

Walter René Fuerst and Samuel J. Hume,
Twentieth-Century Stage Decoration (London, 1928): XIII–XV
Volbach, pp. 187–9; Bablet, 4, pp. 498–500

This attitude should belong to all of humanity. Instead, we have consigned it to the creator of a work of art, turning it into the specific personal property of the artist. The history of art therefore has become a chronological listing of forms of art and their various techniques. There is music, architecture, sculpture, painting – as if by necessity art were carved stone, sound, colours – even words. Our museums, concerts and libraries appear to confirm this. Barely twenty years ago such institutions seemed to represent art, serving as its depositories and glorious protectors.

This is no longer true today.

We have finally abandoned our seat as spectator and are prepared to struggle with all our might to participate. We seek art, and hope to find it within ourselves. Breaking down the barriers, we rush up the steps that cut us off from the platform, and climb without hesitation into the arena.

The beginning of any work dedicated to the theatre demands this positive attitude.

This naturally involves our entire mind and body! To be 'a part of art' we must, like an initiate, search out the point where the work of art and our entire personality will converge. As far as the theatre is concerned, this altogether new gesture places in our hands the key to the scenic problem.

... Sport and the conquest of spatial distance have made us conscious of the effectiveness of our body ... how can we therefore continue to remain calmly seated, observing bodies like our own becoming abject servants in the space in front of us? For on the stage of our theatres, the highest object of the arts, the living body, our own body, is still violated and degraded by the scenic settings.

Thus, properly posed, the problem of stage production is solved ...

Let us assume two opposed poles: on the one hand, pure dramatic art lacking anything additional, and on the other, any spectacle which is presented simply to please the eye.

The more dramatic art approaches spectacle for its own sake, the more it will diminish its dramatic value and, vice versa, spectacle loses its grandeur as well as its variety the more it tends towards the dramatic.

When dramatic art is deprived of the pleasures allowed to merely pictorial art, what is left? The living body of the actor! But this living body is solid and moving. The setting painted on flats has only two dimensions, and depicts illusionistic objects, highlights and shadows. The actor, a *living* reality untouched by such painted lights and shadows, can never come into any organic relation with painted objects. The lighting required to illuminate the painting is not intended for the actor even though it falls upon him. Lighting meant for the actor detracts from the painting and distorts its pictorial quality.

Such obvious contradictions force us to determine a rational hierarchy amongst the elements of scenic expression.

The actor rightfully occupies the first position. Next comes *the spatial arrangement* . . . then follows the all-powerful *lighting*. The last place belongs to painted scenery, the role of which is definitely inferior to the other three elements.

. . . This hierarchy imposes on the stage director a number of conclusions, which are independent of his own imagination and free choice. The setting, and in particular its lines and rigidity, must be in opposition to the living forms of the actor, for it is precisely by providing resistance to these forms and their movement that space takes on life and contributes to harmonious presentation.

These principles . . . are not dogmatic; on the contrary, they are flexible to respond to the various desires of the dramatist. There is, however, one rule that must always be dominant: the indisputable supremacy on stage of the actor. Everything must be provided, everything sacrificed to him . . .

I began this introduction by stating that we wish to 'participate'; that we have rediscovered our body which has been lost for centuries, and that we have perceived a new sense of responsibility, a feeling of solidarity like the sudden revelation of a categorical imperative. *We have ceased to be spectators!* . . . Now therefore we look for change, and our old formulas disperse in all directions.

The dance, the animated plastic art, forms part of an imprecise repertoire that tends to overlap with sport. Music, speech, spectacles, simplification or stylization, splendour and excess, alternate and mix with one another. Such anarchy is disturbing, because we perceive what its outcome will be: the issue will *depend upon us*, on an aesthetic resolution achieved organically, gradually and smoothly.

Since we wish to 'participate', we desire to be free; and thus we have become free! This is absolutely true! Let us attempt to use our freedom nobly.

The time approaches when theatre professionals and the dramas written for them will be completely obsolete – a time when a liberated humanity shall sing of its joy and pain, its thoughts, labours, struggles, defeats and victories. It will sing about them in moving, more or less dramatic symbols agreed upon by all. And the only onlookers will be those whom age and infirmity will arrange around us in shared and avid sympathy.

Then we shall be artists, *living* artists, because that is what we wish to be. I welcome this time with all my heart.

Living Art or Dead Nature?

(1921)

Wendingen 9–10 (1922): 7–15
Bottega di Poesia, 1923
Theatre Annual 2 (1943)
Players Magazine 33 (4), 1962
Volbach, pp. 191–7; Bablet, 4, pp. 62–8

... Dramatic art – the theatre we wish to exhibit[9] – begins with movement ... [it] is above all the art of life, and this life can be expressed, if necessary, without any building or scenic elements, for undefined space and time are adequate for this art ...

Earlier stage settings were composed entirely of painted scenery on vertical flats, which were arranged so that they suggested a perspective vista. The job of the theatrical director consisted simply of placing his performers and their actions within this vertical painting, bearing in mind the conflict between two-dimensional flats and three-dimensional actors ... Soon the action itself became realistic, and scene painting was incompatible with the actor's performance. The question of two or three dimensions became ever more pressing; on the one hand the director retained scene painting from established habit, while, on the other, he called enthusiastically for the solidity that painting denied him. Consequently, playwrights severely restricted their choice of locale in order to place their action within a frame that could readily be depicted on the stage. We had reached this point when dance – doubtless influenced strongly by sport – slowly liberated itself. The living and moving body has asserted itself – and has done so, as a matter of the greatest significance – outside the psychological realism of a particular dramatic plot. It has assumed the role of a means of expression. From that day on, scenic painting began to die ...

For everyone who takes theatre seriously, the actor and his action, and the rhythmically motivated three-dimensional dancer, determine the scenic elements, including the arrangement of the auditorium and the entire theatre building. We are free at last!

... Although movement on its own is independent of all surroundings, it is nevertheless advantageous to provide it with a space broken up on various levels that enhance the moments of action and display its detail to best effect; in other words, the setting should provide some obstacles to the movement . . . Since a space thus conceived is dependent entirely on the movement of the actor, our settings must be designed exclusively for him. The actor cannot himself determine anything without the dramatist. Thus, the normal hierarchy will be author, actor, space. But do not forget that this hierarchy is organic: the author cannot handle space except through the medium of the actor! . . .

Most designs for settings and models displayed in exhibitions focus on plays which are already familiar, and attempt to realize a picture that has emanated directly from the imagination of the author or scene designer, without passing through the actor, as demanded by the hierarchy . . . The actor is patronized with a place in it, but he is clearly an inconvenience there. Sometimes designs when exhibited do not even display the settings as they actually are – a mixture of solid and flat elements – but as they would be were it not for this embarrassing dilemma! The drawing of a setting ought always to give the observer a precise impression of its reality as it will appear on stage, without hypocritical modifications . . . Otherwise the drawing is a fraud and significantly adds to the confusion of the visitor's judgement . . .

Since the importance – and therefore the expression – of such spaces is dependent upon the moving presence of the actor, simple sketches or models will give the strong impression of being incomplete, and awaken desire in the visitor for the presence of the living body which alone has motivated them . . . So the settings should include their natural comp-lement, which is movement.

It therefore follows that a comprehensive theatre exhibition should show on the one hand the spaces designed for movement, and on the other the movement that inspired and shaped those spaces. One without the other is incomplete. But movement and space juxtaposed are not yet theatre . . .

The visitor, surprised by the display of lifeless spaces, feels the beneficial need for them to be filled, and this sense of emptiness is the beginning of wisdom![10] Then, once the move-ment of the performers lends life to these spaces, and when they fuse before the visitor's eyes into a living synthesis, his doubt and former prejudice will be dispelled . . .

In my book, *The Work of Living Art,* I examined the type of structure required for space if it is to be employed for the form and movement of the living person, and I concluded that space does not share the life of the body by assuming its form, but, on the contrary, by opposing it. To accomplish this spatial composition employs only a few lines. These are the horizontal, the vertical, the oblique, and various combinations, such as a staircase that provides the body with a type of support that no other combination can rival. This simplicity allows the material to be handled easily. There will be modules of different sizes constructed carefully to

Figure 15 Appia's rhythmic space design of 1909, 'The Staircase'.

allow them to be combined and joined to make staircases, platforms and ramps, supported, if required, by pillars located evenly at right angles; perpendicular curtains, screens, etc.; a quite elaborate set of components based on right-angled forms in opposition to the rounded shape of the body, and the curved lines of its movements. Such modules can be shifted manually by an intelligent and properly trained stage-hand. I should add that the demonstration will be all the more effective if colour and costume are kept plain so that space and movement can be emphasized on their own, without the distractions of essentially minor elements. The modules are covered in canvas; the costumes are simple, either black tights which leave the neck, arms, legs and feet bare . . . or a short tunic over the tights. During these demonstrations light comes entirely from above in order to reveal clearly the forms of the body in motion and the three-dimensional nature of the setting.[11] No footlights, ever! . . . These solid pieces should be shifted in full view of the spectator; no curtain is required, since we seek to demonstrate, not conceal . . .

Halls created for such synthesis will be a place for experimental investigation; the art of staging will never cease to be empirical . . . The exhibition of such experiments will certainly encourage [playwrights] to take part and from there a productive understanding with the audience is only a step away! The theatre exhibition will have become a living organism! . . .

Our very attempt to reform staging practice raises once more the whole problem of dramatic art, for clearly the two are closely related. Currently one of the mistakes is the wish to reform the one without the other, and even to apply new principles to plays for which they are totally inappropriate . . . The liberation of the body has freed us so far as performance is concerned, but not yet with regard to dramatic art itself . . .

Ours is a transitional period, and to exploit it we have to be clearly aware of this. Today we understand that movement, forms, lines, light and colours are at our disposal. The dogmas of traditional staging have been displaced but we do not yet realize how greatly they have influenced our very conception of theatrical production, and have continually suggested or forced upon it the same practices . . . It is a mistake, therefore, to employ the same buildings both for the contemporary dramatic repertoire and for new experimental work. Their unyielding frame and prescriptive power greatly hinders our attempts to liberate ourselves. So let us abandon such theatres to their dying past, and construct new buildings designed simply to provide a shell for the space in which our work will take place.

There will be no stage or auditorium, only a bare and empty hall, which waits . . . convenient places to store the set pieces; and a complete lighting apparatus. So much for the technical aspect. As for the rest – actors, singers, dancers, eurhythmicists, writers, musicians, artists – all well-intentioned people offering their talent to the new challenge without rivalry over their individual professions; they will cooperate for the good of the common cause, and will direct, offer suggestions or perform, each according to his ability. When we feel sufficiently confident to offer a worthwhile demonstration, tiers of seats can easily be improvised for a public anxious to learn, and this public will naturally wish to contribute its advice and support. Gradually we shall begin to conceive – undoubtedly with the help of the public – new interrelated productions, and to increase or temporarily limit the importance or extent of one type of expression in favour of some other. This experimental field will serve as a sort of nursery for dramatic art, the development of which will no longer be curtailed by inappropriate conventions. It is easy to anticipate productions in which the public participates either in the music or action, and where only the old or infirm stay seated and inactive. Then art will live amongst us!

It is this art for which all our theatre exhibitions must prepare; towards it all our efforts should be directed, in whichever field they may be expressed. Then we shall realize that, in its most noble form, art is a gesture of mutual subordination, far surpassing our narrow individual aspirations.

The influence of such an institution is incalculable; it will reach out across our entire culture, bringing order and vitality. The painter, the sculptor and the poet will not attempt to express through their work what alone living art can achieve. And the dramatists and artists taking part in our demonstrations will avoid borrowing from the fine arts and literature themes which are incompatible with movement. The taste of the public will be purified; this will refine its judgement and enable it to take part more fully and effectively in the great task. This is a dream for the future! But nothing need prevent that dream from being realized some day if we begin now to prepare for it. Theatre exhibitions are taking on an avant-garde quality, and writers rather than stage directors continue to suffer under the dead weight of a moribund tradition and old habits. For, as I have said, the conception of theatre must be liberated. Our dramatists are still unaware of their freedom and continue to regard the theatre suspiciously or submit to it passively. How can they be encouraged to change their attitude? The responsibility for persuading them lies with us, the stage directors, and our projects must all bear witness to a joyful emancipation.

Theatrical Production and its Prospects for the Future

(1921)

Il Covegno 4 (10), 1923: 483–510
Theatre Arts Monthly 16 (8), Aug. 1932: 649–66
Theatre Arts Anthology New York, 1950 (abbreviated)
Cahiers de la Compagnie Madeleine Renaud, Jean-Louis Barrault
3 (10), 1955: 98–115
Volbach, pp. 199–219; Bablet, 4, pp. 72–86

Dedicated to the pupils of the Jaques-Dalcroze Institute

... I feel obliged to ask that you erase from your memory as well as your imagination everything you understand about, or have seen, in the theatre ... I go further yet, and urge that you follow me: we have to make a clean sweep and forget the auditorium, the stage, even the very building that encompasses them.

The title of this talk must not suggest anything firmly set.[12] I repeat: we must make a clean sweep!

... Once an author has completed his play, what element does he deem essential for its enactment? The actors, of course. Without actors there can be no action, thus no performance, thus no play – except on our bookshelves ... In space which is 'without form and void' the actor represents three-dimensionality; he is plastic and therefore occupies a fragment of space upon which he imposes his form. But the actor is not a statue; he is plastic, but also alive, and he expresses his life through movement; he possesses space not just through his mass, but also by his movement within it. His body, isolated in limitless space, measures that space through gestures and movements ... remove him, and space once more becomes undefined and elusive. In this sense his body creates space.

... Measuring space involves measuring time ... From our point of view ... in the hands [of the playwright] the actor is a compass for space, a pendulum for time. The author controls space and time; that is his formal power (using the term in the sense of external form). An organic hierarchy arises from these facts, which we may define as: the author, the actor, (scenic) space. Notice that I have not mentioned time. For in fact, if the presence of the actors affects space, which the author can only measure through him, then time remains in the hands of the author. In other words, the author imposes upon the actor the temporal duration of his role, while having to depend upon the actor to realize that duration in space.

. . . But does the author have any means for determining the time value of his text so definitely as to impose it on the actor? No, he does not; the duration of speech is indefinite; it may be spoken slowly or quickly; it may be interrupted, and so on . . . In short, the author, who ought to control time, does not in fact control it at all; speech does not supply him any means for such control.

. . . The written word on its own does not dictate the time required to deliver it. The duration of a word is approximate and left to the free will of the actor . . . This rule of wilfulness is endemic in our modern theatre. The director, designer, electrician, technician, etc. . . . they all work only tentatively together; a procedure which is intolerable in any other form of art. The will of the author ought to be law, but we know he does not hold all the strings. All too frequently he merely prevents them from becoming too tangled.

It is claimed that the art of the theatre is very complex. This is true. And in the light of that, let us make a comparison by using the example of the conductor-composer of a symphonic poem with chorus and soloists . . . The singers, having studied their parts in advance, are entirely familiar with them, as too are the members of the orchestra. This is comparable to the preparation of roles by the actors in a play, and the advance work carried out by the scenic designers . . .

The orchestral score is written out just like the author's manuscript. The conventional musical signs are analogous to the letters of the alphabet, and the composer seems to be as much a human presence as is the playwright. Where is the difference? . . .

The conductor of the orchestra possesses in the score, and independent of his own will, the means required for translating those signs into the performance in terms of time duration, or a series of such durations, perfectly and completely determined in advance. If those taking part do not obey, they are no longer executing the score! Where is the controlling baton of the dramatist? And even if he possessed one, who or what could lend it authority? His text? Does it provide any directions for the baton? And should the actors, director or others prove absent-minded or neglectful, does this text have any power to pull them into line again? And suppose the piece is spoilt by the incompetence of the leading young actor, or of the scene painter? Alas! Here we have but a kingdom of whims. A false note, a missed cue, and the music ceases to be what the score dictates. Have the myriad stupidities during a stage rehearsal the same effect? What

125

then is it which gives the score its tyrannical influence, this sort of categorical imperative which makes everyone sense that here the question is 'to be or not to be?'

Time! Yes! Time is determined by the score but not by the play text . . . We must concede that the difference between the written work of the playwright and the written work of the musician is substantial, so great in fact that they do not even appear to be in the same category. And yet both claim to be works of art. Is the claim justified? . . . To be an artist means, after all, to conceive and create a work of art . . . The work he offers an audience is his own; otherwise it doesn't belong in the realm of art. The musician retains control of his composition all the way, right up to its performance. This essential privilege is denied to the dramatic author. The work he offers an audience is not wholly his own; he has no control over it, and cannot therefore, be an artist. Whatever influence and authority he may have is not implicit in his text.

. . . The problem of staging can therefore be stated categorically: how can the playwright become an artist, and who can provide him with the means to attain this goal, since he cannot supply them himself?

We can come up with an answer only when we no longer conceive the dramatist's task as divided into two parts: on the one hand the manuscript, on the other the stage. The challenge is difficult; but we shall manage it. Let us recall the musician's work and its performance in a concert. The same integrated performance must be acquired for the playwright.

. . . The challenge is to capture the mobility of life for his own use. Space by itself is like a canvas next to an empty palette. The canvas requires colours – and with regard to life, such colour is movement, which is to say, time. Our would-be artist will be able to choose with his brush the time durations of movement and then project these on to his canvas, i.e. into space . . . Today the musical score is the only text we know that implicitly contains such time values. Let us therefore offer it to the dramatist, to whom nothing could be more precious . . .

Music has set the dramatist free, but what relationship has it to staging? Movement, we said. Do its time patterns match the usual movements of the actor? No, not at all, and there lies the problem! . . . The movements of the actor indicate his emotions, but they do not express them. Our forefinger indicating a command does not in itself express burning ambition; nor does a frown express long-silent suffering. The actor observes these signs in himself and others, and uses them as well as he can in his role as part of developing a characterization. In a similar way words are indications, symptoms; the phrase 'to love' has never expressed what we feel when we love. We may love all our life long, and never say a word about it . . . such is the temporal value of words; it bears no relation to the temporal value of our feelings. A dagger thrust does not express the enduring hatred that leads to this action; it is merely a demonstration of

126

that hatred. In our daily lives we lack the means for direct expression so we must indirectly infer the feelings for which the external life is no more than a symptom. In the absence of music the actor is thus a bearer of symptoms, nothing more . . . For the author of the spoken drama, time serves to augment these symptoms. In that sense he does use it a little, and the higher the plane upon which he places his drama, the greater his freedom to employ time.

If music controls time, it must have valid reasons and sufficient justification for doing so . . . We ourselves are this justification . . . We happily admit that music expresses what our words and gestures are unable to express . . . Music has nothing to enlarge, or prolong; it simply expresses . . . Music reveals to the listener the form and intensity of his inner life in proportions that he accepts because he understands their origin . . .

Music can provide a remarkable medium connecting the playwright's manuscript and the stage. Moreover, by controlling the continuity of time durations, music also determines their relative intensities; i.e. their dramatic values . . . In short, music takes command of the entire drama, projecting only so much of it as is required to motivate and sustain its expression. Music therefore becomes the ultimate regulator of the integrated work of dramatic art; it holds the balance. The hierarchy with which we began contained only three elements: author, actor, scenic space. Music provides the fourth. In fact, by controlling time, music takes its rightful place between the author and the performer.

Because of our clean sweep, which led, I must confess, into a barren landscape, we were able to perceive the essential elements of dramatic art and distinguish them separately prior to their use. Now we can approach the modern theatre free from fear of misunderstanding.

The liberation of theatrical art took place only recently, so recently in fact that habit still retards the most progressive experiments. On the very same stage, simplified modern settings are frequently seen to follow hard upon those of the old-fashioned opera. We therefore live in a transitional period; in the past as well as the future, with the present fluctuating between the two, often in a void! We notice, however, that reform is applied most frequently to the spoken drama, while musical drama has preserved the operatic scenic tradition more or less intact . . . The playwright has begun to realize his inferior position and the arbitrary staging of his work, and is attempting to regain the place he had earlier and secure it for the present; having escaped from the yoke of literary traditions, he wishes to be rid of the scenic shackles as well . . .

Musical drama, on the other hand, appears to us to be merely a continuation of opera, and we can see no need to alter its staging method, which was derived from opera . . . In doing so we disrupt the flow of musical expression and prevent it from being projected into space. On the one hand we have the orchestra and singers; on the other, painted settings. Under such an arrangement the poet-musician is a monarch whose power has been overturned, even though we continue to honour him. His position is painfully unnatural, and our magnificent orchestras and splendid soloists only underline this irony. Everything is lavished on the musical score; nothing on the stage. Our presentations of Wagnerian musical dramas are no more than concerts in which the singers move about without motivation while changing backdrops are displayed before our eyes. The orchestra stops playing, the voices cease; the concert is over, the curtain falls, the setting vanishes: thus concludes one of these unfortunate exhibitions. Sometimes it almost seems that the music is performed in one hall and the staging in another.

. . . Let us return briefly to the literary play! It tries to supply what only music could give it, and with true instinct grants sovereignty to the actor. Painted settings are banished; all the scenic elements are finally placed in the service of the living body. And about time, too! But the remarkable thing is that music has entered into the realm of the spoken drama! Who amongst us has not felt the shock, quite unique, when the sounds of music suddenly ring out in a play? Pure, unadulterated truth seemed then to appear gently and free the actor of the tinsel that obscured him, of the inessentials that thwarted him.

Then truth appeared to whisper, 'You have permitted me to make this brief revelation. Very well! But I could say more, much more!' And if the spoken word is imposed on the music, we sense at once how powerless words are. Music always tells the truth: when it lies, it says so – but words! Therefore any scene into which music is introduced, no matter what it may be, is immediately ennobled . . .

During the brief period when the incidental music is heard, [the actor's] gestures are modified, he perceives the divine element penetrating his body, and he would be unfeeling not to be affected by it. This is a step in the right direction; music has its foot in the door. For example, if a scene during which music performs its unseen role has been rehearsed without music, the first rehearsal including it will reveal that the entire scene must be reshaped from a different perspective. The capricious quality of the earlier rehearsals has found its master.

The drama without music will survive for a long time to come, perhaps for ever; and its staging, corrupted by dead tradition, will be invigorated by contact with a less specialized art, and will adopt at random new elements from it. But the art of stage production can be a true art only when its source is music. This does not mean that a spoken drama may not sometimes be excellently performed; only that the extent of such excellence must remain a matter of chance . . .

To take music as the source of drama does not suggest that musical sound must itself be the origin of the dramatic idea, but rather that the

Figure 16 The 1882 Bayreuth setting by Paul von Joukowsky for the flower meadows of *Parsifal*, Act III. Cf. Appia's setting in Figure 17.

object of the music should also be the object of that idea. It means moreover the internalization of dramatic feeling, inspired by the certainty that music is able to express the inner life without restraint, and need not leave anything to media that can only indicate inner life . . . If the dramatic artist understands that he can express to the very fullest the conflicts of inner life (I say 'express', not simply 'indicate'), that awareness will inspire in him an action quite different to that suggested by words alone. If, in addition, he can rely as we have seen, upon externalizing such conflicts in an appropriate space, his entire dramatic vision will be transformed.

Schopenhauer writes that music does not express the phenomenon, but only the inner essence of the phenomenon; therefore it expresses nothing related to the story, geography, social conditions and customs; no actual objects of any sort. In regard to all such things, music expresses only the Idea. Human passions are eternally the same: music proclaims this. The more the passions that the dramatist seeks to express are stripped of the transitory quality of our existence, the more he will find in music a benevolent ally . . .

Let us move on to the actor! We have observed that musical expression fundamentally modifies the external form of our gestures, i.e. their successive durations in time, and that therefore the actor need no longer interpret his part, but rather clearly present it as it has been entrusted to him. The value of the actor will be his cooperation; music transfigures him, making him unable to resist. The bearer of an inner action obviously behaves in a different manner to one interpreting an action dictated by external circumstances . . .

Our final problem is to enliven space through music using the actor who is himself transformed and transfigured by musical qualities . . . The chief element of contemporary staging is, we know, painted settings, cut up into pieces and arranged in segments, one behind the other, to suggest perspective. And because the pieces of this setting must continually make way for others, these bits of canvas are hung in the flies or are stored below to be readily raised or lowered on to the stage . . . Some stage floors even have a built-in revolve whose diameter is somewhat larger than the proscenium opening, on to which several settings are simultaneously mounted and can be rotated to appear sequentially in the proscenium arch. A play with several settings can thereby be arranged entirely in advance and then unfold like a picture book before the audience . . .

Upstage the setting is closed off by a painted backcloth, and the flies above can be masked by canvas to form a ceiling virtually at right angles to the flats and wings . . . The setting thus resembles a sort of empty box in which to catch flies . . . Only the practicable pieces are actually *three-dimensional*; these are arranged in front of or in between the vertical flats for the actors to use; the term 'practicable' applies to everything that is solid and hence conforms to the plasticity of the human body. But, alas, what is impracticable about these practicables is the job of making them harmonize with the artificial painted setting. No device can conceal the incongruity.

Lighting alone remains . . . There are two types of light with regard to a painted setting: one is fixed on the canvas itself by artificial painting; the second is installed in order to make the painting visible. The painted light cannot fall upon the actor, although it concerns him; the actual light hits him, but it concerns only the painting! And in such an environment we put the living, solid, moving body of the actor. A light not intended for him falls upon him, while on the other hand he moves about in front of painted light! He is visible, but that is all . . .

After light comes colour. A painting is able to employ whatever colour is appropriate, while even the best-equipped theatres hardly have more than three or four colours on tinted glass for their lighting effects. Everything else is haphazard.

This is the scenic material available to our theatres. It is hard to conceive of a more contradictory setup, and it is a miracle that we achieve with it the visual effects to which we are accustomed. But whenever the curtain opens on a setting without the actors, or when the stage picture remains empty for a moment, the overall effect is generally acceptable. The painting, properly illuminated, fulfils its function; its artificial relief and perspective create an illusion, and the cleverly arranged flats are combined to good effect . . .

We notice that by changing one of the elements of production, we distort all the others. If light should be directed only upon the actor, the painting would suffer to such a degree that it might just as well be discarded . . . The slightest effort favouring the actor would tend to banish the painter. But the actor cannot be dispensed with! What is the solution to such a dilemma? This is the ultimate problem: either the actor or the painting!

Those of you listening who think only of productions of drawing-room comedies are probably astonished. For the most part the rooms in which their actions took place were compatible with their sets of furniture and with the presence of the actor . . . The theatre is therefore a place for conversations, and it does not matter a great deal where the persons talk, so long as they can be adequately seen and heard. Then why have a stage at all with its fictions; why separate the auditorium from the stage? Why not just have a simple place that is well lit, and has good acoustics? Cost would be so diminished that theatres could be built all over the city. The theatre would become the last refuge of conversation.

There is really nothing to be said against this; but it means the deliberate singling out of one form of dramatic art and its espousal to the exclusion of all the others . . . So let us concede that the drawing-room comedy poses no problem scenically, and take a somewhat broader view of the situation.

Reform was first applied to lighting . . . The actor, already immersed in

131

Figure 17 Appia's 1896 design for the flower meadows of *Parsifal*, Act III. Appia wrote of this design: 'We are again on the holy ground of the Grail. The tree trunks and the general appearance of the countryside make this clear. Utter calm is doubtless indicated; but the lines of the mountain imply a striving toward a final resolution' (Appia 1960: 94). Cf. the Bayreuth setting, Figure 16.

a general illumination that eliminates shadows, finds himself at the same time struck by footlights from below which quite destroy any trace of shadow that might have remained. Without plasticity his whole body resembles a flat painting. Thus everything is done in order to reduce the actor to two dimensions! But the mobility of his features is three-dimensional! . . . And we dare to invoke theatrical perspective in order to excuse this criminal betrayal of humanity! Anxious to see all of the actor, we end up by seeing very little of him . . . Gradually the use of the footlights was substantially reduced . . .

The scene painter, in the ordinary meaning of the word, is nothing but an expert with an instrument that has been cast on to the rubbish heap. He will survive for a time because of traditional inertia, but will then vanish like the artists who composed historical and narrative paintings.

Let us reiterate: lighting has dictated total stage reform, and come to the aid of the actor. So we are compelled after all to view him as the first element in the hierarchy of presentation; the insubstantial wavering setting, as pointed out, cannot stand up against him . . .

We still lack the technique, but no longer a guiding principle. Heroic efforts on the part of Pitoëff, Gordon Craig, Stanislavsky, and Copeau prove this.[13] Each of them in his own way and within his particular field places the living person foremost amongst the other elements! . . .

It is remarkable that reform began in the theatre with plays, dance and pantomime. In the case of dance and pantomime, the human body is itself the medium of expression together with music, but without speech; in plays it interprets the spoken action without music. In the former case music reigns supreme; in the latter, the visible action of the drama is raised to the same status as speech . . . The other forms of theatrical art, however, kept more or less to the old tradition. When we leave a production by Pitoëff to attend *The Valkyrie*, we tumble from extreme modernity into the most sordid routine . . .

The inevitable conclusion is that music has not yet been recognized as the fundamental controlling element, unique in its type of power, while the actor has acquired a supremacy that is not justified by the spoken word alone, since speech cannot control . . . In short, despite Wagner and those imitating him, the lyric drama does not supply us with the firm basis we expected it to provide, and music will triumph in the theatre only by means of the intermediary of bodily feeling, separate, for the time being at least, from the dramatic element, which we originally considered to be the indispensable source of inspiration . . . Thus, in the end, we are once more face to face with music and the living body, but now in the full knowledge of the reason, and with no other concern except to unite them forever in that harmony whose supreme importance and happy prospects we already anticipate . . .

The union between the body and music is essentially a question of procedure: we can observe then whether this union will not considerably expand the very idea of theatre. All of us are aware, I am sure, of the value of the Jaques-Dalcroze method! . . . It is a human discipline that sets up within us a harmonious balance using the medium of our body. It affects our entire being and thus accords with the musical art which affirms the coordinated unity between body and soul through harmony and rhythm . . .

To take up our theme again, why should production be exclusively the prerogative of the theatre? Does our body really need to tread the boards? Must it actually display itself? Without banning the well-intentioned spectator who is anxious to know more, let us not think of him as indispensable to living art, for which in the end we alone are responsible . . . Here you learn precisely not 'to perform'. Nevertheless, nothing prevents you from taking control of space and subordinating it to the harmony and balance you have achieved within yourselves. If you obtain satisfactory or remarkable results, you will not desire to exclude any who do not themselves enjoy such substantial privileges. This will not in any way be a theatre. On the contrary, it will be its negation; for your desire to share your pleasure opens wide the curtain and causes you to step out across the footlights once and for all! . . .

The future of our theatre is based upon living art. You are the happy bearers of this art. Its future is in your hands. Upon your efforts and integrity depends an extraordinary rebirth of dramatic art.

Monumentality

(1922)

Revue d'esthetique Oct.–Dec. 1953: 349–68
Volbach, pp. 221–34; Bablet, 4, pp. 142–56

When we arrive in Florence, is our attitude any different to that which we have when entering a museum? Can we not perceive that, despite all the profound impressions we receive, an attitude like this leaves the soul empty? Before we even arrive at these real places which, after all, are altogether concrete, we have transported them into the past. Why, then, are they here now under our very eyes? Why do we concern ourselves with visiting them if we deny them their reality? . . .

Our conception of art remains that of the collector and historian. It does not much matter that architecture cannot be confined to galleries open only at specific times; we are quite happy to fashion such galleries in our imagination. Who would dare to claim that he returns with a living and harmonious synthesis of Italy? On the one hand we fill ourselves with what we term art; on the other we manage to enjoy or be interested in observing the Italian people . . . Where then do we locate the idea of the present that is undeniably evident? Within ourselves? Can we really feel able to establish the slightest trace of harmony between the Signoria and ourselves?[14] . . .

We arrive in Italy burdened with luggage that hinders our steps and limits each of our impulses. Then we return home, and when we unpack all our presumed treasures we are quite astonished to find our suitcases contain nothing new! Excuse me, I am mistaken: all the documents we took along with us are wrapped in a tight bundle, leaving an empty space. Our everyday life will never fill it. And yet that empty space is waiting for Life. We took everything with us, brought back everything, except Life! . . .

The intellectual has been compared to an old-fashioned purse in which the gold is confined to one corner by a ring, while the rest of the purse hangs loose and empty . . . In this sense all of us are intellectuals when confronted by a work of art. We wander aimlessly through the picture galleries, the sculpture halls, like matchstick puppets suffering from swollen heads. And we extend our unselfconscious insolence to the point of contemplating the architecture with this lifeless body – an architecture conceived for the living body! Our display cases provide appropriate protection for the Greek amphorae, but where is the wine with which to fill them? Where are the lips to touch them? . . .

We ought often to have two buildings in front of us for comparison: the cathedral at Florence and the Parthenon. Commentary would then be superfluous. So long as the human race survives, the Parthenon will never be an anachronism; for it sprang from the human body that will always be perceived in it. But what is to be done with buildings distorted from the very start by an artificial and moribund culture, or else so particularly designed for a single period of human existence that their survival into subsequent ages is achieved only through corruption? One who thinks the Florence cathedral beautiful is a collector; one who feels comfortable in the Piazza della Signoria is a barbarian. The Parthenon is not beautiful, it is living; and life does not require a descriptive title. I choose these examples because they are familiar and particularly suggestive.

And sculpture? Those who detest museums would like to display it in the streets, and fill our public buildings and homes with it. Why should sculpture be there, and what would it do? Does sculpture in the least concern us? And even if we attempted to concern ourselves with it, what would be the basis for our judgement? . . .

And painting? Since it remains immobile, it too belongs to the monumentality of art. To make painting movable, we cut it into segments of flat surfaces; and in the absence of any architecture to enclose them, we place these fragments within gilded frames. Then we arrange them against walls, also flat, and lacking even frescoes . . . and we gaze upon this beautiful arrangement! Within our own homes this absurdity is just conceivable, since even under the most favourable conditions our daily life is itself fragmented, detached and uprooted. But in our museums?[15] . . .

I have concluded that monumental art as we know it has reached the end of its life; it is no longer alive, only vestigial. We are entering a new period in which art will demand that we live within it and we, in turn, will require that art live in us. When this magnificent reciprocity has become firmly established, and when it has become so natural that we can no longer imagine art without it, then there will probably develop, as the ultimate expression of this reciprocity, a monumental art form. It may be thought that after a period of intense development this art form, like those preceding it, will run the risk of stagnation. However, because this new monumentality will have been created by artists aware of their responsibility – which has never before been the case, except in Greece – their works will in all probability bear the mark of this awareness, and will thus enjoy a certain immunity: their reality will no longer be merely historical like that of our buildings, but will retain sufficient positive and contemporaneous vitality to guide taste instead of stultifying and corrupting it . . .

Greek artists . . . openly began with the living human body, convinced that the architect must serve the body and be justified by it. Consequently their buildings are immortal! The architects recognized their responsibility towards the body. Art will never endure unless it is based upon an awareness of close human solidarity. The Greek temples and theatres provide typical examples of this. The Romans fashioned theirs with the fundamental triviality of the Latin race. Our own cathedrals provide the last majestic echo of the principle of solidarity; their existence amidst our dwellings is like a silent challenge. It is significant that today we speak of the cathedral of the future.[16] The survival of these impressive buildings keeps our memory of their basic function alive, and challenges us to renew this function at a time when we desperately aspire to come together . . .

The concept of monumentality, which we have expanded to embrace sculpture and painting, can and must be extended further. But to do this it must be carefully defined so that it applies almost entirely to the present. We shall see why.

Every work is monumental which relies on its duration rather than upon its immediate usefulness; therefore monumental works are intended to stimulate men's admiration rather than their gratitude. This idea has a certain obvious application in all human activities. The music of a patriotic festival is monumental when its composer sacrifices the immediately desirable effect to the creation of a score which, he believes, must outlast its ephemeral moment of performance . . .

A committee is monumental when it sacrifices for its prestigious existence the efficacy and initiative of a manager who can act on his own. A theatre is monumental when its construction exhausts all the available finance, leaving nothing for the presentation of good productions, which, after all, were the sole purpose of the building and should have been given priority. A de luxe edition of a book is monumental when the cost prevents the book from being widely accessible or when its binding makes ordinary use of the work impracticable. Finally, and above all, we create the monumental whenever we give a fixed plan to a building that, on the contrary, ought to lend itself to continuous transformation in order to encompass in space the evolution of works whose very nature is to remain resilient and tentative . . .

Let us assume that [an architect] is commissioned to construct a people's theatre. For many this term will evoke an image of a modest, inexpensive building. If we consider the details, the auditorium will have to be provided with cheap seating and the stage equipped for low-budget productions . . . And here the principle of monumentality can provide support as much by excluding certain arbitrary fancies as by encouraging bold innovations which we would probably not have dreamt of in its absence . . . 'People's theatre', although it appears to be a simple term, encompasses two ideas, both of which are on the verge of undergoing complete change. Dramatic art has burst the frame that had held it rigid for so long, and the very concept of theatre has so expanded that it gives us vertigo and a slight feeling of anarchy. The idea of 'people' too is no longer tightly defined, and has come to take on the shape of something amorphous, far-reaching and nebulous.

Do we understand 'people's theatre' to be a place for presentations which all can afford? Or a stage operating under a more or less autocratic censorship with either a cautious and conservative policy or, on the contrary, a radically progressive one? Would such a theatre have to exclude works which were expensive or difficult to stage?

Such considerations do not even approach the problem as it currently exists; consequently the term 'people's theatre' is a misnomer. There can no longer be a 'people's theatre' for the two words have become meaningless; they denote a 'monumental' form of the past. Unable precisely to grasp the demands of the present, we have to realize an idea of the future, which will naturally appear to be 'monumental' until social and artistic evolution justifies it and, catching up with it, discovers in it a ground already prepared . . .

However, my project would be rejected unanimously were I not to take the present into account . . . I should de-emphasize the elements of the future which it does not include but which it must suggest . . . Where can I begin? What direction should I take? This is the point where I return to our two types of building – the Florentine cathedral and the Greek temple! How can we hesitate? Obviously the Greeks have given us the direction for ever. Let us therefore begin, like the Greeks, with the living man, and re-examine the question in these terms: the people and the theatre! . . .

By beginning with the people we have defined it; by subordinating the concept of theatre to the people we make ourselves masters of this concept. My task as architect must then start with an attempt to discover the type of theatrical space needed by a modern community, and, at the same time, what mission this space should suggest to the community . . .

Before anything else we must begin by recognizing that a modern community is no longer passive. The theatre, as it has been understood, has schooled the spectator in passivity; therefore it can no longer serve a modern audience. What part of the theatre encourages audience passivity? Undoubtedly, the actors. The position given the actors directly influences the spectator, and we must begin by changing this position. Its most characteristic quality is the remoteness of the actor from the audience, emphasized inside the auditorium by the footlights, outside by separate entrances, and throughout by a mode of behaviour that is far removed from that of the spectator. The audience, for its part, idly perpetuates the custom of paying for and selecting its seat, then expecting the actor to do all the rest. But such conditions are anachronistic, and both the actor and the audience can no longer agree to these humiliating relations.

Between the two is the play, the production, whose existence up to now has naturally depended upon the activity of the actor and the passivity of the spectator. The concept of production has gradually changed, however, as the formerly legitimate conditions of its existence have been transformed. The actor now attempts to bridge the gulf separating him from the audience in order to satisfy his desire for activity, which is easier for him than for the audience, since the actor is active by definition. Such an effort depends on the playwright and the director, and these two individuals have assisted the actor in various ways to enable and even to encourage a new rapport between actor and audience.

Returning then to the original name of the building, I have been requested to design a people's theatre. We should note that the architect must collaborate with the actor, the author, the stage director and the audience to provide each with the greatest possible stimulus in order to bring them more closely together. It is only a step from this preparation to an acceptable fusion in the future! The structure must anticipate this union, but not overtly . . .

As you see, my task is becoming evident: its monumental aspect is to anticipate, without revealing the coming union between actors and audience in a collective action; its immediate and expedient aspect is to prepare for this grand future through an arrangement that stimulates the audience into activity, and allows the actor to advance further and further towards meeting the audience. We have noted that everyone is quite ready to understand and support us, if we employ a bit of diplomacy. Our role is thus that of a teacher, for it is clear to me that a modern architect must be an educator . . .

Let us remember that our life creates the principles of art. If, during a period of perfect and happy equilibrium, life has been able to develop a new aesthetics – that is to say, Greek art – out of stultifying traditions, this art owed its development entirely to this equilibrium. Why then do we demand such a creation out of our murky, confused and turbulent period of transition? If we imitate, our work will be dated and inorganic; if we look for some sort of style to arise within our sick imagination, deriving its detail from our active life, we will only create a monstrosity, for in any life a monstrosity is that which deviates from the norm of that life. Thus we would be surrounded by monstrosity had modern technique not come to our assistance . . .

This technique gives the architect what he requires to adjust himself to the boldness as well as the uncertainty of a confused and distracted period, or, alternatively, to rise above it as an informed teacher. I have chosen the latter role, and since everything is relative in education, I approach the problem of the structural elements not from an aesthetic principle alone, but also from a principle of social aesthetics similar to that which directs us in the education of our children.

My 'people's theatre' will be conceived with the intention of encouraging people to come together and enjoy a sociable atmosphere within a building which is dedicated to that purpose. For my part, the theatre will be the basis for this task, while for the people, it will be the bait . . . Therefore I shall look after this bait by setting up the educational installations so that they seem to be a part of the theatre, and not merely associated with it. I shall attempt to give them as much importance as my duplicity can provide. Finally, I shall bear in mind all the different possibilities for expansion and transformation that modern technology can supply. The auditorium of the theatre will not be located at the centre, for the rear and the sides of the stage house must be equipped so that eventually they will allow performances to be given more or less out of doors. For this purpose, gardens set out with shrubbery instead of trees will ensure that this space remains available, without yet revealing its eventual use.

While appearing to be rigid, the proscenium arch can be widened or narrowed as wished, and may even disappear entirely into the walls and the ceiling, thereby allowing the stage and auditorium to merge into a single architectural unit. The area designated for the orchestral pit will be readily covered, and the seating in the auditorium, set out in the form of an amphitheatre, may be turned down to form a horizontal floor, level with the stage. The floor of the stage, therefore, will be arranged as sections resting upon hydraulic lifts. There will not be either galleries or boxes to the sides; to the rear of the auditorium, at the back of the house, I will probably position two large and deep galleries, set up in tiers, which may eventually be joined to each other and the house itself by stairs running along their entire width. These galleries will not have a different admission price – there will be one price for the entire house – and will provide an approach on to the terraces through side and rear doors. Both auditorium and stage will receive ample sunlight, and can therefore be used throughout the day. At night the lighting will not be provided by visible sources such as chandeliers or the like, but will simply pervade the space; modern technology has recently provided the means for such indirect lighting.[17] I shall also retain the potential to open up all or some portion of the auditorium's lateral walls (and, as noted, those of the stage) in order to connect these two areas with the lobby and promenade hall, and the gardens and terraces, thereby creating an atmosphere of the greatest sociability, which will quite readily encourage performers and audience to mingle during the intermissions. The décor generally will be beautiful in design and colour, but will have no high relief, and as little fabric as possible, since good acoustics must come before all else, even in the lobby and promenade areas.

The materials used for construction should be fully evident in the

Figure 18　Appia's rhythmic space design of 1909, 'Moonbeam'.

building ... my structure will be architectural only in its function; its monumental quality will thus remain minimal both now and in the future. This is desirable. The people must receive the strong, unforgettable impression that they, their living bodies, are creating and defining the space. The living body must feel able freely to modify at will the actual space and its limits. The crux of the issue thus consists in fully preserving an ideal flexibility in a building, which, nevertheless, must awaken a sense of strength and permanence. I am confident the solution is possible.[18]

It would be interesting to carry out this project and observe it being used as our so-called 'people's theatre': to imagine the things taking place there, the performances and entertainments presented, the festivals and very diverse events which such a space might inspire, to discover in what ways and why the premises will have to be altered; finally, to guess the term that will be given to this entire complex as that most generally appropriate to its functions. But although the architect has the responsibility to foresee all these things, his official duty does not extend so far; his intuitive work, his personal initiative as a pedagogue is fulfilled with the building. Afterwards, the architect is simply a collaborator with the authors, actors and the public, to whom he subordinates himself. He will doubtless have to be consulted, but the centre of gravity has shifted; he has produced his work; it is the task of others to prove that they are deserving owners of it ...

To summarize: the centuries of unconscious and carefree labour for the artist are past. If at one time he might be certain of remaining one with his contemporaries, he can be certain no longer; and has not been for a long time. In our day Life moves quickly ahead; it speeds past the work of art so quickly that it has no time to look around to see if the artist is following. Moreover, it displays no wish to do so, since it has lost the total confidence it once had in him. Yet the artist requires some point of departure. If he continues today in looking for it within himself, he will be lost, and left behind as Life will increasingly outpace him. How can he protest? Was it not his blind pride that led him into this impasse?

'Art for art's sake' – that is what we have now, and understand it thoroughly! But what nonsense! Does one ever say 'Life for Life's sake'? Would this have any meaning at all? We have 'abandoned' the artists, leaving them sullen like naughty children, as we proceeded on our own. As soon as they stop sulking, we shall happily welcome them back; but until then they must learn through hard experience, and we will not assist them in discovering themselves by buying their paintings and figurines, by accepting their out-of-date and thoughtless designs, or their fickle music. On the contrary! Their only salvation lies in a sincere confession of their inadequacies. Then Life, active Life, will reach out its hand and, returning to purely human emotions, the artists will be forced to acknowledge that this Life alone can provide them with firm ground upon which to place their springboard. A work of art is an artifice; if active Life does not provide it with lasting substance, then the work is diffused and lost in space, and vanishes like the pyrotechnician's rocket in the night sky. The artist is therefore forced to turn to Life!

Conservatism, like any form of indolence, is afraid of effort, the unknown, potential sacrifice, unavoidable shocks, and therefore keeps us where we are. The modern artist understands that his art is in need of reform. An intelligent artist is no longer able to doubt that a picture contained within a frame is a childish object. A musician composing his symphony now definitely senses that the ground upon which his feet rest is not the same as ours. All this makes them suffer, poor chaps, but instead of looking for the source of Life within Life itself, they continue attempting to discover it in the clouds out of which we forced it down some time ago!

The spectacle of Life is not, however, the active Life. This Life must still be lived, and the artist recoils from this . . . Surely we are all too often still incorrigible spectators; but the artist goes much further! He desires to remain a spectator of spectators; he looks to them as his models! No circle could be more vicious! – Ah, if only the artist were willing! But there it is, he is not; therefore it is now left to us to compel him . . .

We must bear the responsibilities which the artist refuses to accept. We must ceaselessly prove to him that we are capable of this, and are worthy of the task; and because of this we must refuse to be eternal spectators, or allow ourselves to be the spectacle.

Let the artist come to live our Life; otherwise our door must remain closed to him. We do not need what he has to offer us. It is now our turn to give! Let him understand this and be content! There will be no reason for him to regret it, nor for us to regret having compelled him.

The Art of the Living Theatre[19]

A Lecture for Zurich
(1925)

Volbach, pp. 235–41; Bablet, 4, pp. 472–8

In a production of *The Misanthrope*, Célimène's drawing room was suggested by simple tapestries; only the greatly simplified costumes and the equally demure furniture indicated Molière's period. The purpose was to de-emphasize the historical milieu of a plot so purely human, and at the same time to underline the characters.

My companion, visibly shocked, grumbled: 'How curious that Célimène should furnish her house this way!' That appears to me the perfect opinion of a realistic spectator; the type who prefers to see the place of action precisely as anyone transported there would find it. Highly cultured individuals share this attitude. It is important, therefore, to examine its origin, the underlying source of this attitude, before condemning it. It may after all be justified, and scenic idealism may not suit everyone.

To begin with, is the *mise en scène* itself a work of art, whose conception can ever be determined before it is applied? Does it have an independent existence that simply needs to be adapted for each new play? Of course not; if this were so, we should not even discuss it. Staging, briefly, is the method used by theatrical personnel to present a dramatic action visibly. It is not even a technique habitually adopted; instead it is determined by the dramatic action; without such action, staging makes no sense as an idea; in a real sense it is nothing – nothing at all.

Our definition, however, contains an unknown factor, our eyes, whose differing requirements cannot be altogether or implicitly predicted by the text (whether it has music or not); in other words, staging includes elements which are necessary for the visible presentation of a work, but not contained in its printed text. As a consequence, the prerequisite for a production is the dramatic action, but the staging is nevertheless determined by our eyes, which always create it afresh. In this sense we can assert that we ourselves are the *mise en scène*, and the work remains only a text without us. We are therefore responsible for the production, and since we do not intend to let it unsettle us . . . we have the right to criticize its particular appropriateness.

144

The question therefore takes on a new dimension. We must in the first instance know who we are in relation to the dramatic text. It is not the play but we ourselves which must be examined first. This viewpoint may seem novel, but it is as old as the hills. The surprising thing is that our attention must be called to it.

When we use a microscope we adjust the position of the lenses according to our vision, and not according to the nature of the objects we want to examine. The same is true of the theatre. The play is the given object; it is up to us to adapt ourselves. Staging is precisely this adaptation.

The visible world does not always strike our eyes in the same manner. We can regard it as a spectacle separate from ourselves: this we term, 'to look at'. Or it permeates us involuntarily, and mixes with our inner life, where it exercises rather a tyrannical influence on our unconscious, which is in turn modified by whatever our mood is at the moment. Our ultimate view of objects and individuals fluctuates between these two extremes: on the one hand, the objective or realistic way of observation; on the other, the subjective or idealistic, which feels through seeing. Therefore if, given our definition above, we are and desire to be the creative producers of some play or another, we have to start by questioning ourselves about what goal we pursue in the theatre and what we look for when we enter the auditorium. Are we asking dramatic art or the playwright to present life to us as a spectacle which we merely observe – just as the scientist observes nature – or do we desire to identify in the theatre with the characters and thus perceive ourselves in them? Does dramatic emotion consist of curiosity and its product, which is gratification, or of sympathy and its product, the stirring of the soul?

We may not yet suspect it, but we have formulated here the entire problem of staging, and its resolution depends upon us. I shall go even further and assert that our dramatic art in its entirety depends upon the spectator, that is, on the quality of his vision.

Is the audience the same everywhere? Is it an entity, and does internationalism also standardize our dramatic art? If the play alone is considered, it might seem so, but we have already observed that this is not the primary concern of staging, since this is actually determined not by the play, but by us. The taste for an imaginary world of some sort is common to all humanity. Those who are timid about or despise the theatre satisfy this taste through reading, the fine arts, or in a thousand other ways considered moral and respectable, the true significance of which evades their undeveloped sensibilities. Honest men acknowledge their irrepressible desire to forget themselves in order to be enriched through viewing a performance which daily life does not offer; passions and suffering they do not have to experience; joy and triumphs that transport them beyond ordinary life. In short, by fiction that is animated and presented by creatures like themselves.

Dramatic enjoyment, however, is a question of reaction: a Russian reacts fferently to an Italian; a Parisian to a Scandinavian. The production ..ney desire and which they must create themselves, as we have noted, will be different therefore for each of them. The interest a European displays for a performance from the Far East shares nothing in common with that which the natives experience. A Spaniard watches a *corrida* through different eyes than those of a Scot; a Norwegian reacts to a piece by Ibsen differently to a Florentine . . .

If therefore on the one hand we are the spectators, the creators of the *mise en scène*, on the other there is a genius peculiar to every race which determines the actual form of the production – its presentational form, as we shall term it. And because this form in turn inspires and determines what form the dramatist will choose, the chain appears unbroken. This is not really the case, however. Theatre people are well aware of the sheep-like habits of their audience, which they use as an excuse. Without complaining we put up with the continuous violence inflicted on our good sense by such habits, and to our taste, our need for harmony, proper aesthetic behaviour, and so to our dignity. We endure on stage what our art exhibitions, concerts and lectures would never dare offer without provoking explosive revolt. More than that: we allow the imposition of a dramatic and scenic art completely at variance with our heritage and our own genius. How are we to understand who we are in relation to the theatre, and what we require of it? How is the dramatist and stage director to know and satisfy our true desires? We have positioned ourselves outside the question and forfeited the right to criticize, since we do not even know what we want.

Internationalism in the theatre is the death of dramatic art . . . It cannot touch the work of art; but it is causing its source to dry up, and the responsibility for this rests entirely with us, as spectators. Have we not the right to protest? The courage to do so would not be lacking if we had the slightest idea of the demands we could make! In the situation as it is, however, the dramatists look vainly to us for the suggestions so vital to them. In the absence of these, they throw themselves into destructive internationalism.

To summarize: the *mise en scène* is nothing in itself. The spectator creates it, and in the process inspires and determines theatrical production. Therefore, to deal with staging means to observe this aspect of ourselves, and attempt to find, in our heart, the origin of our taste for dramatic art and the appropriate form to bring this art into harmony with our basic heritage and the particular genius of our race.

So our point of departure is clearly suggested and defined. To start with ourselves undoubtedly promises us a more pleasant voyage and wider horizons than we should have if the curtain, wings, border, lights and spotlights of our stage were our only guides and informants . . . !

146

I have spoken of the realistic and idealistic visions. If we want to define these two concepts solely from the point of view of staging, we must first of all assert that the realistic vision does not directly proceed from the text of the piece (whether it has music or not); while the idealistic vision is entirely inspired by that text. I shall explain.

The playwright provides the dramatic action with an historic and geographic environment, or, in a work of pure fantasy, he indicates its setting imaginatively. The objective realist, deeming these directions independent and self-sufficient, depends exclusively upon them, expecting the stage director to follow them. When such settings have been realized, he locates the dramatic action within them, convinced that the proper harmony between the two elements – the play and the production – is established as automatically as in actual life. The subjective idealist moves in the opposite direction. For him, only the text of the play is important; all suggestions outside this are approached with caution, and his staging is primarily inspired by the text itself. Only after this has taken place does he give thought to the scenic directions and consider their appropriateness. For the realist, the only scenic possibility is the precise historic and geographic replication of the locale chosen by the author. For the idealist, it is a matter of balance. The realist rather crudely places the dramatic text within the reality of a pre-existent environment. The idealist surrounds the text with those scenic elements necessary to illuminate it, discarding any that are superfluous, and would therefore diminish its intensity. To repeat: for the idealist reality lies within the text of the play; for the realist it is in the predetermined locale. In the theatre the realistic conception separates man from his milieu; the idealistic conception sees the milieu entirely in terms of its relationship to the inner life of the characters. The drama of *Parsifal* takes place for the realist in Spain; for the idealist it occurs within ourselves.

Perhaps someone might ask me: why not show greater respect for the express intentions of the author? Does he not understand what is needed for the visible realization of his text better than we, and is his place not arbitrarily usurped by the idealist? The question is vitally important, since it concerns our sense of responsibility towards the theatre. The dramatist today must take into account the fact that the great majority of our spectators are realists. His concept is closely tied to our vision, just as a teacher's mode of expression is tied to his pupils' response; the ties are so strong that even when the dramatist conceives his work without regard for the realist's view, he abruptly changes his mind the moment he decides to let his work be produced. To indulge us, he violates his dream, and, alas, finds in our theatres accomplices only too compliant with his cowardice or lack of technical knowledge. They give him no choice: all stage technology is designed for scenic realism, i.e. for a form of art with no direct or profound relationship to the actual text of the play.

147

it really an art? Do we dare talk of scenic art with a straight

 line informs us that 'the aim of a work of art is to reveal some ential, salient character, consequently some important idea, more clearly and more completely than can real objects. It achieves this through a group of parts whose relationships it systematically modifies.'[20] Are our painted settings a voluntary and systematic modification by us? Do we not, on the contrary, desire a realization that is even more accurate? Is not the technique of the scene painter in fact attempting to diminish these troublesome modifications as much as possible, in order to give us an illusion of reality? But to give the illusion of reality is to negate art. By its very nature dramatic art is a modification of real life, a systematic concentration of a type that our everyday existence cannot offer us. No one therefore will ever doubt that it is an art. The *mise en scène* alone is still viewed with suspicion and subjected to endless debate. To have attempted to turn it into an independent form of art is a serious aesthetic error; yet we continue to cling to the technical elements of stage settings instead of allowing the play itself to guide us. Of course this does not satisfy our eyes. So much for the spectators.

What about the playwright?

This unfortunate creature is aware of the inflexible rigidity of our stages; he also knows our incredible tolerance for this situation and the distortion it has inflicted on our taste. The contest seems to him too unequal: to reform the stage might be relatively easy, but how is one to count on the support of an equally reformed audience? Above all, how is one to make that audience accept that such reform is not merely a technical development on the part of the stage director, but an inner and most profound change required of the spectator himself?

At the beginning I said that we are the *mise en scène*. Our staging remains therefore in a debased condition because we are too warped to be capable of formulating our desires, and, childlike, we accept what we have as inevitable.

But for over twenty years we have had an incomparable basis for assessing the quality of our tastes in regard to performance and to enlighten us about the nature of dramatic art: film. Absolutely nothing at all opposes it; and it is widely acknowledged that nothing can compete with the marvels it can offer to our eyes. What is it therefore that makes the theatre so fundamentally different from film, even when sound can be accurately matched to the image, which, by the way, is hardly desirable? It is, of course, the immediate presence of flesh-and-blood actors, a presence that elicits an immediate emotional response. With regard to everything else, film possesses means with which by comparison our most refined and sumptuous productions are childish diversions. Why then demand from

148

the theatre that which it cannot provide, and which is so liberally offered elsewhere?

Art survives on sacrifice. Painting does without plasticity and living light; sculpture without colour; pure music, without space; architecture, without the expression through time sequence which is the particular secret of music; even the poet refrains from appealing directly to our eyes. Should dramatic art alone sacrifice nothing? Its ephemeral existence ought, at any rate, to alert us. But no, again and again we demand an illusion from it that is foreign to it, instead of the one it has supreme power to give us: the great and divine illusion of life, the life of our body and soul, the only illusion of real value, and the only one admissible as art. Here, as everywhere else, Man is the measure of all things, as Protagoras points out. Thus Man, his body and soul, will be the 'measure' of the environment dictated by his presence on the stage. And everything not measured in terms of him, or of no significance to him, must be banished; that is, the dross which still clutters the theatre and all too often hides the matchless treasure of our human nature . . .

The artist who deliberately chooses the living body and soul of the actor as a means to express himself renders himself dependent upon the technical requisites of that living body and soul and, where art is concerned, technical requirements are irreducible. So the dramatist's technique is concerned immediately with the actual presence of the living body and with its expression of emotion. The former pertains directly to the form of presentation; the latter to the conception of the drama. On the one hand, the playwright must be able to depend upon an appropriate arrangement of the space in which the characters of his drama will move; on the other, he is aesthetically required to select a narrative whose scenic environment will not overshadow the presence of the living actor. And both of these requirements directly concern the spectator. It is not sufficient for the director to follow the playwright, and the playwright to agree to the sacrifices required by the dramatic work. These sacrifices must have our consent as well, the consent of the audience. Since the bulk of spectators are disinclined to consent, it seems evident that obstacles prevent them from doing so; it is vital to identify these.

Certainly we all have inside ourselves a very secret, very profound feeling for that which constitutes dramatic art. Our life provides it with nourishment and accurately defines it; we may say that our soul is a theatre that has no equal. All of us remember moments in the theatre which caused us to tremble with so much happiness that we were moved to tears. Schopenhauer, the artist-philosopher, assures us that the origin of the purest tears lies in that compassion which our own suffering arouses in us once it has ended. He offers by way of example Ulysses at the palace of Alcinous where, during a banquet honouring the unknown guest, the bard recounts Ulysses' adventures without suspecting that he is praising them in the very presence of the hero himself. Ulysses slowly covers his face and weeps into his cloak.[21]

Schopenhauer could have chosen no better example; it is so eloquent that one has to believe in it. In its purest essence, dramatic emotion would therefore arise from an encounter between the theatre inside ourselves and that in which we are the spectators. Let us emphasize, however, that the dramatic themes need not be the same as our own; sufferings or joy we have never felt can create emotions in us of the same quality as those we know from direct experience. I shall go even further: the very fact that we view our inner life presented in a form that is liberated from those petty and insignificant things that always cheapen our life is sufficient to stimulate emotion for our human condition. This is what Schopenhauer had in mind. The tragedy of our existence lies not so much in our condition as, so often, in our inability to intensify our emotions and raise them to the heights of exaltation. In this sense dramatic art is a liberating force. And we would betray this art by dragging it into the limitations and humiliating influences of the environment in which we struggle . . .

It is termed the mirror of manners! What nonsense! Where in all of Molière's Paris would one discover an Alceste or even the affected young ladies as he portrays them in such farcical synthesis? Manners can provide a pretext or simply a frame to be broken by the genius who touches it. Shakespeare was well aware of this and did not burden his plays with the tinsel with which we still encumber them. For him the weakness of a character confronted by the necessity to act was not to be found in Denmark alone.

The result of all this is that we turn against the enjoyment of drama when we burden our stages with arbitrary and incidental elements, the very ones from which we would prefer to escape in the theatre . . . Some imagination, therefore some faith, faith in ourselves, in our value and nobility, would be enough to impress those who exploit our negligence and indolence. Anyone who takes the initiative will see how quickly the already shaking structure of our traditional staging practice will crumble and, along with it, probably three-quarters of our dramatic production. How can we estimate the importance of this blessing?

Once we have obtained an inner conviction we have only to compare it to the realities all about us; in other words to test it. So far I have been careful to avoid giving examples of the theatre as it exists; they would have distracted attention and extended the length of my argument. But the issue is now clear: we are without doubt sufficiently well informed to be able to learn to recognize the enemy.

Part IV

Aesthetic and prophetic writings

Introduction

Appia always insisted, throughout his creative life, that no art, least of all that of the theatre, could be adequately described or evaluated without constant reference to its ethical function and social context: to the manner in which it grew out of and, in turn, expanded the lives of those in contact with it. This principle, which provided the touchstone of Appia's work – its point of vital connection with a reality from which predominantly theoretical investigations might otherwise have estranged it – took on increased significance in the last decade of his life. As the conditions and prospects of conventional theatre (even one reformed along the lines he had himself set out) interested him less, the potential role of new, hitherto unknown or only dimly conceived developments took ever greater hold upon his imagination. Technical advances, new art forms, new architecture and performance places, as well as a radically altered awareness of the nature and potential of art to enhance and fulfil human life – Appia's thought reached out prophetically, and seems to encompass it all.

Along with other artists of the period, Appia responded to the vastly altered conditions of a society whose social, political, spiritual, aesthetic and psychological bearings had been violently disorientated by the First World War. Supremely sensitive and prescient as he was, he became one of those whose 'antennae' perceived with dreadful clarity the factors that contributed to the continuing crisis in so many areas of twentieth-century culture. Although he analysed the nature of the crisis and sought solutions primarily within the field of art, he insisted that, properly understood and redefined, art had vast implications for achieving a happier condition *generally* for modern man.

Appia's prophetic analysis and many of the ideas he advanced for confronting the dilemma of art in modern culture – ideas expressed in their most concentrated form in the writings in this section – became widely relevant as society and its art grew increasingly preoccupied with a perceived state of alienation and social disharmony, a breakdown of communal values and relations, and a pervading sense of existential isolation. The therapeutic response to these conditions was to a significant degree anticipated and outlined by Appia. 'Art will never endure unless it is based upon an awareness of close human solidarity', he had asserted in the essay 'Monumentality'; the challenge was to develop the new art forms that could encompass and express this solidarity. These could only be dimly

153

perceived as yet; indeed Appia called the realm of such new art 'the Great unknown',[1] while pointing out (in the same essay) that 'dramatic art has burst the frame that had held it rigid for so long, and the very concept of theatre has so expanded that it gives us vertigo and a slight feeling of anarchy'.

In the light of this perception, it is not surprising that the examples brought together in this section which comprise the core of Appia's final aesthetic writings are only marginally concerned with traditional dramatic art: he had, he believed, left it far behind. His concern now is with 'the New Presence', which he defines in what today would be described as 'holistic' terms: a condition of reciprocity between life and art, and, in turn, between artist and public. Above all else, the note heard throughout all these works is that the passive role of the public (variously described as consumer, spectator, collector, voyeur and so on) must at all costs be transformed into active engagement with the work of art. Moreover 'Living Art' would, ideally, abolish the distinction between artist and public altogether: all would join in creating and, in the process, *becoming* the work of art themselves.

Before dismissing such notions too readily (or cynically) as the naïve musings of an ageing but still innocent dreamer, one should consider how widely Appia's early and articulate call for new forms of art, for a new relationship with the audience, and above all for a greatly enlarged conception of the role and extent of art within society, has found echoes in our own era. The performance art groups, environmental and laboratory theatres, happenings, improvisations, and other experiments of recent years, all taking shape in a variety of new forms and formats, were distantly perceived and predicted in his evocation of 'study sites', communal and collaborative art, and new modes of creative activity, 'with or without an audience'. The connections may inevitably have become tenuous, but they are there.

Of course, many of the ideas that Appia explored and espoused after the war had been evident in his earlier work, particularly that undertaken at Hellerau. The yin-yang sign so prominently displayed in the pediment of Appia's great theatre had not been placed there for purely decorative effect, but to symbolize the idealism and vision immanent in the activity taking place beneath it. As Wolf Dohrn had stated at the dedication ceremony, it was anticipated that at Hellerau 'we shall witness how its people will present celebrations and festivals, for themselves and others, of a type that no other place can offer, because nowhere else will there exist a population so widely and equally educated and invigorated by such a sense of community' (Giertz 1975: 131).

These concerns, further developed and given greater urgency by the cataclysm of the war, provided the basis for much of Appia's subsequent agenda: more advanced formulations of the ideas associated with Hellerau occur repeatedly in the essays. Hellerau was to be universalized or, more accurately perhaps, society was to be transformed to embrace and protect its ideals. A dangerous and endangered world was to be made safe both by and for eurhythmics.

However, the original impulse and inspiration for the ideal of broad physical and spiritual renewal of humanity through movement and music was far older than its most recent incarnation in the eurhythmics of Dalcroze. Motivated as he was in part by a desire to recreate the ancient Greek *orchesis* – to express inner emotion through the union of music and movement in dance – his work, and its subsequent refinement by Appia, was one more expression of a Greek-inspired movement for artistic reform that had long been evident and influential in European culture.

The radical proposals and criticism that Appia puts forward in these writings must be seen not as the isolated, semi-mystical musings of an eccentric visionary, but in their broader cultural and historical context as the latest (and arguably a most advanced) attempt to reform society in the light of ancient precepts and models: an endeavour that has character-ized many of the most innovative and far-reaching developments in West-ern arts and letters since the Renaissance. Appia draws on this context and this tradition constantly in his writing, sometimes explicitly, more often as an informing sub-text and implicit commentary. His work is 'revolutionary' in the truest sense: it seeks to *return* society to a former and happier state.

In 1919 Appia completed the book he described as his aesthetic 'last testament', *The Work of Living Art*. In this he presented ideas systematically and at length for the first time which he later continued to explore and develop through the essays written during the final few years of his life. The early chapters of the book are devoted for the most part to a restate-ment and refinement of his earlier wide-ranging (and already widely influ-ential) principles – those contained in the writings included in preceding sections of the present volume. He discusses the essential elements of theatrical art, and analyses their use, employing the headings 'Living time', 'Living space', 'Living colour' and 'Organic unity' to sketch out his model of a reformed theatre. But running through these chapters, somewhat ambivalently, before rising to dominate the final portions of the book (including those excerpted here) are even more advanced ideas, which, in the end, overwhelm any remotely orthodox conception of theatre – even a theatre reformed along the lines Appia had laid down earlier and summar-ized in that very book!

So in the very process of consolidating his earlier work, Appia's restless and prophetic thought surges beyond it. The final chapters, 'The great unknown and the experience of beauty' and 'Bearers of the flame', border, as their titles suggest, on mysticism and the ineffable, while yet conveying

155

through their sometimes extravagant imagination a sublime and inspiring vision.

Appia passionately believed that art was a basic human need, not peripheral but at the core of existence: it must resume its place once more as a fundamental human activity shared by everyone. Art must cease to be merely the record or distillation of human experience; it must be renewed and reformed to become part of that experience through the individual's active participation in it. In the theatre, he pointed out, it was not so much the drama or method of reproduction (the reform of which had first motivated his work) that was ultimately at fault, but the very audience itself: 'It is the passive reaction of the audience that makes the stage fictitious; without an audience, scenic action enters the realm of actual existence, and the actors are human beings who, at one and the same time, create a work of art and take part in it; relations have become normal.'[2]

This redefinition of the nature of the performance was predicated on Appia's analysis of the basis of theatrical art, which he had come to believe lay not in the enactment of fictive stories but in the immediate physical activity of living, moving bodies, motivated by light and music as they in turn express inner emotion. Previously he had been concerned to free and externalize the expressive elements of theatre as they were contained in a musical drama and conveyed through the medium of a dramatic plot. In enacting such stories, however, the actor is constrained to take on imitative and representational qualities, which are not themselves purely 'expressive' elements but constitute instead what, as noted earlier, Appia termed 'indication'.

If the dramatist and, in turn, the actor, were to renounce these fictive encumbrances altogether, to use the expressive elements of their craft in their purest and most direct form, would it not be possible for them to create a theatrical art analogous to abstract painting or sculpture, or indeed to music?

In his essay of 1921 (not included here), 'A dangerous problem', Appia details his belief, mentioned earlier, that (once it has been reformed) contemporary art, like its Greek antecedents, can provide the most vital and immediate expression of the human spirit. Directly echoing countless assertions by the Greek philosophers,[3] he states that 'music expresses the reactions of our soul'. A little later he evokes Plato to suggest the process by which such initially personal expression is linked to the well-being of the larger community; first through the enrichment of the individual's capacity for perception and self-awareness, and then, the imagination enlarged, through the development of compassion, empathy and a sense of shared life with others. In describing this transition he makes use too of the Platonic notion of ideal form, which because of the decadence of modern music must again be derived from the idea of the body itself. The body alone can inspire music's revival – its 'return to basics' – and through it, the renewal of society.

'The gesture of art' takes up the theme once more of society's salvation through art and, if that is to occur, the need to transform the role of the individual from onlooker to active participant. In the process, a sense of reciprocity both between the individual and the work of art towards which he 'gestures', and between that individual and the larger community of which he is a member, will be engendered and nurtured. In the second half of the essay Appia turns his attention more specifically towards theatrical art, and again evokes the concept of a 'living art', which uses the body not in its costumed and fictive *role*, to convey stories, but as a means of direct expression akin to music which, in turn, must motivate it. 'Evidently another art form expressive of the living body must exist. The body is alive only because it moves; therefore this new art form will have movement like dramatic art, but will otherwise probably have no relation to it.'

Appia does not further specify this new art (beyond emphasizing that its redemptive social value requires that it be open to all to participate), but he identifies eurhythmics as its embryonic form. Although eurhythmics did indirectly engender theories, movements and schools which in aggregate resulted in the diverse species of modern dance, it is unlikely that any of these later manifestations could fully embody Appia's ideal. Yet, like Artaud's concept of the 'theatre of cruelty', Appia's vision of 'living art' has profound importance as a provocative *idea*, and has exercised real force on the artistic imagination (and thereby upon tangible works of the imagination), even though the thing itself remains elusive and unrealized.

The particular role of the concept Appia termed 'solidarity', which had been an important component of his aesthetic creed for many years, is dealt with comprehensively in 'Picturesqueness'. He points out that once art and artists have become separated from their ancient and exalted task of directly expressing humanity's collective spirit, they become alienated, esoteric and, ultimately, irrelevant. If the modern world is to recover and repossess its art it must return to the original source of all aesthetic endeavour: the human body. In the meantime, the primal impulse of art has been displaced by a decadent preoccupation with sentimental and materialistic concerns: art as a souvenir or nostalgic icon of the past, or as mere commodity. Such deprivation from the vital spiritual nourishment which art alone can provide is unhealthy. Appia concludes in a polemical tone, by citing contemporaneous examples to illustrate the point.

Somewhat similar concerns inform 'Mechanization', arguably the most political of Appia's essays. In a strikingly prescient passage he notes the peril inherent in scientific development: 'We shall venture as far as our faculties will allow, and catastrophes warn us of the limits it is perilous to exceed. But the moral problem implied by mechanization . . . is exclusively concerned with our conception of life and its solution depends on our free will.' Technical advances have brought a particular burden of responsibility to ensure that the power of science is used ethically and with great restraint. Appia sees a disturbing correlation between the notion of 'art for art's sake' and that of 'science for the sake of science': the power of the imagination can be used well or villainously in either sphere and only an abiding sense of 'the New Presence' can determine the outcome for society's good.

This, Appia explains once more, derives from a sense of solidarity and reciprocity between the individual and the larger community; an attitude to be engendered and put into practice through new forms of art: 'Our modern weakness results from our consistently passive attitude as spectators and, in particular, as spectators of works of art.' The basis for such art will be the human body, set in motion by music to express our collective selves. Such expression must, he insists, be guarded and exercised with great responsibility, 'lest mechanization, escaping our control, gain supremacy; and God knows how far it might take us if we let it go'. The massed, carefully coordinated and highly dramatic ranks of moving bodies which characterized the Nazi rallies a decade later provide a chilling example of the misuse Appia warned against.

In 'The former attitude' Appia identifies sports as one relatively harmless example of how the dishonesty of art, and its failure to link up with human reality, compels society to find other more genuine expressions of itself, even if they fall short of providing an ideally sensitive and creative alternative: 'Sport . . . is sometimes disagreeable or rough, but nobody will deny that it offers us the pleasure of candour not found elsewhere.' Its integrity is derived from the human body itself. The gradual alienation of society from its art means that it has entered a period of transition and experiment, and Appia states that his purpose in composing these essays has been to 'clarify the question a little', while suggesting the technical basis for future investigations. Modern painting, music and dramatic art have lost their way, and without recourse to basic principles of the type Appia has identified, art will become nothing more than a 'series of experiments in a vivisecting room, more cynical than anything imaginable'. The subsequent history of twentieth-century art does not lack examples to verify his prediction.

In considering these writings, one is conscious in the end not only of their remarkable foresight, but equally, and with some sadness, of the extent to which aesthetic evolution and reform have failed for the most part to advance very far beyond his ideas or, indeed, to solve some of the problems he had identified and described so long ago. Perhaps this is inevitable, given that Appia began in the 1890s by seeking to reform the theatre and ended his life calling for the transformation of society itself.

Theatrical art in the first decades of this century developed very rapidly – though sometimes randomly – through a spectacular range of innovative and experimental work. The dislocation of traditional theatre – particularly the displacement of its scenic basis, which was due largely if indirectly to the efforts of Appia – left a vacuum, which a great variety of new aesthetic forms rushed to fill, some more substantially than others. In the resulting confusion of ideas, styles and techniques, Appia's influence is more easily identified and traced in terms of the guidelines and principles his work provided than through any particular individual, movement or school.

In the realm of conventional theatre practice, his contribution was nevertheless decisive. As Jacques Copeau acknowledged,

> It is he who has brought us back to the great and eternal principles . . . We are at peace. We can work with the drama, with the actors, instead of worrying eternally about more or less original decorative formulae, without searching for new processes, new and startling methods; a search which leads us away from the main point.[4]

Appia's more visionary calls for social reform and 'living art' have had a mixed response, having at best identified an agenda and basic principles while providing a stirring manifesto reminding us of the potential of art's high office in contrast to its sometimes degraded contemporary role. Appia has sometimes been called a mystic and a dreamer, but he was never that. The gift of his genius was to formulate distant, difficult, but attainable goals. His theories and the changes in attitude and practice he demanded were rarely immediately convenient, but they were always desirable, and never impossible. Above all (and as a contribution separate from the question of the worthiness of particular elements of the reforms he conceived), Appia's certain and uncompromising assertion that the subject was not peripheral, but lay at the centre of human endeavour and achievement, remains a source of admiration and inspiration. From it we may still experience what Gordon Craig termed 'that strange joy which is desperate and tragic because of your peculiar *powerlessness and power*'. He was, as Craig better than others could judge, 'the very noblest expression of the modern theatre' (Beacham 1988: 276).

Figure 19 Appia in the last decade of his life, the period when many of his essays were written.

Theatrical Experiences and Personal Investigations

(1921) [Excerpts]

Volbach, pp. 47–72; Bablet, 4, pp. 36–56

The art of the body, as my dreams would term it long before I was aware of Dalcroze's eurhythmics, applied only to the actor. I have always been and still am a theatre man. Auditorium and stage, one opposite the other, seemed to me something normal and self-evident; so did the curtain; and that the director's preparation of the feast should not be noticed by an audience that is to be offered only hot and well-prepared dishes. My most advanced ideas always were concerned exclusively with the *performance*. And if I ever thought about the audience it was only to hope that it would comprehend my efforts. The darkened house and the invisible orchestra at Bayreuth filled me with delight.

In a fanciful little story from that period I went even further, imagining a rich man who invites his friends to spend an evening with him. In a large parlour these gentlemen are seated on cushions on the floor; coffee and cigarettes are provided on low, small tables. Gradually the light fades, one of the walls opens and very softly and slowly there appears the beginning of a miraculous spectacle of which the host's friends were entirely ignorant, just as they had been completely unaware of the elaborate installation arranged by the owner on a vast site adjacent to his residence. The passivity of the spectators could not be carried further, nor could the absolute separation of the place of action! It seemed to me at the time a dream: impossible, of course, but desirable! . . .

[Appia relates how his encounter with eurhythmics opened up a new vision to him, 'communion in art, not art brought within the grasp of all, but art lived together'.] Today in the light of subsequent experience I understand that this revelation, however suddenly it took place, was already immanent in my earlier vision. My passionate concern for the fullest development of the actor betrayed a way of feeling that surpassed the egoistic satisfaction of the spectator. Whenever I explained my scenic vision to others I acted it out, quickly arranging the furniture at hand not for someone else, but for myself as I required it for my performance; and often it was said I was quite convincing. My discomfort during Wagnerian performance became ever more painful to me, because, identifying with the actor, I suffered with him, for him, and in him; I myself was the actor, who longed for better treatment.

I shared in the existence of eurhythmics almost from its birth, helping its development and struggle to survive . . . Now I can speak of a past that was followed by the blossom, ng of a cultural principle recognized by all and assured of life.

First of all, eurhythmics shares the condition of all living organisms; it never stands still, but constantly evolves in perpetually renewed, never crystallized forms; its study is solidly based on a method, but this is subject to constant change; . . . it is a microcosm, and a little world within the larger one. This little world is based on an educational principle and dominated by an art, music; movement is its element and its medium of operation is obedience. Obedience to what? Communion of ideas implies subordination . . .

Hierarchy is not an invention; happily, it is a discovery. I have discovered the mutual subordination through which the elements of expression under our control acquire life, or rather, the right to exist. Here, more than anywhere else, the law of solidarity applies. Theatre is undoubtedly a creation, but through its hierarchic requirements this creation becomes a meaningful symbol. The composition of a piece and its production appear at first glance to be at the mercy of the whim of the author and stage director. But in fact this is not so, and if one or the other violates the laws controlling him, his work is no longer truly viable. Indeed, it slips into anarchy or turns into mechanical movement, which is the opposite of true art, and that is precisely what our current repertory theatre is.

Art is an instrument, created by our hands, which records thoughts and emotions collectively experienced; theatre is the symbol of these thoughts and feelings in a fictitious form; it is their indication, but not their reality. In the theatre, fiction is, after all, in the auditorium, not on stage. It is the passive reaction of the audience that makes the stage fictitious; without an audience, scenic action enters the realm of actual existence, and the actors are human beings who, at one and the same time, create a work of art and take part in it; relations have become normal. One can easily observe the fact during a good rehearsal.

It is normal to look at a statue or painting since we cannot simultaneously see and create them; it is, however, abnormal to yourself to be the art object and display yourself to others, who, although they are just as alive as you are, do not want to take part in your creation. I deal with this entire problem at length in my book *The Work of Living Art*: a painting enclosed inside a box does not exist as such. A moment of living art with no one viewing it except the performers themselves exists fully, and with more dignity than when reflected in the eyes of passive onlookers. The living body, when it is itself a means of expression rather than the mere bearer of a dramatic action (an actor), is independent; but it is not alone, for henceforth it participates in the rhythm of other bodies. Even if isolated, it will sense and always feel the solidarity that directs it. It has become social within the forceful grip of art. This remarkable fact is perceived by everyone who has submitted their bodies to eurhythmics.

Theatre, therefore, would be a transitional form linking the static fine arts and living art. It should not be considered a completed and fixed form. On the one hand, it aspires towards literature or pure music, on the other it instinctively seeks to free itself from the control of the audience and evolve in an unrestricted atmosphere. The audience still restrains it and will probably continue to do so, for mankind is lazy even in its diversions, but eurhythmics and its rich promise for the future have liberated us from the restrictions forced upon our imagination by an exclusively representational form. We can now conceive a nobler form which, since it no longer isolates us in passive reaction, will bring us into living contact with our fellow human beings. This is the revelation of eurhythmics. One can easily assess the influence it would have upon a man of the theatre!

The designs I first prepared for Dalcroze were still in essence oriented towards a spectacle presented to the eyes of others; they therefore only partly encompassed the auditorium. Today I have reached extreme conclusions with regard to the hierarchic principle of stage production. Reaching beyond theatre, it will serve all living art. I imagine a rectangular, empty and unadorned hall equipped with complete lighting installations. On either side are large annexes for storing sections of three-dimensional units. These would be built with lines and proportions appropriate to the human body and broken up into segments that could be joined together to form every possible arrangement of levels, whether horizontal, vertical or sloping. They would be combined with curtains, folding screens, etc., and everything would be covered with canvas of a uniform type.

This would be called the 'study site'. Its various elements would be light enough to be shifted by a few students. The walls of the hall should be kept an unobtrusive neutral colour, close to, or the same as, those of the platforms; the overall effect of the arrangement should make the performers feel at ease, encountering no obstacles except those they place on themselves. Whenever a series of exercises or a piece is to be presented to a group of people, movable rows of seats can easily be set out, first on one side, then the other. But, as a general rule, the entire hall belongs to the students, with no suggestion of an audience in it. Music contributes to the overall flexibility; there are one or two pianos, or other instruments up to an entire orchestra, sitting together or dispersed in small groups. Soloists and chorus can be similarly distributed at will, all the more so since the singing may be entrusted entirely or in part to the dancers themselves. Since the studies are focused on movement, whose expression emanates from the body, near nudity is essential. Short tights, preferably black, may be selected in the first instance (arms, neck, legs and feet left bare); but whatever costumes are chosen, they should not retard movement during rehearsal nor conceal it from whatever spectators may be present. The latter will concern us for a moment.[5]

Today it is actually the audience which determines the position taken by the performer both in the theatre and in the concert. We are used to being *offered* a concert or performance. This is an integral element in our overall view of the situation; music played on one side and heard on the other. In the same way, a performance is presented on one side, observed on the other. We cannot even imagine any other setup, and yet this one is arbitrary. One might object to having the chorus with the orchestra presented one way or another, to avoid disturbing the acoustical effect. Very well, but who will be disturbed by the effect? Certainly not the performers, I should think! Or, for example, a play will not be understood if the actors whose every facial expressed has to be seen and every word clearly heard, turn their backs. The actors can see and hear each other very well. The principle of facing one another is embedded in us: the book *and* its reader; the picture, the statue *and* the public! . . . but can one imagine a building existing solely for the eye? . . . Or music? The shepherd singing in his mountains, does he not create music? Does the tourist listening to him contribute anything to the singing? Does the little dance performed by young girls in a meadow greatly gain by being heard and noticed? Quite the opposite! We confuse living with feeling; he who has taken part as a singer in the opening chorus of Bach's *St Matthew's Passion* and the listener who has heard the thundering message are two quite different beings: the singer has lived the work; the listener has felt its effect; and if he assures us that he too has lived it in the depths of his soul, he uses the word living in a figurative sense.

Experience always surpasses everything else. So all of us must experience art, the living art, each according to his gifts and the measure of culture granted him. Is the experience of living art necessarily so superior to the impression of the spectator-listener, which can sometimes be so extraordinarily alive and moving? That is not the question. We are always basing our scale of values on egoism. Art is, as its name indicates, an artifice which we learn to use for the purpose of doing greater justice to life than we could by arbitrary means. Egoism is a second artifice within the first; it is forever demanding more from art, forcing it to strain its capacity and therefore to diminish its power. All our arts provide evidence of this. We preach simplicity, but egoism will have none of it; though satiated, it desires ever more; it is the corrupter of art and recognizes no limits, or, at least, confuses them with its own demands. Egoism therefore violates the divinity of art yet never blames itself for art's inadequacies and failures.

To live art means to offer oneself to its artifice, as it is, without adding anything to it; the gesture of art is giving, not taking. Therefore the presence of any audience is not necessary for living art, and the performer's gift of his work and effort to an audience does not directly concern the life of art; it is derived from the particular circumstances of our culture and civilization. To speak of egoism is to be sentimental; all of nature teaches us egoism. To overcome it one must have something to offer, and consequently one must first have acquired something. If we wish to offer art to those incapable of living it, let us first live it ourselves. The apostle Paul had first to endure the frightful experience of the flame himself before he could communicate it in a beneficial form ... To live art is to live in a grand manner. Art must not be measured or limited by our sensitivity, any more than a sick man's desire for a necessary medicine should determine the dosage. Appealing solely to this sensitivity, that is the desires of the audience, turns art into poison. Alas! that is what has happened; our resilience is worn out; it takes violence to make us react. . .[6]

Our current civilization, opposed to culture, divides both our attention and our work; we cannot follow it as a whole; each part goes forward under its own impetus and in its particular direction; the most disparate things go together. The situation was never better suited to every type of experiment; yet never before was there less faith to move mountains, because modern obstacles are not opposed by any conviction, and only the presence of the obstacle itself suggests the faith necessary to overcome it.

The obstacle to living art is the audience. We are in it, and it in us! Therefore the very concept of an audience, the expression of passivity, must be neutralized through an effort to overcome this passivity. Yet to forgo everything that suggests and maintains passivity in our time would mean the abolition of three-quarters of our public life! So we must mark time for the moment and allow our attitude to work from within. Then we shall understand how and why art is a supreme instructor.

Culture recoils from our civilization, which resembles a large cardboard filing cabinet with a great many differently labelled drawers. The distinctive sign of any true culture, by contrast, is mutual penetration. In the growing mechanization of life, only art has retained its flexible independence; art protests and objects, but it also waits; and it can afford to wait, since it is confident of its power and expansive strength. We must not attempt to make it fit into the compartmentalized elements of our civilization. Nothing with its origins in art is fragmentary, everything is integrated; the discipline of living art, far from being an isolated phenomenon, exercises a general influence ... it does not matter which aspect of art is used to provide guidance, so long as the artist has a sense of responsibility that integrates his work with all other activities ...

The fact that the actor has been taken as a point of departure is indeed significant. Man is the measure of all things, said Protagoras. If we are certain of this (and how can we not be?) then our scale of values will not deceive us. Yet it can be true only under one given condition: that man, who supplies this measure of values, is not a mechanical but a *living* organism.

The Work of Living Art

(1919) [Excerpts][7]

L'Oeuvre d'art vivant, 1921
The Work of Living Art, 1960
L'opera d'arte vivente, 1975
Bablet, 3, pp. 355–411

An artist who has once sensed – in his own body – the spark of aesthetic movement, will feel the need to conserve that spark, to express it in permanent works of art, not simply in piecemeal demonstrations, and he will therefore have to face the problem of *choice* in all its importance. He will perceive quite clearly that to attempt to transpose subjects appropriate only for inanimate art into *living* art would be destructive; clearly the source of inspiration he craves cannot be found there. He will have the same experience whenever he attempts to give movement, life and solidity to an object that could appropriately serve any other art. The touchstone is there. His subject will be *himself*. He had already known this; now he experiences it bodily. What art will he be able to develop entirely on his own, without the aid of literary, plastic, sculptural or pictorial subject matter?

For the sake of simplicity we have thus far always referred simply to 'the body'; we have placed it in isolation in an undefined space. Obviously it is the Idea of the living body that we have therefore deemed to be the essential element. It is clear that in attempting to practise *living* art, one finds oneself in the midst of bodies – including one's own – and that if this art is created by the body, the artist in possession of the Idea of the living body implicitly possesses all these bodies. Consequently he works, as it were, with the life that he creates – with the life of living beings whose collaboration is essential if he is not to create mere marionettes.[8] The idea of Collaboration therefore, is implicit in the idea of *living* art . . . *Living* art is social; it is in its very essence, the social art . . . This is simply repeating that *living* art will be the result of a discipline – a collective discipline which, although it may not affect all bodies, will at least affect all minds, by awakening a bodily sensibility. And just as the Idea of the body – the ideal body, if I may so define it – has proved that its reality is aesthetically possible and desirable, so the Idea of a bodily sensibility will be able to guide and orient those who have not yet actually experienced plastic movement . . . In *living* art . . . the forces employed by those engaged in bodily exercises will be automatically transfused into the responsive organisms of others, thereby producing a bodily awareness that they would themselves be hard pressed to achieve on their own . . .

Living art affects the entire being, and the more that its collaborators can involve their entire life with it, the higher its mission can be. The *living* 'craft' is both quite simple and very complex. The theory is simple since it demands only the total gift of oneself; but its application requires a complex study that only a few will be able to accomplish fully. From this arises the principle of Collaboration, or cooperation. And one can perceive how this principle in itself guarantees the purely human quality of the work . . .

We have mentioned the fact that a work of *living* art is the only one that exists completely without spectators (or listeners), without an audience because it already implicitly contains the audience within itself; and because it is a work *lived* through a definite period of time, those who live it – the participants and creators of the work – assure its integral existence solely through their activity. Coming with good intentions, we might find it persuasive and be able to contemplate it, without contributing anything to it; the specific input, the personal activity so dear to the artist in regard to all other works of art, is no longer asked of us. On the other hand, however, *living* art does not condone the deadly passivity of our theatre audiences. What then ought we to do in order to take part in its life? What should be our attitude when we are face to face with it? Above all, we must not feel that we are *face to face* with it. *Living* art is not a representation. We know that already; now we must prove it. How? By turning away as if the work were unapproachable? Yet we cannot do that; from the moment that it *exists*, we are with it, and in it. If we turn away from it, we would disown our very selves, alas, just as we already do on so many occasions in our social life. Let us not, at least, allow this miraculous thing merely to flower and blossom before our eyes! Let us attempt the great experience and beseech the creators of the work *to take us with them!* Then they will seek some connecting link that will kindle the divine spark in us. Though our collaboration *in* the work be small, we shall live with it, and we shall discover that we are artists.

The author writes these last words with feeling. In them he encloses all his thoughts and sums up his highest aspirations.

Work is not only the source of contentment and therefore of happiness; it is also the only means of achieving any profound desire. Consequently, in whatever sphere, the *technique* of the work is of utmost importance. The masterpiece of an expert artist in the ancient guilds was, above all, the proof of technical mastery. These ancient artisans understood how crucial this alone was for achieving beauty. The search for beauty was self-evident for them; they probably never even spoke about it. Technical mastery alone was the object both of their discussion and effort.

The author is convinced that only the path of *technique* can lead us to a collective universal beauty for which the work of *living* art is the model . . . To desire the end, without achieving the means, is perhaps more dangerous and illusory in art than elsewhere, since art conceals a demon which can easily transform itself at our thoughtless command into an angel of light – a demon that only scrupulous technical integrity can keep in subjugation. Many attempts at a unified art with more or less universal appeal have foundered, and founder still because of inadequate technique; one takes for the whole work what is only a fragment, and applies to this fragment processes that are inevitably ineffectual. We have improperly created a type of classification and deem, for example, all technical attention directed at objects different to that concerned with individuals. We even wish to term the one practice, the other theory, while forgetting that human theories may equally become techniques and be transformed into tools for work. In sociology, psychology, etc., contemporary efforts have recognized this, and perceived the value of the *tool*.

Anarchy still reigns in art, and hoping to place the human being within a hierarchy of usable elements – as one of a set of technical tools – may seem utopian and childish. Indeed, the artist still considers humanity – his brothers – as a mass distinct from himself, and to which he presents his completed work. The aesthetic conversion of which we have spoken, which consists, as we have seen, of [the artist] taking himself as art object and tool and then extending the resulting feelings and conviction to his brothers – this conversion is still unknown to the artist. Even those with the best intentions still imagine that they engage in acts of social solidarity and display their desire for communal art by placing under the nose of the poor spectator a work never intended for him, and which, moreover, he cannot enjoy in such a form.

The technique of *living* art is conditioned by precisely this same poor spectator; without him there is no technique.

And if the author appears to have been obliged to begin at the end in his analysis, it is because we still live under an aesthetic misunderstanding which results from a false hierarchy. Had he begun by attempting to present the Great Unknown, he would perhaps have run the risk of being misunderstood himself. Now, however, fortified by our knowledge, we can retrace our steps in order to achieve an overall view, since it seems that a misunderstanding is no longer possible.

By this quick backward glance, the author will try to answer the questions which the reader undoubtedly has long been asking him. What should be done? How is the work created? How can the problem be grasped and solved?

THE GREAT UNKNOWN AND THE EXPERIENCE OF BEAUTY

In an age when, in every sphere of knowledge, we are seeking to understand ourselves better, how can we not be shocked by the ignorance of our own body, our entire organism, from the *aesthetic point of view*? Marvellous developments in sports and general hygiene have given us a taste for movement, fresh air and light; with good health, physical beauty is certainly enhanced, and physical strength lends an unmistakable air of freedom which may even border at times on an indifference that is slightly insolent or inhuman. The body begins *to exist for the eye*; we clothe the body not just from necessity, but according to taste. And although many prejudices still persist and display themselves in regrettable cases – such as viewing the unclothed body with suspicion, or maintaining out-of-date customs of dress which we think good education or social or professional circumstances demand – still there could hardly be a middle-class person of fifty years ago who would not be greatly surprised by our tolerance in this area now. We *feel* our body beneath our clothing, and when we undress we sense the anomaly of deeming a moral precaution (in this sense our morality is always sexual) what is simply dictated by climate.

The result of all this is that the beauty of the human body is beginning to re-enter our culture. Hypocritically, we still relegate it to our museums and artists' studios with a sigh of tolerance and embarrassment, but we are nevertheless reassured: these bodies do not and cannot move. Art immobilizes them, and in this sense they are completely at rest; public morality and censorship can gaze upon them. Yet if they could move, or were to move, would they be of marble, or designed and painted? No! They would be beautiful living flesh, and that, it seems, is precisely what we do not want. Do not the unease and curiosity inspired in us by a wax museum arise from the fact that the body is represented almost as if about to move, or even beyond that point? And that to make such movement plausible it was necessary to imitate this body to the point of deceiving the eye? On the other hand, acrobats frozen in groups termed 'plastic', do they not coat their bodies with a uniform colour, usually white, to imitate inanimate material, and hence to make themselves 'morally' inoffensive? And when they change their stance before our eyes in order to adopt a different frozen pose, is not the moment they do this – because of their movement – puzzling and upsetting? Why coat oneself with colour if one moves? Just as immobility in a living body is an aesthetic nonsense that no polished surface can justify, so mobility in a polished body is repugnant because it animates a form which ought only to be represented as inanimate. Both the one and the other are profoundly immoral because they pervert our aesthetic taste by employing for their own use that which should be a most sacred object.

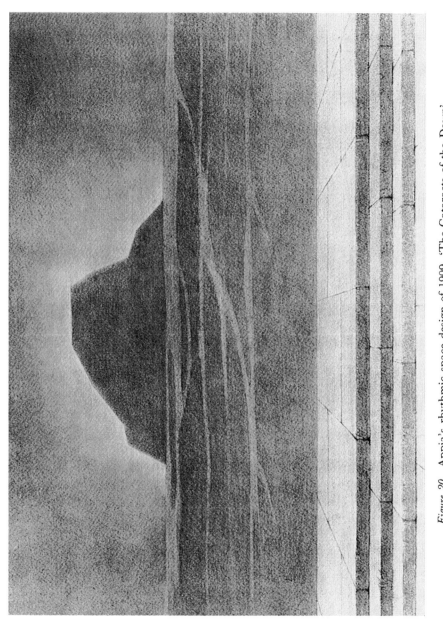

Figure 20 Appia's rhythmic space design of 1909, 'The Cataracts of the Dawn'.

For the great majority, bodily beauty – and consequently the naked body – is only tolerated in art because there it is inanimate and transformed by its context. And despite what is termed sexual 'morality', we tolerate in art the most overtly lascivious scenes; some because we may thereby mitigate something of the impoverishment of our public life in this area, others to avoid the charge of not understanding the fine arts.

Our modesty arises from the embarrassment we feel when we expose our own body and because we feel the same type of unease in the presence of other naked bodies, since we understand quite well that these bodies are our own. If we maintain this type of feeling – to put it no more strongly – we must renounce *living* art from the very start, since this art depends upon a feeling for the communality of human bodies, and for the well-being that this communality brings about. Therefore we must renounce every trace of purity and ingenuousness in our general artistic attitude, for art in whatever form it takes is only the expression of ourselves. No compromise is possible, and the entire history of art attests to our deep confusion. To be an artist is above all not to be ashamed of one's body, but rather to love all bodies to which it belongs. If I said that *living* art will teach us that we are all artists, it is because *living* art inspires in us love and respect – not love without respect – for our own body and from that a communal feeling: the artist-creator of *living* art perceives in all others his own. He feels in all the movements of other bodies, those of his own. He lives, therefore, *bodily* in humanity. He is its expression; humanity is his own; no longer in written, spoken, painted or sculptured symbols, but in the supreme living symbol of the living body, freely alive . . .

The inhabitants of Tahiti could not conceive of love or friendship unless the two people concerned had been afraid *together*. Their life was so calm that a very vital impression, experienced *in common*, was necessary for the union of their souls. In our life – placid and monotonous to the point where the worst disturbances, the cruellest sufferings are insufficient to upset our social torpor or to illumine our accumulated egoism and our barbarous dilettantism – the ineffable joy of art *experienced in common* can consecrate our fraternal union. However, to experience in common does not mean merely having the same pleasure together as in a concert hall or theatre, but being animated through one's entire being – both body and soul – with the same *living* flame, living and active; it means having 'been afraid together' in the all-powerful embrace of beauty, and having accepted together the creative impulse and its responsibilities . . .[9]

When we recognize ourselves in our brother, it is in another body than ours; moreover, dramatic illusion is not an indispensable condition for our union; the aesthetic modifications prescribed by music are sufficient to set up the current which unites our souls by uniting our bodies. The Great Unknown, our body, *our communal body*, is there: we sense its silent presence like a great latent force that waits; perhaps at times we feel a bit of the

172

joy that we can scarcely contain . . . Let that joy overflow; art wants to give it to us!

Let us learn to live art in common; let us learn to experience in common the deep emotions that bind us together and urge us to be free. Let us be artists! *We can.*

We are accustomed to think of the artist's existence as more independent than ours; we pardon him nevertheless and mix a certain protective kindliness with envy and admiration. Our admiration is inspired by the disinterested character of his art, which we trace back, without thinking about it, to the artist in order to find there an excuse for his many failings. Then we envy him after we have granted him the right to live more or less marginally and in a very advantageous light. We all clearly observe that the result of this is that he develops a capacity we do not possess, and that exercising this brings him happiness and an enviable influence. However, we do not perceive that all those activities whose details we cannot master, but of which we have only the results to judge, tend to inspire in us the same admiration and envy. The person of a great thinker, astronomer, chemist, etc. is separated from our own by the mysteries of his work. An unusual activity evidently must exert a most singular influence on the character; we believe so at any rate, and tend to ascribe all originality to the effect of this influence. An unfamiliar activity therefore fills us with admiration, but it also separates us from the individual; we see ourselves equally set apart from the thinker, as from the artist. Socially we occupy the role of spectator with regard to each. We are forever extending a hand to take from them – as we do everywhere – and although we would never ask for money from a businessman because we deem ourselves his equal . . . yet we beg all our life from those whose activity seems sufficiently to differ from ours to permit it.

It is altogether clear that we always expect something from the artist, without a thought for what we might offer in return. If money is the means of exchange, we remain the artist's debtor. We know that a pair of shoes is made with money, and so, once we have paid the cobbler, we think no more about it. But when we contemplate a purchased work of art we feel that we have given nothing in return to compare with it, and that this work of art, after all, is not really ours . . . Nothing can be offered in exchange for a great discovery; nothing in exchange for a work of art; each remains still the property of the artist and thinker. On the contrary, the function of money as an intermediary simply emphasizes yet again that we are incorrigible spectators.

Whenever we purchase a ticket for a concert, the theatre or a lecture, our lamentable relationship is clear; to stand in a zig-zag queue at a box office is always humiliating; everyone tries to ignore it . . . Yet our life is a perpetual queue before the ticket counter of the artist, the thinker, the man of renown. We persist in supposing that things are bought, but if we open our purse to do so, with or without money, we only deliberately padlock our individuality. The only thing we can offer in exchange is the gift of ourselves; we know this only too well, and refuse: the same contemptible shame that prevents us from uncovering our body keeps us, likewise, from exposing our soul. And we complain of isolation! . . .

Ah yes! We are isolated by the bars of our jail; we receive our pittance through the grating of a tiny window. How then can we know what takes place on the other side of that window? There is the mystery which commands our respect, there the freedom that fills us with envy! The artist? But it is he who lives beyond the window and beyond those limitations and our pathetic dependence.

Such a situation has, inevitably, created abnormal forms of art. Our contemporary art is an art destined for prisoners. And the artist can no more give himself to prisoners than they can give themselves to him; a locked door bars the way.

Our contemporary art forms can serve as neither norm nor example. We want to escape from prison, to breathe pure air, and to breathe it collectively. All that work inspired by our captivity we leave behind, in those sad corridors wherein we languished. And our freed hands will no longer be stretched out to take, but to give. What matter if they be empty: other hands will come to grasp them, to fill them with the same living warmth that they receive back in return. And the immortal pact will be sealed. All of us will want to *live* art, not merely enjoy it! Face to face with each other we will no longer oppose one another as before in our theatres and libraries, but will permeate each other, and pale reflections from outside will no longer dazzle our eyes . . . No! Our eyes will cast their own flame into space, and create in their freedom *living* light, across *living* space, in the transfiguration of time. And what does it matter if our first steps falter? We *will live* art; or better, we will be learning to *live* . . .

Our touchstone will be the experience of beauty, experienced collectively. All of us will be *responsible* for our own works, and will no longer try to understand the rationale for works created without us. Our works will be the supreme result of our entire life, expressed through a body – our own – and subject to the austere discipline of beauty. Our goal lies in this same activity; when it is attained we shall pass beyond it. Life exists in time: once it is realized the past engulfs it, the future claims it, and time grants it no leisure for idleness . . . In this sense, above all, art must be lived!

Let us leave behind the art collectors and book dealers to their cobwebs. A book, a musical score, a painting, a statue will have only a relative value: that of education, information, sentiment, to remind us of or preserve the past. Schopenhauer has assured us that every great man in whatever sphere of human activity has always said, or wanted to say, exactly 'the same thing' . . . We feel this 'thing' beating within us, ever more insistent, more inspiring; freed from the shackles of form, we shall loudly proclaim – this 'thing', each in his own way! As certain of its supreme reality as we are of the conquest of our entire being.

The Experience of Beauty, in giving us the key to our personality, will make us conscious of the limitation of our everyday life, and will teach us patience and serenity. For within the dreary or unhappy conditions of life it will kindle a fire of hope, like that of the artist when he witnesses the destruction of a beautiful work of art – perhaps even one of his own – and yet feels within himself the power to create another thousand more.

But the new power will not be simply a feeling of joy. The development of a power implies the development of responsibility; and the gift of the self will oblige us to assume new obligations. We shall have to perceive that the gift is not enough, and we shall seek to discover the value and quality of that which we have to offer.

Because the experience of beauty is the result of a *new* awareness of our body the idea of the body acquires a dimension we had not suspected, or had forgotten.

Up to now the author, concerned with the technical requirements of his subject, has limited himself to designating the *body* by that name alone, and more than one reader, perhaps, has been offended by that insistence, and may have been surprised that I failed to qualify it in any way. In fact, our morality has accustomed us to take the word only to mean an organism, threatening such peril for our spiritual existence that a strict line of demarcation had to be drawn between them. It is useless to recall the extremes of hypocrisy and ugliness to which this criminal principle has reduced us. Yet, on the other hand, it has become necessary to remember here that we mean by 'body' – the human body – the only *visible* form of our whole being, and that this word therefore encompasses one of the noblest meanings our life can grant to language. Consequently, although the author has repeatedly used it to identify simply a movable form in space, he has never lost sight of its higher connotation.

The moment to affirm this has come; we have arrived at the point in our study where the responsibility for our entire being – including the body – takes on a very special significance . . .

We have seen that the artistic dignity of the body in movement consti-tutes an important technical problem to resolve for the future of our culture. We have now only to convince the reader of the obligations this dignity imposes on our whole being in its outward existence, and then it will be time to bring this present study to a close. Then each can assess for himself within the limits of his age and social position, and of his cultural and personal ability, the place he occupies or should occupy in order to be a *living* artist, a representative of the *life* of art.

This life confers on its disciples a radiance that no professional limitation can diminish. It is a fire that has definitely been kindled within us. It is

175

a real Presence moreover, personal and integral, possessing new worth which can *directly* project on its own and without any intermediary this divine radiance, with or without words, with or without any fixed form. The slightest gesture reveals it.

Therefore, by developing our capacity as much as possible, by taking an active or sympathetic part in every manifestation of our public life, and by giving ourselves unreservedly and without recompense – but also without compromise – we can prepare for the joyous future of *living* art.

The author intends to return to the subject of the social influence of a *life* of art and examine its consequences in a subsequent article.[10] He is already noticing remarkable anticipatory signs. For example: public halls of every sort are becoming more flexible, as anyone can observe. Political meetings, religious gatherings, concerts, conferences, etc. are often taking place in a circus or theatre; at the same time, theatres are freely transformed into circus halls.[11] The labels so rigorously attached to the facades of our public edifices are being scattered to the four winds. Music and dance have entered into the Comédie-Française and drama into L'Opéra. Our private and public lives are no longer so strictly separated as before. The family hearth intrudes into the street and the life of the world outside bursts in through our windows; the telephone makes our conversations almost public, and we no longer fear to display our bodies – and therefore our souls – to the light of day.

We are, moreover, beginning to sense an ever more compelling need to unite with others, whether outdoors or in a hall not restricted in advance to one or the other of our public activities to the exclusion of the others, one which, on the contrary, exists solely and simply to enable us to come together with one another, as once we did in our cathedrals . . .

The term escapes me! I cannot recall it. Ah yes: it is in a *cathedral of the future* that we must take our vows. Let us refuse henceforth to rush from one place to another for activities that we must observe but cannot enter into. Let us seek a place where our newborn fraternity can clearly assert itself in space; a space flexible enough to allow us to realize our every desire for an integrated Life.

Perhaps then other labels in their turn will drift away like dead leaves: concert, performance, conference, exhibition, sport, etc. etc., these may become names never again to be used. Their shared and mutual functions will have become a fact of life. And we *shall live* our life with others, instead of watching it trickle away in disparate channels, between impervious walls.

BEARERS OF THE FLAME

In carrying my study to the furthest limits of its implications I fear that I have overstepped my rights as far as the reader is concerned. Yet this seemed essential to me, for if one intends to grasp an object firmly, he must reach beyond it. It is the same with an idea – we have taken possession of *living* art, of the Idea it represents and the responsibilities it imposes, and we may now investigate the practical use it requires to be of benefit to our modern culture.

So far, through making one sacrifice after another we have arrived at the essential idea of what Movement – which is to say *Life* – represents in art.

We have proceeded negatively on almost every front in order to grasp each idea as securely and firmly as possible; and now we stand before ourselves, and those like us, with no intermediary except the desire for an aesthetic communion. How are we to express this desire with regard to its practical realization, and how can we share it with others in a concrete and persuasive manner to encourage them to join with us in achieving the Great Work?

A purely restrictive attitude, a passive renunciation of everything in our contemporary life that contradicts *living* art, would this not discourage and depress those who wished us well? Would we not be taking the letter for the spirit? Who then would provide a lead, and who would orientate us if those who hold the key lock up its meaning in a secret chest on the pretext of avoiding all compromise?

Living art, as we have seen, demands a new *attitude* from the dramatist, and the attitude requires the concentration of his imagination entirely on the living being, to the exclusion of all else. In a sense we have all now become dramatic authors, and our attitude must reflect that title. In his work the dramatic author accepts aspects of human behaviour of which he disapproves; it is precisely out of such a conflict that his work draws life. Our dramatic work is our public and everyday life, and if we renounce every subversive element we thereby renounce straight away our dramatic work; a work of *living* art. Our attitude to this reveals everything: just like the dramatist – but aware from the start of the *living* elements – we must master the conflicts and our reactions in the interest of a higher purpose. Our direction certain, we bear a torch of life that must illumine all the recesses of our public life, and in particular those of our artistic life. We cannot place it in our private sanctuary before idols which we alone love, and still guide our fellow men. I have said that every sincere Christian follower is an artist; he is that because he gives of himself and does not disdain contact with those whom he wants to know, and may be able to comfort.

Like him, let us be sincere followers. Like him, let us jealously guard the source that nourishes our torch, but let us bear its flame aloft like a great emblem. And wherever we are, or wherever we might hope to be, let us brighten the space for those who are there; it will awaken unknown splendours, it will cast revealing shadows ... and thus we will prepare, together in our truly fraternal struggle, the new space that our vows require, a *living* Space for our *living* beings.

In order to kindle the flame of aesthetic truth we have had to extinguish along our path the deceitful torches of a deceitful artistic culture. Now it is our own fire – that of us all – that will rekindle these torches.

Let us not finally abandon them to a pathetic smouldering existence. Our only right, henceforth, is to spread light, not abandon it. If we wish to be happy together, we must first of all suffer together. For this, as we have seen, is the essential principle of art, and the strongest reason for *living* art.

In our day *living* art is a personal *conviction* which should be collectively joined by all. And so we must preserve this conviction in ourselves, wherever life brings us together; to forsake it is the only compromise that cannot be condoned.

The Gesture of Art

(1921)

Volbach, pp. 277–303; Bablet, 3, pp. 439–76[12]

I *VIS-À-VIS*

There are some who die as they were born: *vis-à-vis* the external world. The unconscious assessment that the child forms of his environment remains for such people the limit of their capacity to adapt themselves. When they have reached the limit they stop, then decline and vanish. They depart, the door of their box at the theatre is shut once more, and the performance continues, quite indifferent to their absence, and to the carriage that arrives to transport them, elsewhere ... They have received, but given nothing; up to the end, they think of themselves as instruments of observation. Eternal *onlookers*, they are not surprised to observe the same spectacle taking place both in front of and behind them, on their right as well as their left, because life for them is a panorama of which they are the centre; they move only to observe things better. When they do so, undoubtedly the panorama changes its appearance slightly; but this hardly concerns them, so long as they are *offered* an uninterrupted view and a seat at the centre.

In spite of all this movement, they are immobile.

The role of forever being *vis-à-vis* the world which these immobile beings maintain from birth to death obviously reveals itself in a variety of ways ... But the author considers the subject unpleasant ... he believes that the purpose of life is an attitude and therefore it is more important than anything else that one come to terms with oneself before death, and that all other problems are of no real importance, indeed probably of no significance, except in relation to this attitude.

I spoke of coming to terms with oneself before death. There is therefore a distance to cover, a road to follow; what can they be?

... It is clear that no sensitive and creative person believes that his own works exist by themselves and for themselves alone: all agree that they are symbolic. Because we live in terms of action, the only means we have of approaching the self-awareness that should be the purpose of our existence ... is clearly through perceiving the symbolic value of our activity ...

179

To interpret a symbol, which is to say to purge it of inessentials that attach to it and give it its shape, it will probably be sufficient to determine the exact difference between the inessentials and its eternal content . . . (As philosophy has it, the phenomenon and the inner essence of the phenomenon.)

In every field of activity the inner essence of a phenomenon can only be identified with our own self. Humanity is the only immortal thing we can perceive: whatever is only tangential to it is not essential, whatever is inextricably bound to it is eternal . . .

Let us therefore begin by examining these diverse activities in order to measure the inessentials they contain.

The study of nature in all its aspects seems to us dominated by phenomena. The aim both of the scientist and of one who makes use of science is to observe, ever more carefully and extensively, these phenomena: the laws governing them, their mutual interaction, and the conclusions to be drawn from such observation. Imagination and intuition undoubtedly draw scientists beyond such observation and allow them to determine phenomena before their existence can be proven. Still, such study can concern only phenomena, unless as an intellectual exercise it slips into the domain of philosophical speculation.

Psychology and its branches together with their useful or destructive applications (education, politics, etc.) enquire into the human phenomenon. This is essentially an experimental activity, although the experiments are done with our fellow human beings. The teacher stands before his students, the leader of men before individuals or assemblies . . . in such fields, the nature of the observer is the same as the object he observes: he is an ant observing other ants.

Art occupies a place apart, which it has always done, and for good reason. Whereas in everything else the phenomenon and its observation tend to become confused, at least in the case of art, the phenomenon is always subordinated: acoustics are never confused with a symphony, nor colours with a painting. In art, the centre of gravity is not occupied as elsewhere by phenomena, but is displaced by a central concern which seems to ignore them . . .

The role of the technician is to assist the functioning of phenomena as much as possible; his task is always concerned with certain phenomena and is entirely directed at serving them. The artisan has no such obligation: he has the opportunity to select the combinations of the materials, that is to say, of the phenomena he uses. In this sense his profession is free by comparison with the totally dependent profession of science and its branches . . . The free man is one who is in complete charge of the *purpose* of his work, not one who spends his day as he pleases! . . .

As we consider the different activities of men, solely from the viewpoint suggested above, we identify two ways to think of phenomena and, more importantly, two different ways to make use of them. One appears to correspond to the attitude of the *onlooker*, the subject of this chapter. Here we approach the phenomenon by scrupulously respecting the image it presents to us, in humbly attempting to understand it, or making use of it either for purely scientific aims (knowledge) or utilitarian (technique). Intuition may be of precious use in this undertaking, but it must always be strictly based on observation of the phenomenon as given, if it is used at all.

The other attitude discovers a new element (or new challenge) which is independent of the phenomenon and dominates it . . . It is an element outside the central axis of that panorama which is exclusively displayed to our eyes as spectators. The intrusion and function of this element destroys the tenacious charm of observing *vis-à-vis*, and almost violently installs a new order . . .

It is characteristic of a panoramic view that it spreads out before us and that we do not see anything except what the spectacle *offers* to us. We may change our position, but our attitude remains the same; as a result only our reaction to the sight of the external world makes us aware of ourselves. When we close our eyes, nothing remains. Some distinguished men have remained permanently in this state, although they correctly inferred that there must be something else; intellectually they even explored this (philosophy is pitiless in this regard), but wherever they looked, they were only able to push their own horizon further away. Some termed this 'expanding' in a complacent euphemism, but few were able to maintain the illusion in the face of death.

Art is the force that acts upon the duality of our personality.[13] This is its very essence. Its goal is to remove us from the centre, to pull us away from an altogether unfavourable position and to free us for ever from a paralysing centrifugal force; if only we would let it act.

I have spoken of art alone, without referring to the individual artist and his work . . . contemplating a work of art and allowing it to sink in is an activity. We have therefore on the one hand the artist, the creator of the work, and on the other the person for whom the work is conceived. The distinction is somewhat arbitrary; the artist creates as much for himself as for the beholder; if the latter achieves a healthy duality only by approaching as closely as he can, the artist, for his part, will obtain freedom only by resolutely going to meet the beholder. The two activities are different, but their goal is the same, as we shall see.

The game of mirrors persists. Many artists make use of sound, form, colour, and even words, just as the electrician uses current. They are manufacturers. On the other hand, for many amateurs the work of art is merely an ornament in the panorama they enjoy. They are customers. Art has nothing to do with either of these two groups. Hardly a step separates them from the indolent. The indolent, however, may be relieved from

181

their misery, while the manufacturers of art and their consumers deceive themselves to the end, thinking to escape the nothingness that snares them.

Therefore the essence of art lies in fostering the duality of our personality, and its aim is to free us from paralysis, not all at once, but in an evolution which is almost miraculous. Consequently, whenever such complete or partial duality of our personality is achieved the *presence* of art is evident, with or without the actual presence of an art work. And whenever we firmly wish to escape the paralysing syndrome, we are moving towards art.

Art is therefore not a work: above all, art is a *decision*, from which all else proceeds deliberately. Who would prevent us from believing that this decision is relevant to any human activity? . . .

If we agree that art is not the work itself then we must distinguish art from other activities. This returns us to the assertion that the decision which is peculiar to art can in fact be taken in every human activity; therefore an artist is not merely one who creates what we term rather simplistically a work of art, but, on the contrary, we can all become artists to varying degrees. We all have the means to produce this power within ourselves. But our decision must be unselfish, and its value lies in this. Yet such disinterestedness does not function within a void. The word implies abandoning the centre that has been of interest entirely to us *alone*, and so we abandon ourselves to enter the panorama and become part of it. Duality operates here; to be disinterested in something does not mean to obliterate it, but to pay less attention to it. Art, that is to say the decision which defines it, allows us to see ourselves reflected in the spectacle of life . . . In this sense, art enables us to recognize ourselves in our fellow men, and then to strengthen the decision in order to apply it to other activities . . .

The exceptional position of the artist misleads us; we forget that his activity, like all others, is a symbol; and we stand *in front of* a work of art as if before some object detached and discarded, which we need only contemplate. This is where misunderstanding begins . . . Why? Because artists stand alone; we refuse to collaborate with them, we who ought to be their models. And thus, far from wishing to recognize ourselves in them, we are reluctant for them to see themselves in us. This activity, which above all and almost by definition wishes to shift us from the centre and unite us with our brothers, we place in front of us like a painting on an easel . . .

Everywhere and always we take the symbol for its divine reality. If I am not mistaken, this is termed materialism, or at least is the mental attitude which leads to the most degraded materialization of existence. The years as they pass have borne witness to the fact, and the sad state in which they have left us is not unrelated to it. 'Thou shalt not make for thyself any graven images!' We have done precisely that, and we have adored and served them hypocritically . . . This is what has become of our love for our neighbour. Like barbarians we have lived and live still within a forum of degraded material symbols before which we march, endlessly. We address our prayers to them, but their hearts are of stone, and they do not hear us.

I have lingered on the subject of the spectators who refuse to change. Let us now turn to one who has experienced the duality effected by art and wants to surrender to it entirely, in order to free himself: the artist-creator of a work of art. At present his situation is tragic. The artist, detached from the centre and placed facing both himself and the rest of humanity, now tries desperately to unite these two visions so intimately that they blend into one. This is his goal, though perhaps he may not always be fully aware of it, or at least not able to express it. He wants to reflect humanity and find himself within it. He has the means, but for a long time humanity has eluded his efforts. Exhausted by the struggle, he renounces the *living* mirror and creates through artifice one that only reflects his own image. Without any doubt at all, he is aware of the distortion. It distresses him and he attempts to relieve the discomfort, just as the photographer tries to reduce exaggerated perspective. But in vain: the *living* mirror alone can receive his life and reflect it back to him, transfiguring it in the process. The glass merely reflects a deformed image; the expression on his face remains lifeless . . . The artist, defeated, grimaces at his own image, and we have too many examples at hand to doubt it!

But what about us? What have we done to justify sitting in judgement on him? Nothing! Absolutely nothing! . . . Everything must be *offered* to us, of course, while we remain at the centre.

Art is everywhere the liberating force. It *is* life, unencumbered by what-ever paralyses or arbitrarily colours it. Undoubtedly geographic or historic circumstances act upon it, and these are significant influences, but far from disproving our assertion, they only make it more obvious. In fact, art requires a certain amount of circumstantial material to achieve a positive and complete work, but it can nevertheless always affirm its independence in a symbol surpassing all the contingencies of its immediate milieu . . . The *actual* presence of the symbol is independent of the quantity or relative quality of the elements employed by the artist, and as a result art is independent of the direct influence of milieu. In this case as elsewhere we confuse the phenomenon with its inner meaning. The specific means of which one artist or another makes use are no more part of art than is the potter's clay. Art begins at that point when the potter introduces into his work the expression of his freedom, regardless of how modestly this may be done . . .

Now, when we criticize the form alone, while ignoring the divine pres-ence that called it into life and its sense of solidarity, we corrupt the symbol and at the same time the entire activity of the artist . . .

We therefore find ourselves in a vague and ill-defined area. Again and again, tempted by the form alone, we return anxiously to the centre, which we deem the most favourable viewpoint for contemplation. Then, however, becoming conscious of our responsibility, and disturbed by it, we once again abandon this ominous centre to become wandering adventurers. The artist, however, does not seek us in this vague realm, and so we never encounter him. Many are not bothered by this, and consequently readily give up a happiness which they cannot imagine, and which therefore does not concern them.

Others, ill-prepared, suffer a sense of injustice. Still others despair; they have an awareness of duality, but search in vain for their reflected image . . . How well certain faces, seen at exhibitions, concerts, or gazing at our buildings, betray this troubled condition, which no pretence can mask! They have introduced learning and refined taste into their lives, everything except the power to give themselves. Therefore they are for ever in search of themselves . . .

It is obvious that a landscape, a moving body or any such subject chosen by the artist does not have the power to project itself into the realm of art. It can even be asserted that the subject resists his interpretation and that there is always a struggle between the artist and nature. The blank page expresses this struggle in that it waits . . . The artist knows that he must use force, for the external world no more contains the germ of a picture, statue, poem or building than acoustics contain the germ of a symphony. The subject which is merely *represented* by the work of art is independent of the quality of that work as art. So the artistic interpretation participates in a mode of existence different to that of material reality, and in this sense every work of art is the symbol of a victory over nature . . .

And here the miraculous duality of art comes into play: the artist hears an echo to his cry of victory; he has forced the external world to become his sounding board, a complacent surface that can reflect his own image, the creative artist, back to him. And now it is he himself, the conqueror, who is able to *give*! But to whom?

Ah, the marvellous and tragic quality of the blank page! This virgin but demanding space is the motive for the sacred exchange without which the work of art is stillborn. The artist is powerless *vis-à-vis* the outside world on his own; he imitates and compiles and cries out again. From our modern art galleries, concerts and many other events we hear this monotonous and pitiable cry; we come to fear it, or to greet it with cynicism. Yet the artist-conqueror is able to create something that resembles himself, thereby establishing a contact. But alas! It is now that he feels his new and painful solitude: he gazes into his own eyes now, and not into the artificial mirror of his arbitrary fantasy and search for technique; and he misses the presence of others. The image of himself contains the indispensable condition of his art, but not yet the *object* of his deepest desire, the look from

184

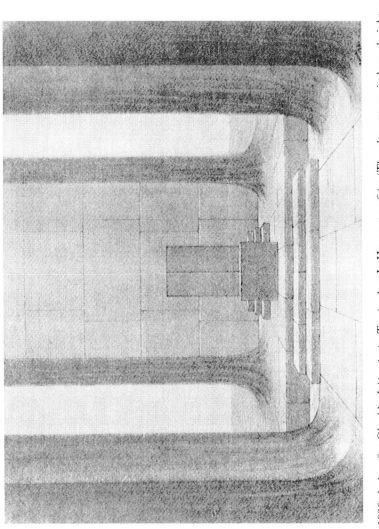

Figure 21 Appia's 1926 design for Gluck's *Iphigenia in Tauris*, Act I. He wrote of it: 'The downstage is bound right and left by two successive wings of very dark green drapes suggesting cypresses . . . The facade of the sanctuary is of rigid material to the height of a man, so that one can freely lean on it. No particular style of architecture; the pediment cannot be seen; the lines in the stone are inconspicuous and *insignificant* . . . When the door opens, the interior of the sanctuary shows a vague *chiaroscuro* in strong contrast to the light atmosphere outside . . . The character of this setting is perpendicular, which is favourable to the presence of the living human being . . . This arrangement accentuates the presence of the performers so strongly that the setting, barely noticed, vanishes from the consciousness and memory; the dramatic action alone triumphs' (Appia 1989: 426).

another which offers the ultimate affirmation, in saying to him, 'It is I!' . . . Deprived of that look, the artist resolves to cry out in his agony; we have forced him to do so.

The straightforward artistic recording of the external world that characterizes our modern works of art is an ephemeral product that is actually neither science nor art; its appearance of disinterest hardly sets it free . . . By contrast the cry of anguish of the artist before his own image, in whatever form he chooses to give it, is a true work of art, but one as painful for the artist as for us.

Here the author touches – not without apprehension – the realm of the inexpressible. Yet as he noted at the beginning of this study, the symbolic form is alone capable of guiding the spirit to the mysterious depths of the unconscious. The reader may forgive him therefore for adopting this approach and seeking beneath the cover of words invisible realities that elude rational analysis.

II THE REFLECTED IMAGE

In his chapter on tears, the philosopher-artist quoted earlier [Schopenhauer] assures us that our purest tears have their source in the compassion inspired by our own suffering, and arise, therefore, from a sympathetic enquiry into ourselves . . .

This is the origin of dramatic art and the source of the emotion we demand of it. All our suffering and our joys as well are reflected in the characters of the play, and they return to us in a plausible form that we *recognize*. This reappearance of ourselves moves us and transforms our actual emotions into a symbol that endows them with lasting value. Those feelings are mingled with admiration; we expand the scope of our feelings in the theatre; it is incontestable that our aesthetic pleasure there arises from the momentary communion with all our fellow men. Dramatic art thereby brings about the liberating duality, but does so *artificially*. The image reflected to us is offered *without* our actual involvement . . . and to continue our example, we observe how in leaving the theatre we feel a painful jolt in once more encountering the spectacle of actual life; we were able to weep over imaginary joys and sufferings, and now feel ourselves closed off from the real thing. Confronted by fiction, we first exclaimed, 'It is I, yes, I!' – then at last, 'It is we, *ourselves!*' – but we deny this when confronted by reality, so our liberation is impossible. We shall not enter the 'Kingdom of Heaven'.

The creative artist has a similar experience. He sings forth his agony and thus offers it to us as an entertainment. Ever more insistent, he expects an echo. The performance of his work undoubtedly gives solace to him; he feels a tenderness approaching love . . . he admires his work and finds himself within it! But if that is the limit of his experience, the work remains a monologue: however beautiful or impressive it may be, and however much we may hear and view it with sympathy, because of this quality it does not move us. This will only perpetuate the isolation of the artist and his work . . .

No; the artist feels that he must not dwell on private and completely personal admiration; it is beneath his dignity. 'Of course, it is me,' he will say, 'but is it not them as well? Those whom I cannot do without?' . . . He wants to offer to others the mirror that reflects his image, so they too may recognize themselves in it; he wants to free himself from it . . .

As we have seen, we refuse this offer.

The reflected image is thus the last resort of the artist; it displays the quality of his work prior to his total liberation. Dramatic art gives us an artificial example; we should understand its lesson, though it is a negative one. But our passivity leaves us with this example alone, and we cling to it. It is forever the symbol which we set up like a statue to worship, as if Dionysus were made of marble.

The end of all this is that artists are not free, that their creations have no significance for us, and that art has no meaning in our life. Many accept this state of affairs. It is not to them that I speak.

These pages seem like an indictment. Their intention, however, is to allow new construction; but not with dilapidated materials. The ground must be cleared; ruins provide a poor foundation, and the author wants to reach bedrock on which to construct the new edifice . . .

Dramatic art . . . is a burning issue: everyone senses the immediacy of this form and feels constrained to come to terms with it, and here we come to the heart of the question, where nothing could more readily persuade us of our responsibility. And this, evidently, is just what we dread. Let us confront it.

A play is written to be performed. A purely literary dramatic art is a nonsense. Otherwise, why create such expensive temples and raise such a fuss about it? The answer will be that the majority of literary people disapprove of such temples. Perhaps, after all, in this they betray an enlightened taste. But it is less a question of taste than of principle. Never to attend the theatre because it is badly done is quite acceptable, but to condemn production as such under the pretext that reading a play is more intriguing is to commit a boorish blunder . . . The reason for this is that . . . words allow an intellectual comprehension that thereby gives an illusion of a complete, and purely literary, work. Nevertheless, dramatic art, because of its origin, is an art form which appeals to the eye as much as to the ear.

It is the deliberate neglect of this fact that has plunged us into anarchy in regard to dramatic art. The performance of a work is the only normal form of dramatic art. Currently, performance requires on the one hand the stage and actor, and on the other the auditorium and spectators . . . Thus in our theatres we have the spectators and the actors rigidly separated one from the other. The former are totally passive, and this passivity is enhanced because everything is presented to them. To entertain the spectators, the actors enter into a contract whereby they imitate the external behaviour that arises from the confrontation of the characters with their circumstances. This fictitious game only makes sense if we can recognize ourselves in it, and that is what we term verisimilitude.

So we have, on the one hand, a spectator who temporarily abandons his own circumstances in order to take on those presented to him by the actors; while the actors shed their own personalities to adopt imaginary but psychologically plausible characters. Fiction can go no further! Not satisfied with its grip on the stage, it forces the audience and actors to lose temporarily that which gave dignity to their life: the living and active awareness of their own personality. At the conclusion of the performance everyone recovers and puts on again the vestments of their individuality . . . The intermission always finds us in a morbid condition; we drag our body about hardly knowing where to locate our soul. Notwithstanding our pretence, it would be interesting to capture in photographs our facial expressions at just this moment . . .

All this is quite normal in itself. The example of dramatic art would not function if some part of our everyday life became mixed up in it; the whole must be an entirely imaginary creation. It is the only art form that forces us at such a price to leave ourselves in order to recognize ourselves. The dramatist and his interpreters lull us into a hypnotic sleep to hold us in passive obedience; and because it is pleasurable to forget ourselves so long as we can retrieve ourselves later whenever we wish, we welcome this oblivion in the theatre.

And the actor? It is clear beyond any doubt that his pleasure is immense. In spite of the difficulties and serious deprivations attendant on a life in the theatre, all actors enjoy it, and leave it with regret only when they have to. Such constant self-forgetfulness is too powerful an opiate to give up before one has to! For them the sleep is not hypnotic and passive; on the contrary, it is the imitation of an activity pursued to exaltation. We should not forget that the fiction for the actor goes well beyond the duration of his performance; he must study his roles, plan and rehearse them, and thereby hold himself for much of his life in a constantly imaginative atmosphere. Moreover, actors *offer* us the product of their labours. Is this not in fact the defining characteristic of their profession? Other artists do the same, but with the essential difference that they offer it through their works, and not in person; their works are their mouthpiece. The actor, by contrast, expresses himself directly through his whole personality, body and soul. It is because of this that the work of dramatic art is the only one whose very existence depends not only on he who conceived it, but also on those who perform it. Its material is *living*. Colours, marble, words and sounds do not live, nor do they directly arouse our interest in *humanity*; the actor arouses it for himself, for his own person, and rejecting him is a crime that we all commit . . .

Dramatic art, as we have noted, is the only art which makes use of the human being, the *living* being, to convey its work to us. It does so through the medium of actors. But can the living being employ only this form to express itself in a complete work of art? Is it necessary that our living body assume a dramatic fiction in order to enter the realm of art? What about statuary? Or paintings? Is not their most noble and perfect subject precisely the body? They immobilize it, to be sure, but perhaps this immobility is not a necessary condition for the aesthetic presence of the body. Actors are not immobile! Can we not imagine a work of art that is liberated from dramatic fiction and yet presented by the *living* body? The beauty of this body – which fortunately none dare deny, though quite a few disown – can it not have its own value, an independent existence in the realm of art, without thereby being immobilized? If this is the case, dramatic art may be only an application, possibly a misuse, of the aesthetic life of the body – which I termed *living* art in my previous book – and we are justified in seeking a different and very probably less harmful application for the living human body . . .

The costumed body is merely the bearer of fictions; it depends on these and cannot do anything that separates it from that role. In this sense dramatic art *makes use* of the living body but is not its direct expression. Evidently another art form expressive of the living body itself must exist. The body is alive only because it moves; therefore this new art form will have movement like dramatic art, but otherwise will probably have no relation to it . . .

We call everything that is not of practical value a luxury or a distraction, which is to say, anything that might relieve us temporarily from the one thing we consider honourable: practical activity. Theatre is the supreme distraction, because it constrains others to do things for us. In this sense it is both sleep and dreams; instead of lying in bed we occupy a chair, but that is the only difference . . .

In the theatre we remain outside the dramatic dream, which is to say, in the auditorium but not on stage, and this dream must therefore be presented to us as a fiction in which we can recognize ourselves. But this will no longer be the case: freed from materialism and the conventions it demands and we accepted in order to find the thing believable, we shall identify ourselves both with the actor and his audience; and it is quite unlikely that we will fail to recognize ourselves in a being that will be our own person! Thus, we shall be totally freed because everything will be plausible to ourselves . . . The actors have always deported themselves according to the demands of verisimilitude; their movements did not express the dramatic action, but simply made it recognizable to our eyes. Now verisimilitude, which has dominated and conditioned all dramatic art up to now, will be displaced by a new principle drawn not from external reality but from our secret existence, the life of our soul. Our concern for verisimilitude will be replaced by concern for the superior truth that comprises and expresses our personality. Movement is an external phenomenon; it joins time with space. We therefore require a principle that will determine our movement in regard to both time and space *without being derived from external reality*. If it prescribed only duration (time), we would not have the element of space, and vice versa. It is therefore essential that we discover this principle within movement itself . . .

Music is presented and expressed in time, but only in time; and because it is able to determine precisely successive durations of time, it is the art of time *par excellence*. If we can find the means to unite it with space, we will have found the principle we seek. Movement is related to music through its participation in time; our movements have duration, but this remains arbitrary so long as it is not definitely controlled by an art. Music has the power to do this, since it is not simply a continuous sequence; its duration is broken, then resumed, then broken again; the time sequences used successively by music are variable and subject to infinite combinations. Controlled and determined by the composer, they constitute the phenomenon of *Rhythm*. Our body offers primordial examples of rhythm in its heartbeat, in breathing and in walking . . . By applying musical rhythm to the body's movements, by subordinating them to this rhythm, we transfer time into our organism *through the medium of art*, and thereby discover the principle that orders and controls our movements. For music is not the expression of the external world of incidental phenomena (which we want to avoid); it arises from the most intimate life of our inner existence. And because rhythm gives music its form, it is rhythm alone that can externalize time sequences through the medium of our moving body *and only through this body* . . . Our body – alive and therefore mobile – thus offers us the joining of time and space within the realm of art; and music possesses the indispensable authority to effect this conjunction which leads to a kind of metamorphosis.

The problem assumes another aspect. Dramatic art is subject to verisimilitude: the actor's movements convey to our eyes the meanings that result from this principle. Although the conflict of our inner life is one of the objects of dramatic art, the *representation* of such conflicts can only be conveyed through the actions of the actor in an external visible form which is intelligible and familiar to us. There is no question of expression; we all know and feel that our gestures and attitudes only very approximately convey the inner fluctuations of our emotions, and that without speech they remain ambiguous.[14] Verisimilitude thus only joins time and space in a juxtaposition which is incomplete, unequal, and subject to diverse interpretations ... The actor's mobility bears within itself an arbitrary quality; it is this that gains the actor his credit with an audience. In liberating ourselves from the requirement of verisimilitude we give up movement, which previously has been the only principle applied to the actor; and so we must find a new one. Because our body has no need to be validated by a spectator in a work of *living* art, we must seek in ourselves the affirmation previously accorded the actor by the audience.

We are our own audience; our verisimilitude is within ourselves and the movements that express it will be determined by music, which is the direct expression of our soul. We shall internalize the complex and pretentious displays of our theatre. Through music we will preserve only the inner essence of all phenomena, because music never expresses anything concrete; even its externalization through our own moving body will no longer be subject to arbitrary whim, because it will not be judged by any person, but by ourselves and our own conscience. The incorruptible spectator, now both judge and participant – and certainly not just a mirror – will be our conscience that will require us to obey the dictates of the music.

Art works to release duality more completely than any other human activity. The gesture of art is that of *offering*. The artist wants us to identify with his work; to enable this we must therefore offer ourselves to him, so that in turn he may present to us an image in which we recognize ourselves. Without this encounter, the artist remains confronting himself alone: his work is a monologue. For our part, we remain alone, *vis-à-vis* the external world; then the work of art is for us merely something to look at; we have brought nothing to it, and so cannot identify with it; and centrifugal force soon eliminates us.

This is the condition of the fine arts. Dramatic art, by contrast, provides the example of an art form for which duality is the basis of its existence, but, alas, in a fictive combination! The result of this is a serious danger for both audience and performers. The pleasure of theatre impairs the spectator's awareness of reality and tends to make him incapable of generous reactions. The obsession with depersonalization delivers the actor into an existence at odds both with ordinary social life and with the dignity of his private life. Nevertheless, because he offers himself, body and soul, his attitude is infinitely more respectable than that of the spectator! Thus dramatic art is currently the only one of our arts which uses the *living* being offering himself to us ... Of course the theatre is deadly in deluding us about the part we play in a work of art; and in another way too, as we have seen. To escape it, we must discover for the *living* body, i.e. for movement in a work of art, a principle other than that of verisimilitude which totally governs and characterizes dramatic art. Music is found to be all powerful in this regard, through the medium of rhythm. Under its dictates our body can externalize itself, in a form not subject to our whim, but, on the contrary, by the transformation of music, in a manner expressive of our deepest emotions. Because verisimilitude – which is concerned above all with the opinion of the audience – is not a requirement of this art form it can exist on its own, and with no other spectator than our innermost conscience. The beauty of the human body will no longer be immobilized in a technical symbol (painting, sculpture) but *will live* in both time and space; and because of the ideal quality of musical expression . . . the body will shed the realistic accessories which imprison our life.

Movement, under the command of music, makes our body conscious of the inner essence of phenomena.

. . . The expression of our inner life, which is the object of music, takes no notice at all of the form we spontaneously give to our gestures and attitudes in real life. In fact, these gestures are far from *expressing* our feelings; at most they are able only to suggest them, and the entire drama of our inner existence takes place within us and in a different pattern of time. A quick frown, for example, *signals* that we suffer, but our suffering may go on for hours; we have not therefore expressed it. This inner duration is taken by music and modified according to its own will and independent laws. Rhythm and the expression activating it together impose themselves on our body in order to determine its movements. Anything other than music would lead to arbitrary modifications which could have no value or justification in a work of art . . . We can trust it without reservation; and indeed, we must do so out of respect for our body, this incomparable instrument we have ignored for far too long.

Music will suffuse our body with its infinite rhythm and thus endow and enrich it with new life. For a long time our soul has responded to it, but only as an echo; although it has recognized itself in music, it has not been able to express its joy; the encounter has remained locked up within us. Now this echo assumes form in space; our body proclaims it! We recognize ourselves, now both body and soul; rhythm no longer remains in the vacuum of empty space; musical expression no longer remains the captive of sound alone: both now spring forth freely towards the light; their identity is consummated.

The union of the body and music, as a virtual identity, poses not only an aesthetic problem, but a moral one as well. If the *fiction* of the theatre has already convinced us of our responsibilities, the *reality* of our body, together with the modifications that music imposes on it, presents us with an ultimatum. The response we must make to it and its repercussions in our diverse activities, on our art forms, on our whole existence, will conclude this study.

III IDENTITY

The power of a symbol lies in its universality. It sets up a relationship between the limited example it represents and the eternal truths we could not express without it . . . The practical value of a symbol seems greater than the value of logical thought, for the latter can only be applied to objects that can be intelligibly expressed; the symbol concerns realities of which our soul is aware and often suffused, but unable to describe. It is therefore natural that art should be the highest and most important of our functions in the world; the symbol is the basis of its existence, the essence of its character.

The intellectual device, which after all is what a symbol is, and the aesthetic device of art tend to merge . . . These two devices in fact can only unite into a single artifice when both derive from our entire existence and not merely from some fictive artifice like that of the theatre. Then we can feel the deep bonds that join us to nature and to humanity. This encourages us to make 'the gesture of art', to anticipate the artist; and this arises from the desire to identify ourselves with his work. The spectacle of life that surrounds us is a supreme symbol, but we will not discover its meaning if we remain mere spectators. Art says to us, 'It is you, recognize yourself in everything!' – and we recognize ourselves in *it*, which symbolizes all things. There is one step more to be taken: we must enter into the final sanctuary, the '*tat twam asi*' [it is yourself].[15] Yet again we must free ourselves and *dominate* our liberator, dominate art! Only then will we have the power to offer ourselves to it and be worthy of serving it as a model . . .

We have said that art is a decision which, if we take it, results in an attitude.[16] It is an impulse that determines the work of art, which is one of its applications. A work of art can exist without our effective assistance; it is then just a monologue and the exhibition hall is its loudspeaker.

If, on the contrary, we would take up our task, if we would follow the impulse of art, we must abandon the centre and its dangerous passivity and take part in the concert of life, made capable of life; and through the artist and his work become living witnesses of this most beneficial decision. Because of us, the work of art will assume its place amongst the most eloquent manifestations of our culture, instead of being merely its incidental ornament. In a concrete form it will exalt the abstract symbols of religion. Has it not always done so in periods of cultural innovation? And do we not feel that this is its true function? . . .

Musical rhythm made its appearance at Geneva about twenty years ago through the ingenious creation of Jaques-Dalcroze. Experience gathered over the years has demonstrated that the study of eurhythmics (called rhythmic gymnastics at first) can readily be combined with other school work; and that . . . those who spend a few hours every week in these exercises discover an unexpected source of harmony, joy and enthusiasm.

The practice of eurhythmics should continue throughout life as a good and beneficent habit . . . In time it establishes a harmony superior to that of our normal existence; it even delivers us, for a time, from the anxieties relating to our general harmony; we give over our whole being to it, to be returned to us ennobled by having been simplified. After a period of some time in this discipline we acquire in our ordinary life a larger sense of things; we are less sensitive to passing circumstances of only secondary importance and more aware and respectful of higher and more lasting values. It teaches us to see things from a higher point of view. It cannot be denied that such an influence is very desirable! Particularly at the present time when the giddy progress of applied science attempts to place the machine above the individual, eurhythmics instructs us in the supreme importance of our total being, an importance which is undeniable because it is experienced. It appeals to our deepest emotions, and meets with our wholehearted assent . . .

I stated earlier that the work of *living* art – that created by our own bodies – is the only one that does not need the spectator. Although this may seem to deny solidarity, in fact one of the essential characteristics of the lesson of eurhythmics is the confirmation and demonstration of that solidarity. To find some semblance of understanding from some portion of the public, the creator of the static arts exhibits his work; otherwise he has no hope of contact; ordinarily his work only expresses this desire, but does not, alas, realize it. Our body, alone and isolated, has no social existence; it is neither the work of art nor its spectator. It waits; its expansive power remains shrouded and latent. When conquered by music, it sheds the veil of inessentials that particularized and isolated it; it becomes *social* and consequently aspires to unite with those like it. It only remains then for it to find favourable conditions for such collaboration. And here, just when the body finds itself effectively alone, the presence of a spectator is not necessary nor even, in all likelihood, desirable. Alone, the body already sensed its close kinship; joined with others, it has the particular good fortune of combining its own expression with theirs. This is a social communion in the name of beauty or, better still, the aesthetics of physical beauty consecrated by social communion. It is hardly possible to imagine an activity more *alive* and more broadly symbolic. Other activities are only a partial application of our faculties and therefore represent a symbol of limited power . . .

What will be the influence of this supreme symbol on the other arts and our activities in general?

. . . The dangerous position of the *onlooker* alienates us from the outer world. We use our faculties only to understand what is *offered* to them; we assimilate this as we like, and then call the process 'cultivating the mind'. The possibility of an exchange never occurs to us. We believe we do well in being open-minded and curious to learn. Those who adopt this attitude most fully enjoy general esteem, particularly if they juggle with the ideas they acquire, thereby giving the illusion that these have some use. Nature, more humane, does sometimes derive beneficial results from such ideas; in the event such men are the instruments of a more powerful force. But, alas, this is not always so, and too often one wishes that the juggler had confined himself to being simply an entertainer. The play of ideas is held in high regard; the process of toying with serious subjects fills us with respect. Why? We do not know. The obsession with mental labour is not greatly different from any other obsession. We exalt some and denigrate others; and regardless of how utilitarian we deem ourselves, often a completely superfluous labour seems quite valuable to us merely because it involves the mind . . .

The more we cultivate and affirm our individual differences, the more we isolate ourselves. The one and only method for taking part effectively in the concert of life is the intense search for points of contact, for affinities; all undertakings that have this as their goal are therefore eminently respectable. Here, once more, the normal scale of values must be reversed. Selflessness is everywhere the proof of a superior purpose, and there is no greater example of such an attitude than to deny oneself in order to approach others. If intellectual fervour, which is the basis for all individualism and the cause of so much superfluous toil, is not actually dangerous, it certainly does not have anything in common with selflessness, despite its beautiful appearance of self-sacrifice and hard work . . . Because our life is a great symbol we always need to transform the enduring truths into a symbolic form that we can grasp for practical use . . . A symbol is the expression fashioned by us of a reality that cannot be expressed without such assistance . . .

Eurhythmics is a spiritual act. Many of its practitioners have felt it so, and the author writes these words with emotion drawn from his own experience. He believes in the power of selflessness. He knows that principles, like laws, do not change humanity, and that it is necessary to find another means since the source of all progress is within ourselves. He further believes that humanity is lost if it continues to think of the body in opposition to the soul, and persists in living in such irreconcilable dichotomy. Death tells us of the body's destruction, but what do we know about it? Are our eyes, so limited, infallible? We console ourselves with the immortality of the soul; what do we know of this, and what can it mean? Are not our feelings and hopes entirely concerned with our earthly mode of life? Can eternity make sense for us? Let us leave all this; faith in life is the master of death, but not faith in the life of the spectator . . . ! When the spectacle is over, what remains for him? This is why our attitude is so important: in offering ourselves to humanity we are servants of life, and masters of death.

Music lifted from its isolation, the body liberated from its solitude, the plastic sense rendered *living*, the architectural environment in the service of the body's proportions and movements; finally, and above all, the wish to realize *in common* this harmonious synthesis: this, surely, is a splendid programme! And it is evident why we refused to serve as a model to the artist: we had nothing to offer him! Now he will ask us. He is well aware of the boundaries of the work of *living* art and understands that it is at these boundaries that his static work and its synthesis must begin. He will capture in a definite form flowing and virtually infinite movements, from which he will exclude all the inherent imperfections of everything that *lives*. His work will be a perfect whole. His model will not be our bodies in movement, but the modifications effected on our bodies by musical rhythm. The artist has himself sensed them, and has observed the same awareness in his brothers. And his own work, *the work of static synthesis, will henceforth express not the fleeting quality of movement, but its shaping influence on our organism and its repercussions on our entire life.* The artist will bring this attitude to everything around him, and the style, deeply felt, will pulsate in him, in us his models, and even in inanimate nature. His work, which had been merely contemplative, will become *living*, in the true sense of the term, despite being static. And we, we shall recognize in it a new way of sensing and perceiving the external world, our fellow men and ourselves, which *living* art has revealed to us. These modifications, which are qualities of the work of art, will have made us aware within ourselves of the principle of identity, which we know is the principle of freedom.

The gesture of art will have found its symbol.

Picturesqueness

(1922)

Volbach, pp. 349–58; Bablet, 4, pp. 157–65

. . . Our life is filled with situations in which only faith in a scarcely under-stood truth can guide us. One might even suggest that life is the way it is in order to teach us the value of faith (I am not referring here to religious beliefs). As soon as we glimpse a light on the horizon, life enjoys putting in front of our every step a barrier to obscure it. Consequently, the pursuit of truth often resembles a process of demolition.

These barriers have to be knocked down, one after the other. Our neighbour therefore only observes the negative activity of our life, and judges us in the light of this. We must then . . . retain our confidence both in the scarcely glimpsed light and in the rightness of our actions in the face of the sceptical and hostile judgements of our neighbour. The desperate condition of the fine arts forces us to seek out in our collapsing contempor-ary civilization a solid, uncorrupted position that we may safely use as a point of reference . . .

In *The Work of Living Art* I wrote of communal physical feeling; the Great Unknown. It was important to underline this particular point because we have separated our body not just from our soul, but also from the body of our fellow men to such an extent that physical feeling has become so personal a mystery that we reveal nothing. In this essay we can examine this collective feeling – which has created and always will create the beauty of a civilization – as already being completely achieved. Therefore we expand our point of reference by deeming it the communal being, a perfect whole perceptible by all of us. Perhaps this is to anticipate? I think not. On the contrary, it seems that the early indications are of a New *Presence* . . . Its very name must thrill my kind reader who must have felt it arising within himself. Let us all place our faith in the dimly glimpsed Truth! Let us have confidence in it! Light cannot deceive us. In this conviction, I shall proceed.

After the great communal creativity to which our cathedrals bear witness, the work of art gradually became independent. Ceasing to be a simple community artisan, the artist moved out on to the destructive path of individualism that led him into decadence. One of the first principles therefore for a flourishing art clearly seems to be a sense of solidarity. All social reforms, without exception, are derived from this feeling of solidarity and no one would think of denying the sovereignty of this principle. If the artist declines to accept it as a rule of conduct, he will isolate himself from society and forfeit his rights. We might even say he has lost them already . . . Every day he perceives that his reputation is further damaged; soon what will remain of it? As the popular saying goes, 'The house is on fire'. Ah! If it were only fire the artist might rise again from the ashes purified and rejuvenated! Alas, he is sinking in quicksand too, and all we can see of a good many artists is a lock of wildly fluttering hair.

Had artists but clung firmly to the golden chain of humanity, providing a fine example of loyalty and steadfastness to all, they would now be our masters. But instead, what are they? Not even entertainers. But we, what have we done to maintain them in a more elevated position? Nothing, nothing at all . . . Let us consult the New Presence; it will speak volumes about our flaws, our neglect and our squalid egoism towards the artist. We have ourselves created the dilettante, which says quite enough, I think.

Unless we accept the law of solidarity and its duties, we shall fall victim to a far harsher law, that of responsibility; for solidarity implies a reciprocal response that cannot be avoided. With regard to the artist, up to now we have lived as we liked, demanding everything of him and offering nothing in return . . . Tired of waiting, the artist seeks refuge where he is certain not to encounter us. He chooses this freely, but there is nothing human there that could inspire him . . .

Through what miracle has the New Presence been able to manifest itself in such circumstances? The answer is very simple: we have returned to the origin, the point of departure, to the only stable ground – the ground that artists pulled us away from and then forgot. We have returned to ourselves – our essential selfhood, body and soul – and there we have discovered our neighbour . . . But how can we extend this miracle to encompass the artist who awaits it even if he does not admit it? This must be brought about through our own actions. Because what he offers us is not in the least suitable for us, we are no longer prepared *to take* from him: we want *to give*.

However, despite all those moments when that scarcely glimpsed light – the light of an art living within us and we in it – illumines and guides us, too often life interferes and multiplies the barriers separating us from that light. We must, therefore, destroy before we can build, and this demands sacrifices we are unwilling to make . . .

Let us nevertheless make a start in this new direction by, for example, defying what is termed, not without apprehension and some doubt, the *picturesque*. Etymologically this word indicates objects or themes particularly appropriate to the purposes of painting; those which may successfully be depicted by shapes and colours on a flat surface. By extension we apply the term to literature or speech. Yet, and take good note of this, this concept does not apply to architecture or sculpture when a ruin is said to be picturesque; the adjective does not refer to its structure or style, but rather to its decay and age . . .

Picturesqueness is thus a condition we judge in visual terms . . . From this particular point of view, what do we call 'picturesque'? The painter . . . does not hesitate to choose between an old decaying wall eaten away by leprosy and moss and the well-maintained wall whose concrete supports no parasites. Nor does he hesitate between a chestnut tree all of whose branches are normally developed . . . and an old veteran of a tree giving way beneath its years and the weather, and lifting its bare branches as if to accuse heaven . . .

Does the painter favour decay, shabbiness, neglect and dirt (for one must call things by their proper name here) only because neatness, health and strength generally offer fewer themes to be caught in colours and shapes? We realize that notions of veneration, nostalgia, etc. are evoked to justify this taste for things that are old and dilapidated. In such a way people try, more or less deliberately, to mix two motives that are quite distinct . . . Does our incurable preference for old furniture, for example, depend entirely on our cult of the past? Is it out of a sense of sacrifice to this cult that we go to the antique dealer to haggle over rickety tables and ill-fitted cupboards? . . . Let us not fool ourselves: the cult of the souvenir is one thing, but our taste for the old another. The New Presence can easily tolerate the one, but not the other. And we have to ask ourselves why this is so.

Some artists and I have rented an old parsonage in a tiny medieval village beside a very beautiful lake. The whole situation was certainly picturesque, perhaps even to excess! The moment we arrived we white-washed all our rooms and repaired a few things in the house which, although they were really very picturesque, seemed incompatible with our dignity. But we never tired of the dilapidated lanes in our neighbourhood, or their filthy inhabitants. The slightest repair to the shacks, even the maintenance of their streets and walls, wrung our tender hearts. It seemed to be an undeniable crime against art, and therefore against us. The picturesqueness of the locale was of the utmost importance to us . . .

What sort of degraded sense could force us to such extremes? Our concern for this village arose from no historical incident, no personal recollection, and certainly not, alas, from any interest in its unfortunate inhabitants ruined by alcohol and debauchery. Our motive has to be found elsewhere . . .

The sight of a restoration such as the Parthenon in polychrome or the Roman Forum filled with buildings distresses the artist, not because he has any reservations about the accuracy of the restorations but only because he has to concede that he far prefers the ruins to anything new; and that this

199

taste is peculiar to him and would not in any way have been shared by the Greeks and Romans . . .

We therefore have before us two possibilities: either we denigrate the present because it seems less attractive to us than the past, which makes us unworthy of it and therefore unworthy of life; or we split life into two separate areas: the past (its trees, houses, etc.) to which we dedicate all our artistic concern, and the present, which merely affects our material well-being. Undoubtedly the latter attitude characterizes the contemporary painter, which is why he is isolated from his colleagues in the fine arts. Let me observe here that what I term the past is not the historic facts *per se*, but all that arises from the corrosive force of time, and in particular negligence in the face of this corrosion, or even a complacence which sustains it. The sculptor, architect and musician are easily attracted by the painter to this perversion, but never apply it to their own creations. Why? The poet may often become fond of ancient languages, but he writes his own book 'in good French'. The painter alone projects into his own art this taste for the worn-out and dilapidated . . .

The *sculptor's* object is the human body or, more precisely, the movement of this body as expressed in an immobile synthesis that conveys both the preceding movement and the one to follow. No sculptor would select exhausted, debased or sick bodies; he may occasionally employ them, but it would never occur to him to see any particularly beneficial quality in them, as the painter does with the concept of the 'picturesque' . . .

The *architect*, in organizing space, always bears the living body in mind. Even if designing a hospital, he would not give his building a diseased appearance. An architect who builds fake ruins . . . and prefers the use of corrupt material is a sad case, and unworthy of serious consideration. His taste has been perverted by the painter, in inducing him to use old material that impairs the youthful beauty of his work and misleads both the eye and the emotions. The architect would never have conceived such a thing on his own.

The *composer* expresses the impulses of our soul. Without support from a poet, he must work in general effects; with that support, he immediately has the most developed and precise power. But the emotions he experiences are eternal; they are no more part of the past than the future. Music is the perfect art of the present; decay, degeneration and neglect – in short, picturesqueness – is altogether alien to it . . .

The painter, therefore, is the only artist who takes pleasure in dilapi-dation, dirty objects, natural decay . . . unlike his colleagues in the other fine arts, he seems to have no clear appreciation of the dignity of his fellow men, and, consequently, of his own dignity . . .

The object of the sculptor, architect, musician and poet is the *living* human being . . . the wide selection of objects within the poet's grasp causes him to approach the painter, whose accomplice, alas, he easily becomes with regard to the 'picturesque'.

Thus the three artists who deal pre-eminently and entirely with the living human being remain untouched by the infection! This is extremely significant.

We have chosen the taste for the picturesque as our example in order to discover a possible touchstone that can warn us whenever art is in peril of sinking into quicksand. The outcome of this brief survey is conclusive: the artist can depend on the *living* human being and not the historic being, for in dealing with living man a lie will invariably come across as a lie, madness will be madness, neglect will remain contemptible, dirt repellent, and superstition disgraceful. The term 'picturesque' will no longer serve to make them more attractive . . .

Here as elsewhere we are in a transitional period; by turning away from monumentality[17] and its development, the 'picturesque', we prepare the way for centuries of sanity and a vitality that we can hardly imagine in our current state of mind. *Living* art will be its noble expression; what it will allow the other art forms . . . we cannot yet predict; but in our battle against the poison of the picturesque we must start with respect for our contemporary, the living human being . . .

Our painters insist on entirely objective and correct technique, yet they employ this to represent ancient and grandly weatherbeaten buildings with antique furnishings and gardens whose naturalness is contrived . . . There is a persistent absence of feeling for the human body. Like an ostrich avoiding danger by burying its head, we attempt to block out dissonance by disengaging ourselves from our environment . . . Not really understanding the past, we naturally play at inhabiting it. If it were not so, who would ever dream of living in rooms completely at odds with our habits and mode of thinking? . . .

As long as the artist enjoyed boundless confidence, his taste seemed to us unquestionable; we accepted it with our eyes closed . . . He knew that whatever he liked would be blindly accepted by us as the expression of superior taste . . . This gesture of deference was second nature to us; but today it is no longer appropriate to the actual state of affairs; we may still behave like sheep, but have lost confidence in our leaders. None can deny, I think, the sense of unease we feel.

We have to make a clean sweep at whatever price and start to construct again, but not on ruins. We want our life to be healthy; let us therefore investigate a type of art in harmony with such a life . . .

Up to now I have been forced to describe the 'picturesque' in terms of the ideas best understood by us under this label. Now we can define it more accurately to give it a new and more extensive significance.

We are currently suffering from a neo-picturesqueness that is as puerile as – but far more pernicious than – the earlier type. It consists of taking the mental, physiological and social deformities that afflict our age as the proper norm for the work of art. How many artists, for example, consider it a disgrace not to express, always and everywhere with almost insane persistence, the slackness of face and posture currently typical of a certain category of individual? . . . They even enforce this decadence upon nature which otherwise would appear healthy, straightforward and vigorous. They no longer examine ruins and decay; no, they calmly create their own, forming puppets or caricatures of whatever happens to appear before their eyes. They assure us that they desire to be truthful . . . Yet a well-ordered society rejects such truths. Our exhibitions, and more recently our museums, have opened their doors to all this beautiful world. The public is evidently willing to recognize itself there . . . certainly it does not demand much of anyone to resemble that world. Shame on the artists who hold up such mirrors![18]

'Picturesqueness' results therefore from a preference for something unhealthy and thereby offers evidence of a definitely pathological lack of concern for the most basic responsibilities we should feel toward our fellow human beings . . .

The painter imagines that he is in the avant-garde when on the contrary he lags far behind in the past . . . our pace is no longer his. His lethargy belongs in a studio; we are outdoors, in the sun; our health is good and strong, which is how we would like to keep it!

Mechanization

(1922)

Volbach, pp. 359–74; Bablet, 4, pp. 166–80

What do we mean by the term 'mechanization'; what is it that we mechanize? In the beginning man tamed animals to free himself from manual labour. The limited potential of animals . . . then required mechanical assistance . . . This constituted the origins of mechanization which, as the name suggests, is by definition inanimate. Always passive, it awaits its initiative from a human being; . . . the initiation it does not possess itself. Now, Life is this initiative; therefore it is not life that we mechanize, but various natural forces, and mechanizing them is to master them . . .

Today mechanization has two goals: speed, most often identified with the efficient use of our physical and mental resources – and authentic, simple recording. The development of locomotion, manufacture and notation could be termed physical efficiency. Intellectual efficiency occasionally benefits from such developments, but the saving is often an illusion since, alas, our nervous system does have its limitations. Actual intellectual efficiency arises primarily from new methods introduced into our work by mechanization.

Recording . . . has its most familiar and probably strongest expression in the cinema and the phonograph; the latter for time without any spatial dimension, i.e. for sound alone, the former for time in space, i.e. movement . . . In order to *possess* time we must have space, and in order to possess space we must have movement, which is the idea of time projected into indefinite space.

For us mortals, any recording, of whatever type, can involve only time or space or the two together. These are the only conceptions we can record, or, at least, those that must form the basis of all our recording, for through them we have defined, without reservation, the form of our existence. So it might appear that by constraining these conceptions of time and space into our possession by means of mechanization, we will possess life itself, or be on the point of doing so . . .

The elements of the world around us, hardly perceptible to our very limited senses, have become accessible with the aid of the telescope, microscope, or even an invisible ray revealing to us the interior of solid bodies.

It sometimes appears as if our senses were given us merely to control the recording of objects they themselves can neither see nor feel!

Thus we have an ever-increasing amount of recording, the majority of which is mechanized to suit our needs. Does this mean capturing Life? . . . The power of impulse, or as we might better express it, of *initiative* is dependent upon our will. Therefore it will be consistently our will that refuses to be mechanized, since it requires a will to surrender it up to the operator of the machine.

From the point of view of science, the problem of mechanization is solved in advance; we shall venture as far as our faculties will allow, and catastrophes warn us of the limits it is perilous to exceed. But the moral problem implied by mechanization, which is the only one that matters since it alone is a problem, is exclusively concerned with our conception of life, and its solution depends on our free will. To accept as indisputable some recorded scientific observation, and to accept or tolerate its application thereafter in our public and private life, are two quite different attitudes.

The politician and the businessman say, 'I have the power, and therefore I have the right.' But a person who recognizes any moral law at all acknowledges the necessity of choice, not as a right, but as a duty. The possibility offered by one scientific discovery or another does not have to be applied to everyday life . . .

The developments of modern science and its applications begin to weigh heavily upon us . . . and it should be noted that currently, in relating everything to ourselves, we do not yet make sufficient distinction between a discovery and its potential use. The discovery itself need not harm us; what puts pressure upon our individual freedom and causes anxiety is our utilitarian bias, which forces us to find new needs for the discovery. We rightly accuse mechanization, the instrument of utilitarian application *par excellence*, of being the modern disease. 'Where are we heading?' In fact, things will go . . . only so far as we allow them to go. That ought to be the motto for all instruction on the issue. The decline of willpower arises from our assumption that we have to adopt immediately everything offered us.

'Time is money', we are told. With this nonsense we implicitly accept an ever more dizzying acceleration, an ever more overstimulated existence, and the sanatoria that these must bring with them. 'Liberty!' . . .

Our liberty is merely a film projected upon the blank screen of our existence. We are spectators who buy a seat in the dark every day to watch our liberty parade before us in artificial light. Passive as we are, we allow the increasing mechanization forced upon us under the guise of progress, and thus conspire in the intellectual decline, the moral decay resulting from this mechanization. We are on the verge of placing ourselves in the service of technology.[19]

Art for art's sake, speed for speed's sake, force for the sake of force! . . . Like the *nouveau riche*, we hurl our gold out of the window for the sheer joy of throwing . . . Like squirrels in a revolving cage, we earn money in order to move faster and faster, and we go faster and faster to earn money . . .

But let us not be ungrateful: our mechanization is not so blind as it might appear, and there is some rationale for its current excessive development. If we have rediscovered our body (see *The Work of Living Art*), and its latent potential, we have also become better aware of its limitations. It is therefore only natural that we look earnestly to science to extract from it anything that will enhance the expressive powers of our organism . . .

In becoming inured to new instruments for which we are still seeking some purpose we run the risk of seriously impairing our sense of values. This will diminish our awareness of our responsibility and duty towards others. Mechanization as a goal in itself is inhuman – which does not mean it is useless, for even though we may be deceived about the goal, the means we use to pursue it are not necessarily worthless; but these means ought to have a different purpose . . .

The giddiness we experience when confronted by the myriad aspects of mechanization prompts us to draw a general conclusion by inference; but instead we ought to start with our fundamental convictions and use these to test the value and the positive reasons for our use of mechanization . . .

Here, as everywhere else, conscience is the final judge – not in the religious sense of good and evil, but simply our conscientious view of life achieved through meditation; which is very difficult to maintain in our modern world. The new attitude we have assumed towards our body allows us to re-establish in ourselves a sense of awareness of our responsibility as a whole being. We are therefore obliged to protect it carefully from distractions and the narcotics offered it by modern life, lest mechanization, escaping our control, gain supremacy; and God knows how far it might take us if we let it go.

In the previous essay I described the 'New Presence' as a complete personality fully conscious of its responsibilities. Its integrity would not accept the unhealthy notion of the 'picturesque' . . . If our whole self is to be our reference point, then it will have to be the touchstone for everything; we can therefore set up the New Presence as an arbiter of mechanization as it was for picturesqueness . . . It is our being, simultaneously personal and social, body and soul, the deep awareness of the one conditioning the responsibilities taken on by the other . . .

The world war has shown how feeble our imagination was. We continue to locate imagination in the realm of fantasy, literary invention or artistic fiction, and do not consider it seriously, or at least only do so rarely, from the practical viewpoint. To imagine, which is to make for oneself an image of something not actually there, is not necessarily something that is left to our own free will. Everyone now perceives the superhuman creative power of an idea: their faith in being the chosen people created the Jew, and brought the Germans to war . . .

Our intuition, for example, rightly informs us that a work of art is so valuable that it should be accepted with little deliberation. Yet because we cannot know how to imagine a work of art before it actually comes into existence, we ignore everything that led to this existence – which ought surely to be worth consideration . . . Here, if we think about it, is an obstacle encountered by all our public actions; we judge only the results; imagination fails us. And it is hardly necessary to point out that this tends also to complicate dangerously the conduct of our private affairs. One wonders whether it may not be a matter of urgency to designate imagination as a specific subject of academic instruction, or at least to encourage it by *pointing it out* and giving it the high value it deserves . . .

Every positive activity, and not purely the intellectual ones, trains the imagination. Any artisan coming into another's studio immediately realizes in his imagination the route covered, that which is yet to be travelled, and the goal of the journey. His assessment is not limited simply to the outcome, but includes the entire process . . . The intellectual, by comparison, is only interested in the route as an activity, yet he cannot assess it since his imagination fails clearly to reveal the goal to him; he has to wait for it. When the goal is attained, he judges the result but loses sight of the route that led to it. The same thing applies to a work of art: the dilettante sees only the work and expresses his taste; an artist perceives the entire process in his imagination, estimates it, and judges the final work, depending on his assessment of the route. Only he is just and fair.

Our failure of imagination is the cause of almost every delay, procrastination, lack of organization, error of judgement, etc. This amounts in the social sphere to almost perpetual injustice; in our private life this lack is a vice that results in the direst consequences, and it is inhuman quietly to condone it, for it is the source of our selfishness and insensitivity . . .

Imagination can undoubtedly be used badly, as for example by diplomats . . . but however it is used, imagination enriches life enormously and this more than compensates for its dangers. Is there not some cowardice in self-control and the consistency it brings about, both so highly valued by us? Where on earth would we be if the history of humanity, if our own history, were the result of eternal self-control! . . .

The New Presence, as we have seen, reawakened in us the awareness of new responsibilities, to which in turn new values must apply, or at least some older ones must be adapted. The New Presence, as the product of our imagination, sustains the confidence we feel in its prophetic and creative power. We shall therefore only attain its proper realization through a *common belief* in the imagination . . .

Isolated individuals are not able to oppose mechanization; resistance –

assuming it is necessary to resist, which has not been proven – must come from a community enabled to do so through the harmonious use of its faculties. If we exclude art, we deprive this community of the most systematic and regulating element which, more than any other, might bring all the diverse desires into harmony.

Art has always previously been communicated indirectly to us through work in which we had no active part. Our modern weakness results from our persistently passive attitude as spectators, and, in particular, as spectators of works of art. This passivity makes fatalists of us, especially in regard to art, where we have accepted everything offered us. And artists, by habit not overly scrupulous, have made fun of us.

Mechanization also finds us fatalistic. Its stupidest experiments, its most shameful excesses no longer make us wince. We submit to everything, agree to everything, to so great an extent that such words as 'unacceptable' tend to disappear from our contemporary vocabulary; as for 'resignation', we dare not pronounce it too loudly.

In my book, *The Work of Living Art*, I said that art must be lived and not merely contemplated. This *life* in art, which simultaneously renders our whole being both a creative artist and a work of art, grants us an authority which is difficult to achieve in any other discipline. The gift however is *jointly* made to both artist and audience bound together in solidarity. This is its prime condition. Without it, we fall back again into a work of art *opposite* an audience, losing all benefit from our efforts.

We espouse communality in almost every phase of our social life; why should we still hesitate to apply it to the benefit of art, the most powerful source of conciliation? . . . Art has begun to permeate our life, but it has entered it through a back door. The omnipotent fashion of living bows before it; our homes and possessions have been enriched through contact with art . . . It is even found in the details of our machinery . . . And yet a single area remains untouched by this blissful development: our own selves . . .

Our house is on fire, and our bathrooms will never extinguish the flames. Who would deny that music and painting are in peril, that sculpture and architecture need some definite orientation? And why? Because art has wandered into a blind alley from which only our body can rescue it. I deliberately speak of our body, for in taking such initiative our organism naturally will bear along in its wake our mentality generally. We push ever farther the culture of the body; it provides us with strength and health, but not necessarily balance, or beauty, which results from balance. Art will give us this balance. Without it, what would be the authority of the Presence? Let us not be dominated by our habits: *let us have inspiration!*

In *The Work of Living Art* I discussed the aesthetic education of the body . . . we are now collaborating in exercises, in actual practices, communal ceremonies etc., in short, caught up in a current that sweeps our body along, forcing it . . . into constant activity and beneficial reactions.

This discipline sets up within us a bodily awareness that accompanies us in our activities, and obliges us to sense through our own body the presence of other bodies beneath their covering of clothes . . . The disciple of living art experiences the joy of feeling his own body to be at one with the body of others . . .

For the followers of living art this sensation is strengthened further by their common experience and realization of musical expression. Such a follower knows that the transformation caused by this extends such awareness automatically to the bodies surrounding him . . . he has the power to strip humanity, his brothers, of the encumbrances of habit, fashion, professional distortions, etc., to reveal their purely human qualities, untouched by the passage of centuries. 'Modern', that word we so esteem, causes him to smile gently, since he considers himself to be as much a contemporary of Sesostris or Alcibiades,[20] as he is of one of us. His interest in the manifestations of contemporary life is as great, if not greater, than that he feels in any other era, but he has a sense of perspective. He has a point of comparison, an infallible touchstone: the New Presence! . . . Unlike the rest of us, he does not plunge headlong into this or that expression of mechanization, this or that sport, or spiritual speculation . . .

[Appia digresses at this point with an extended account of a musician fooled into thinking that an exquisite recording he heard on a phonograph was actually a performance by living singers. When he discovered the truth he felt compelled to play the voices over again, while accompanying them on the piano: 'he must animate this monstrous recording at any price.'] . . . Of all our machines, the phonograph most nearly attains personality . . . it thus violates the most intimate, the most inimitable and most personal nature of the individual . . . If our musician had heard his own voice, undoubtedly he would not have been so agitated. Responsibility to oneself evidently is always less compelling; honour is less involved, apparently. But there he was, the New Presence forced him to act . . .

Mechanical recordings have two distinct purposes: one relates to scientific knowledge, its popularization and exclusively commercial and industrial uses; the other caters to our pleasure and diversions, or attempts to stimulate our amateurish curiosity . . .

When recordings are widespread they become technical or industrial and are no longer addressed to individuals . . . an orchestral piece, for example, touches directly upon the individual character of every member of that orchestra, whether one likes it or not; for the recording in fact is created by systematically violating each of those individuals in the course of his playing. Mechanizations of this type – film, phonograph, or various combinations – would appear to pose a simple problem to the New Presence: do we acquiesce in this violation, or do we reject it? But reality is more complex; whether someone renounces it and attempts to avoid it whenever possible is of no importance. The violation *is* there. The New Presence will not allow us to behave like an ostrich. Strengthened by its authority, we assert that one cannot escape from mechanization from the very point at which it enters the equation. Therefore we have to determine the nature of our responsibility towards it and how we should approach it.

I have pointed out that the conscience of our whole personality – body and soul united – must be the final judge. This obliges us to preserve its *unity*; the ultimate test of our judgement. Anything that tends to diminish, weaken or paralyse its vitality, to insult its communal dignity, and thereby to injure its authority, must be regarded as dangerous and consequently must be attacked. Now mechanization is not in itself at fault; it only becomes so because of the attitude it demands of us. In the live theatre it is not the stage which must be condemned, but the audience! The cinema itself is a marvel; it is those sitting in the audience whom the film seeks to please, who are guilty. Once we are aware of this fact, we must concede that it is equally true of all our mechanization: its only danger lies in the use made of it, and since we are the ones who use mechanization, it is our responsibility.

The same is true in other fields. If we read something pornographic it is not the book which is at fault, but we, if we can be tempted by it. The inanities of modern music and painting are quite inoffensive in their childishness, but we are willing to welcome them; the disgrace therefore is ours, and, if possible, so is the regret. In this regard we should always look to ourselves and our attitude and intentions, since we are ourselves creating life day by day . . . Here the principle of community and solidarity will be of significant help, since the mechanization of entertainment, which requires our passive attitude and therefore must always appeal only to the individual, cannot surmount this principle . . . Collectivity implies action . . .

An institute of rhythmical and body training is currently one of the places where the New Presence definitely affirms the principle of artistic collectivity and aesthetic solidarity . . . I refer here to the student of eurhythmics, because in him the New Presence is particularly visible and expressive in a way that can be demonstrated, and therefore allows us to examine the source of its strength in opposing modern mechanization. It is easy to deduce that the New Presence will *never* condone mechanization as an end in itself – regardless of what form it may take now or in the future. It will make use of mechanization whenever it might help to secure its own affirmation . . . The New Presence will tolerate recording so long as it allows animation at times . . . and it will refrain from it whenever a violation has no purpose and is therefore unacceptable. It is not possible to deny mechanization; therefore I say 'refrain'. The attitude of vigilant expectancy . . . permits us much more numerous and more effective reactions than the passive attitude of consenting to everything . . .

We too readily consider sports as engaging only the body and ignore the influence their training must inevitably have upon our minds. Our illustrated magazines are quite eloquent on this subject, and their sports photographs require no comment.

As in the example of inanimate mechanization and its recordings, we must also oppose sport for sport's sake, with an aesthetic, socially strong and well-integrated personality . . . It is not necessary to go into detail regarding sports, as anyone can debate them as much as they like, according to their particular taste . . . Courage, especially in war, is about to fall into disrepute for ever. In all likelihood courage in sports will go the same way sooner or later, and it may be quite pleasant simply to assemble for a boxing match, a bicycle race or anything else; even horse races and the questionable sort of people they attract will be viewed as childish . . . So the moment seems to have arrived when it is time for us to stop patronizing all the parasitical and tiresome manifestations of our public life and toss them into the toy box once and for all. The Anglo-Saxon will himself retrace his steps; it is he who has been our leader in physical education, let us now teach him grace and beauty. The notion of sport must devolve into actual doing; to take sport as an end in itself is barbarous and childish.

The idea may be put forward that sport on its own merit is training in energy, courage, endurance, self-control and the rest! Very well! Who would deny it? But unless these virtues are applied to something they are meaningless. The sports professional seems to develop them in order to apply them over and over again to sport. If ever there was a vicious circle, this is it! All the acquired strength, which is developed and then expended, has nothing to do with humanity unless it is used to help humanity on its happy journey through our sad world . . . the outcome of a boxing match is not a sign, I should think, of a superior mentality or an elite human race. It is, rather, the living symbol of man's return to the brute . . . When public opinion will turn away with disdain from such spectacles, then perhaps we shall see how things stand . . .

However, and this is the main point on which I wish to conclude this chapter of suggestions, if we take away, we must replace; if we destroy, we must rebuild. The New Presence is at hand; let us submit to it and obey it confidently. How could we not? Is not the New Presence in every one of us the very power we so admire in others?

The Former Attitude

(1921)

Volbach, pp. 375–8; Bablet, 4, pp. 102–5

About a century ago a cartoonist did a sketch of 'modern man' – i.e. his contemporaries – in the form of an old-fashioned purse in which the entire contents were compressed to one side by a ring, while the rest of the purse hung loosely, empty and useless . . . Only the head seemed to have any importance; the body was at its humble service. Such a concept separated us consistently from beings and objects, and the notion that one might take part in them and participate effectively never occurred to us. We were content with words, assisted if possible by sight; spectators, listeners or actors, we looked at or were looked at. We exchanged points of view; works of art *were presented* or we *presented* them to others . . .

Eternal spectators, we were for ever separate from someone or something, firmly convinced that everyone else was in the same situation . . . Our concept of our own body and that of our fellow humans was either entirely intellectual or based simply on sexual instinct . . . Because social life consisted exclusively of small talk, and solitary life for the most part only of literary writing . . . art was the loser and became merely an indulgence like other indulgences . . .

We refuse to accept our existence as the point of departure and the norm for everything. Only what is of interest to or flatters our intellect seems legitimate to us, and our organism hangs limply like the empty purse below the ring. All of our works of art appeal entirely to our brain – the small, gold-filled section of the purse – and the brain, not having any pressing engagement, accepts it all under the express condition that we do not have to leave our orchestra seats.

We have thus made ourselves into eternal 'spectators' and have forgotten that the performance presented to us, or which we *present*, still has considerable influence on us. If this influence is not somehow controlled and integrated into our way of life, it propels our taste and sensibility beyond all reality into a perpetual fantasy, whose existence in our midst constitutes a source of infection . . . Whatever one may say, we perceive a pressing need for honesty, and since our art cannot satisfy it, we have to turn elsewhere. Sports and mechanization cannot lie without destroying themselves, and because their existence depends upon our body they include us in their honesty. The company of a sports professional or expert in mechanization may sometimes be unpleasant or crude, but no one can deny that it provides us with the pleasure of candour not found elsewhere. The body taken as the point of departure always tells the truth. Why? Because we cannot separate ourselves completely from it . . .

We are in a period of transition; violence alone can set us free. Intellectual exertions have failed us miserably; it is now time for physical exertion. We must at whatever cost recover our organism, our disciplined and, above all, conscious body. The gulf that we have dug is so vast that it is perilous to leap across it . . . That is why we wait; and so the exciting drama unfolds before us, the spectators. Rather than get up from our seats, we prefer to detach ourselves from *living* humanity . . .

Once upon a time, dignity resulted from a carefully ordered existence. We may speak of the division of labour; but we should remember that such division is not really valid when everyone stayed in their place only out of deference to the agreement; a life of dignity was easily achieved. Such serenity is no longer possible; today the question embraces all of humanity, and none can avoid it, for our proper place has become a place shared by all mankind.

All great lawgivers have given their special attention to the role of art, granting it power of the first order. Plato based the state on music. Schiller, the prophetic philosopher, could not conceive a superior form of humanity without a universal education in aesthetics. Our recent experiences one might say have made us aware of the civilizing and cultural significance of applied science and the intellectual training of our youth. Indeed, it seems we have no choice . . .

'The former attitude!' We have abandoned it without knowing which attitude to take up in its place . . . What might be termed the intellectual attitude has been dominant for a long time. It still survives atavistically; a certain respectability, a last glimmer of prestige keeps it among our customs. But those who retain it have no illusions; their rule is over and their grand airs no longer impress anyone . . .

The only professional from the past to keep his dignity is the peasant. Increasing mechanization, commercialism and the love of pleasure cannot keep the earth from being the earth. Whatever his dress or his way of life, one who cultivates the earth always embodies activity at its finest, and preserves his dignity. No one else from the past has survived; the other professions, thrown into turmoil, attempt as best they can to put themselves back together . . . positions have become interchangeable, no longer demanding a specific attitude . . .

And the artists? Is there still a caste that can lay exclusive claim to that beautiful title? Did not this group also undergo a profound upheaval just like all the rest? At the end of his life Goethe lamented that the poet wanted to be a painter, the painter a sculptor, the musician an architect, etc. What would he say today? After all, do not all those 'interesting experiments' of such and such an artist prove that he is attempting to break down the barriers of his art? . . .

That the greatest musical geniuses have dared to conceive mimetic music only demonstrates that music, the divine art, has not yet found its path and purpose. In the theatre we still attempt to create painting, sculpture, animated literature, intellectualization for the eye, etc., etc. as if dramatic art could not depend simply on itself. Modern architecture is often nothing more than modelling through a magnifying glass. The sculptor seeks atmosphere, the painter wants to give movement to his lines and colours by throwing various attitudes and images together on the same canvas. Finally, alas, the musician believes he will liberate the art of sound by bringing to it the sounds and discordant rumble of mechanized life. Having attempted to free himself from the meaning of words, the poet has discovered an intermediary that is no more than an arbitrary composition reflecting his caprice and insolence. Without flinching we combine different means of expression, juxtapose, separate or combine them, pile up or eliminate at random. Art has become merely a series of experiments in a vivisecting room, more cynical than anything imaginable. And the public accepts this; so long as it smells blood, anything is thought good. In all this, where does the artist stand?

What is the origin of this growing anarchy, this contempt for technical integrity, this mad urge to rush blindly into the void? It is quite obvious: we want *Life* and we do not know where to find it. In spite of everything, we have retained 'the former attitude', that of remaining *spectators*. We search outside for what is only within ourselves, like a sybarite who exhausts himself and plunges into despair by searching everywhere for the treasure he possesses within himself.

Appendix

Appia's Commentary and Scenario for
The Valkyrie, Act III
(1892)

The process by which Appia conceived and fashioned his scenarios, as well as their profound significance, has been discussed earlier in this book, and was described by Appia in the portion of the essay 'Theatrical experiences and personal investigations' excerpted in Part I.

The concept of using such an elaborate and effective device for detailing, coordinating and wrestling into a unified work of artistic expression all the disparate elements of production, constituted, together with his unprecedented prescription for technical reform, his major contribution to the art of the theatre. Its supreme value was not, however, immediately recognized. As he recounted in 1925 in a letter to a friend,

> In 1892 I completed my scenario for the *Ring*, together with the designs. I was thirty years old. I sent them to Cosima Wagner, along with a letter. Chamberlain, who was well regarded at Wahnfried [the Wagner household] presented them to Madame Wagner, and warmly endorsed them. She did not even open them – and Chamberlain returned them to me with his deep regrets. Since then, I have not offered them to anyone.[1]

Gordon Craig recorded in his diary that Appia told him how, a little later, he was granted a personal interview with Cosima. She listened coldly while he explained that his designs were concerned with the pictorial aspect of staging, and in no way went against the music itself:

> She turned to those present and said, 'Gentlemen, we are met together for the direct purpose of forwarding the works of Richard Wagner'. Appia attempted to remind her that Wagner himself had written, 'This art of music is not the completed art of the theatre – this art is only in its infancy'. Frau Wagner then turned her quiet head and looked at him while one might count one, two, three, four, and even five. She then dismissed him scornfully, with 'All this has no meaning at all!'[2]

Not until 1983 were these scenarios published, in the first volume of the

214

French-language *Oeuvrès Complètes*. The section of the *Ring* – the scenario for Act III of *The Valkyrie* presented here – was the first portion of it ever published in English, when it was included in the Volbach/Beacham edition, *Adolphe Appia, Essays, Scenarios and Designs* (Appia 1989).

THE VALKYRIE:
COMMENTARY AND SCENARIO FOR ACT III
(1892)

Setting

The setting presents great difficulty due to its contradictory composition, and its use in *Siegfried* and *Götterdämmerung*. The description which is given in the libretto, together with the scenes whose actions take place in this setting, sufficiently indicate these difficulties, and require a further justification here for the two essential ways in which the conception that follows differs from the description.

1 The scene ought to provide for the spectator a lifelike impression of a mountain *summit*, a real summit without which the Valkyrie could not be properly arranged. This impression must not be diminished; it must be created by the setting, without making it an isolated object which in *Siegfried* and *Götterdämmerung* one relegates to a corner like a useless piece of furniture.

2 The trunk of the fir tree, under the branches of which Brünnhilde sleeps, becomes the *subject*, interrupts the harmony of the design, divides one's attention, takes up a great deal of space, and disadvantageously pushes back the rest of the setting. Its importance is minimal, and it ought to be given lesser weight than the overall picture.

Description: The rocks should not rise up but should be sliced through on a horizontal plane with deep hollows, the perspective of which, together with the lateral stones at the peak and the overhang that they bring into view, provides a jutting profile against the sky. This formation greatly enlivens the effect of the actual stage objects and the well-defined nature of its lines does not allow one to imagine a continuation that would lessen the sensation of emptiness a mountain summit ought to suggest. The sombreness of the material and the scenic arrangement will be of the greatest importance.

With the exception of the practicable of the summit itself,[3] the setting is shallow. The distance from the curtain to the rear of the stage will be determined by the lighting.

On the right,[4] four or five feet above the stage, a ridge rises sharply to form towards the middle of the setting an unequal platform, half of which drops sharply towards the audience, while the other half descends in tiers on to a second level a little lower than the beginning of the ridge on the right, which in turn descends to the quite narrow foreground.

From the upper platform the rocks rise in unequal steps, extending to the upper left where they end in an overhanging ledge. This is to the rear of an isolated step that extends to the extreme left in the foreground above the cave, and continues the line of the summit by turning sharply downstage before entering the wings. It forms a gradient sloping upwards back to the right, forming in turn the actual summit located a third of the distance from the left of the visible stage picture, and two-thirds of its height. The line from left to right is continuous, and the detail of the overhanging ledge hardly interrupts it. The mountain is cut through in a segment, perpendicular at the overhang, so that any detail one sees of the slope does not interfere with the clean line of the ridge, except for the vertical elements visible within the slopes, the largest of which is seen in the bend forming the ridge.

At the beginning of the ridge on the right, the ground falls away slowly towards the centre to join the lower platform. In the middle of this platform a gently sloping path on the left descends to the foreground past the foot of the rocks. This extends almost as far as the right wing, where it is enclosed by a low, mossy rock wall, which then continues to the extreme right foreground. At the foot of this wall the ground rises gently (Brünnhilde's 'moss hill') and this formation is underlined by the rocks that extend from the wall on the right, reaching the path along which they stand, and rising back to the level of the lower platform. In the centre of the foreground the path turns slowly to the left keeping to the base of the rocks supporting the lower platform, and then drops sharply to disappear into the cave at ground level.

The entrance to the cave is half hidden by a wall at the downstage wing, which rises to rejoin the upper platform. The second wall, which is essential, determines the bend in the crest, leaving a practicable ledge which becomes larger in turn as it reaches the summit.

In the extreme right foreground corner, masked by a downstage rock, is an exit that is between this rock and the one forming Brünnhilde's hill.

Above the wall that defines the boundary between the lower platform at the right and the hill one must imagine a plateau inclined towards the background up to the ridge along which trees stand. The wings at the right are narrow and set back, possibly representing the borders of the forest from which one or two trees extend branches over the scene, leaving the sky completely open; their trunks are not seen. To the rear an isolated fir tree may perhaps stand to define the perspective and the supposed formation of the ground, but it remains close to the wing without coming forward; the background must remain completely free.

The wall of rocks to the left of the actor emerging from the cave is vertical at its base but then meets the slope of the ridge in a jumbled pile.

Directly above the cave the realistic overhanging entablature forms a kind of vaulting that casts an actual shadow over that entire portion of the set.

On entering the set from the cave, the actor climbs several steps towards the middle of the downstage 'section to the base of the rocks supporting the lower platform. By following the gently sloping path that passes between these rocks and those of Brünnhilde's hill, he can reach the foot of the steps that lead on to the upper platform. From there, by continuing slowly, he can reach the crest and disappear into the wings directly behind the ridge near the first step at the base of the upper platform. This is assumed to extend on to a ledge on the farther side and is not visible. A platform slopes away to the left behind the set to reach stage level (Siegfried's exit in *Götterdämmerung*).

The lower platform begins at one-third of the width of the visible stage from the left, extending up to the wall of rock on the right, which is covered in its second half by Brünnhilde's hill. The upper platform begins at one-quarter of the width of the stage from the right and ends by merging with the levels descending from the ledge.

The steps which straddle the two platforms are of irregular shape, some quite large, leading in an imposing manner to the lower platform. For the audience the impression is of the same terrain in two formations; only the rocks descending to the floor at the left mark the difference in levels.

There are some loose rocks on the path at the left before its descent into the cave; one of them is used to sit upon to the right of the cave as one makes an entrance.

The backcloth shows nothing *but the sky*.

The rocks are of greyish colour, here and there some light turf. The approach to the fir trees is green, and the rocks become mossy. The hill has turf. The trees are old and irregular with thin branches covered with lichen . . .[5]

For this setting, the most important in the *Ring*, one must use the best materials in constructing the practicables to allow easy positioning and movement of a landscape represented three-dimensionally. In particular the function of the rocks requires sturdy practicables that can be adapted to each break in the ridge and *form a sharp profile against the sky*. In the front sections facing the audience the construction can be free, and the edge of the practicable may occasionally disappear behind painted scenery. The rock wall in the foreground can easily be attached to the practicable.

Brünnhilde's hill on the right must be entirely *plastique* and connected to the rest of the setting, and must have nothing in common with a piece of furniture.

The downstage area is slightly elevated, covered at the front with a narrow strip of earth, and dark almost to the base of the incline. Only the direct entrance to the cave at the left and the exit at the right foreground are at stage level. The path is gently sloping but *uneven*, remaining practicable for Siegfried's horse in *Götterdämmerung*. All the other practicables will be very uneven and undulating, and none should resemble a staircase.[6]

The branches of the fir trees throw a light shadow over all of the setting to the right; this painted shadow must be capable of becoming *real* for Act III of *Siegfried*.

The colours will be blended harmoniously, soft, with *nothing of a reddish hue* in them, and the lichens form a bridge between the very *sober* green of the trees and the grey of the rocks. In front of the cave, an area as far as the lower platform and one-third the depth of the stage must be painted in a shadowy blue, fresh and transparent, much deeper than that cast on the right by the trees. The actual shadow of the entablature above will blend with the painted shadow.

The gauze at the back must be painted in accordance with the lighting requirements.

Shadows and patches of light on the rocks must be very lightly indicated and the choice of details must be *more than sober*.[7]

The scenic picture should produce a feeling of calm satisfaction and etch itself on to the mind as simple lines, recalled with pleasure.

The accompanying drawings, more finished than the previous ones, have no purpose but to indicate the setting and the formation of the rocks, and have no pretensions to being a definitive artistic product. The portion which is in shadow only gives a very sketchy suggestion of the effect that should be produced.[8]

Lighting

Two essential elements: movement and repose. In the first the role of light is active, in the second it is of a passive calmness with slight and imperceptible variations, only interrupted by the episode of the Magic Fire, which, because of its magic, has nothing in common with the ambient light.

The sky provides the visual interest until the arrival of Brünnhilde. Then the focus of the drama sets the place of action in the sky that previously served only as a kind of commentary, but now remains, to the end, a living thing. One must therefore treat it as such and consider the projections and the other elements as *actors* whose tasks when taken together have all the importance of an acting *role*.

The act begins during the *day*; it is the storm which darkens the atmosphere; the sky to the rear must remain clear, the bulk of the setting always stands out in silhouette. The foreground is dark with shadows diminishing imperceptibly up to the crest.

After the departure of the Valkyrie, all becomes calm, and everything should serve to create the most limpid sky possible. The projectors have nothing further to do except prepare for the Magic Fire.

The setting of the sun, *very subdued*, diffuses itself slowly and disappears in the same way. The thin crescent of the moon must merge into the surrounding landscape.

Depending upon the arrangement of the projectors, of which there should be a great many, it may be necessary to divide them into two categories: those supplying the backdrop with the vague movement of clouds with slow modulations and streaks of blue sky and those responsible for the *march* of individual clouds in the sky and against the rocks, for lightning flashes, for apparitions (the Valkyrie) and for the Magic Fire. It is absolutely critical to leave as little to chance as possible.

The difficult question will be the arrangement of the lighting itself, to preserve the scenic harmony while rendering the outline of the setting and the actors placed within it, indistinct (with the exception of pp. 210–14).[9] The light must never be so strong as to make the facial expressions really distinct.

An area of diffused light with all the intensity coming from above, therefore striking the slope in the foreground. Natural shadows created by the construction of the set itself cannot be controlled in the alternate light–dark; they therefore contribute to the haphazard effect in the first half of the act. Perhaps towards the end, in order to emphasize the calm and serenity of the atmosphere, one ought to spread a little diffuse light over the scene. The corner of the cave remains completely dark and the shadow of the fir trees on the right, which is a painted shadow, may be taken as *real* because of the diffuse light.

The ride of the Valkyrie

Until electric photography is introduced into the theatre, which in a series of quasi-simultaneous projections can produce an arrangement of movements, the scene of the Valkyrie must always remain incomplete . . .[10] A realistic apparition will always be ridiculous because of the spectators' literal-mindedness, and no matter what projection is shown, it is always imperfect in a drama of this type. The alternative taken in the scenario remains the only inoffensive solution. It goes without saying that an artist of the first rank should be commissioned to create these apparitions.

The magic fire

It is not a decorative but a *mimetic* effect. It is a magic act, completely independent of the natural environment, totally in the service of Wotan's will, and therefore created through his gestures. The scenario gives the process of its development.

Projection will be essential. Very little steam and *absolutely no noise or violent movement* (it is not a volcano!). Perhaps a number of small fireworks thrown by hand and well integrated with the core of the flame might be a convenient method. In any case, part of the floor of the lower platform will be specifically constructed for the effect, and in the composition of the rocks of the upper platform one must remember that channels will be necessary for the passage of the fire.

The light that ushers in Wotan is *blood-red* without variation; the Magic Fire is the colour of *fire*.

Scenario

171/2 Curtain: The set in silhouette. The eye only gradually takes in those patterns of the terrain not set against the sky. The foreground is dark. The sky is bright, a rainy grey, veiled with indistinct and variable clouds. A few isolated clouds move from left to right near the summit, chasing and doubling back upon themselves. Everything is in crescendo until 210 when the projections vanish into the setting itself. Gerhilde is at the highest point of the rock, Ortlinde is below the ledge, Waltraute and Schwertleite near them at curtain rise; climbing during 171/3–4[11] on to the overhang. All four, *erect* facing the sky. 172/1: Gerhilde makes her first cry to the three Valkyrie, then turns towards the sky and her voice is lost upstage. At her call, Ortlinde rejoins Waltraute and Schwertleite on the overhang, all three leaning over the precipice stock still.

The manner of their singing should give the impression of unrestrained savagery and the inflections of their voices should not be coordinated with their movements. They hurl their shouts first to the audience and then upstage. Their movements during the rising flow of the 'hojotoho!' are not formulaic. Repetition would become tiresome and silly. The whole body ought to physically reinforce the shout. Adopting a formal pose is undesirable; on the contrary the impression should be of *excessive* life. The expansiveness of the music should not be ritualistically paralleled by physical movement.

Helmwige's voice is heard as if from far away, lest the audience confuse it with that of Gerhilde. 172/4: The Valkyrie brandish their lances. Menacing clouds gather at the left, grow and are shot through by lightning. The clouds stir, at first slowly, and then ever more quickly moving from left to right. 172/5: A violent lightning flash *emerges from the cloud*. One glimpses a vague colourless form, perceiving only a mane of hair, a cloak, a headband flowing in the wind, a lance, gleams of armour, all shrouded in clouds. A second into 173 a similar apparition is seen coming closer. The two are still only vaguely visible from the lightning, which silhouettes them so fleetingly that one can only sense their immobility, emphasized, moreover, by the rapid movement of the clouds.

173/5–6: Waltraute and Schwertleite descend on to the upper platform; Ortlinde does the same but stops somewhat higher. 174/1: All three are in right profile facing the audience. The cloud reaches the fir tree. Several brilliant white flashes outline the branches, and then the sky regains its initial appearance while, imperceptibly, the number of clouds increases. Gerhilde descends from the summit and stops on the overhang. 174/2: Ortlinde descends, crosses in front of Waltraute and Schwertleite and stops at the right on the edge of the upper platform. Waltraute follows closely and presses against her. 174/4: Helmwige sings from the wings and Schwertleite darts past Ortlinde and Waltraute at the same moment that Helmwige enters through the fir trees.

Entrance of Helmwige

At Helmwige's casual gesture, Gerhilde descends to the upper platform, Waltraute goes to meet her. 175/2: Gerhilde signals Waltraute to stand guard for her; Ortlinde goes off *singing* and disappears. The others very agitated. 175/3: Gerhilde darts *laughing* in the direction of Helmwige and Schwertleite, during which Waltraute quickly reaches the summit. 175/4: Helmwige moves into the fir trees *singing*. At Waltraute's first call, Gerhilde and Schwertleite climb as far as the overhang and all three are in right profile. 177/1: A few lightning flashes on the right. 177/2: A violent white lightning behind the trees. Gerhilde descends a few steps and turns suddenly to the left. 178/2: Schwertleite rejoins her; an enormous shape silhouetted in lightning climbs behind the summit of the mountain, breaking through the clouds.

Entrance of Siegrune

178/4: 'gegrüsst'; in a lightning flash more violent than the others, similar to Helmwige's arrival, Siegrune emerges from the trees and ascends the upper platform while *singing*. 179/1: All face left. 179/2: There is a cloud near the fir trees, the Valkyrie turn, following it with their eyes. 179/2: Two violent flashes in the trees. 179/2: Waltraute descends. 179/3: Gerhilde and Schwertleite remaining above the overhang, descend while *singing*; soon rejoined by Waltraute who has sung, 179/3, on arrival at the overhang. Helmwige quickly turns from the trees and sings while rejoining Schwertleite, Gerhilde and Waltraute on the left above the upper platform. Gerhilde, 180/1, descends still lower nearer to Siegrune and Ortlinde, who direct their first cry from the edge of the trees. 180/2: Waltraute descends towards Gerhilde; Helmwige reaches the rock over the cave and sings, facing right; Ortlinde climbs on to the overhang and almost disappears upstage where she hurls her cries in all directions. Gerhilde, together with Waltraute, ascends, and Schwertleite comes down to meet them.

181/1: While singing, Ortlinde approaches Schwertleite and Gerhilde, who have now rejoined Siegrune above the overhang. Helmwige joins them, moving towards the audience. 181/1: They stand for a moment in a tight group facing right on the steps above the overhang; Helmwige remains alone on her step. 181/2: The group, very agitated, brandish their lances. Helmwige descends, followed by Ortlinde. 181/2: The others, with the exception of Gerhilde, descend. 181/3: Gerhilde follows and quickly overtakes the group who are stationary on the platform, and continues all the way to the right edge, where she shouts into the fir trees. 181/5: The group stirs restlessly while remaining in one place; Ortlinde leaves them to rejoin Gerhilde. 182/1: Waltraute does the same, as well as, 182/2, Schwertleite, who laughs together with Siegrune on meeting Gerhilde as the latter ascends towards Helmwige, who has remained behind. 182/3: Waltraute and Schwertleite laugh as they approach Helmwige and Gerhilde who, descending, reply to their laughter. All four, laughing, rejoin Ortlinde and Siegrune, who laugh in turn. Thus they arrive as a group on the extreme right of the upper platform. 183/2: Grimgerde and Rossweisse are heard singing offstage. 184/1: All the Valkyrie rush to meet them in a single movement, while remaining onstage; then return one by one.

[A sense of how detailed Appia's directions are may be had by noting that at this point the act has been running just under six minutes; approximately four and a half minutes have elapsed from the first cries of the Valkyrie.]

Entrance of Grimgerde and Rossweisse

Grimgerde is first, turning to reply to Schwertleite; Rossweisse in the middle of the group. Helmwige, from behind, comes forward to reply to Rossweisse, whereupon Siegrune moves on to the summit to keep guard. 185/2: Gerhilde, in front, turns back to speak to the others. 185/4: Thus they all arrive together, all on the upper platform to the left and above. At Siegrune's call they stop suddenly, motionless and attentive. Gerhilde, at the head with Waltraute almost on the overhang; Ortlinde last with Helmwige and Schwertleite; Rossweisse and Grimgerde in the middle. In this order (in vocal sequence) they start to move, 186/2; Ortlinde moves quickly in front of the others, and at 186/3 rejoins Gerhilde and Waltraute. Helmwige does not reach the summit until the last bar of 186/3; the others, variously, before her.

Siegrune stays at her post, and everyone sings at full volume, oblivious of the audience and without modifying their voice on account of their movement. 187/4: 'bewegt'; Siegrune descends quickly and stops on the overhang, leaning over one edge as if to see better, and then returns to the summit to talk with her sisters. 188/2: Gerhilde descends, talking with Waltraute; Schwertleite remains on the summit. 188/3: Waltraute arrives on the very edge of the overhang, shouting with all her strength towards the right. 188/3–4: Rossweisse and Helmwige descend, and Ortlinde follows several steps behind. 189/1: While the four dash, *running* into the fir trees, Waltraute, at the second bar, hurls her cry at Ortlinde. Grimgerde and Schwertleite descend quickly; Ortlinde and Waltraute utter their second cry, while moving. Waltraute, in front, pauses, 189/2, on her arrival at the upper platform, to move forward once more, 189/3, while the other three advance quickly towards her. Grimgerde sings while running. 190/1: They disappear into the fir trees.

Entrance of Brünnhilde and Sieglinde

190/2: 'schnell'; The Valkyrie re-enter, half of them encircling Brünnhilde who *sings during this movement and arrives*, 191/1, on the lower platform, at the extreme left of which she places Sieglinde during the agitated ensemble around them. On entering, one of the Valkyrie places Brünnhilde's lance, shield and buckler behind the small mound, in full view of the audience. 192/1: Broad movement of the Valkyrie in a staggered group *around* Brünnhilde, who remains close to Sieglinde. 192/1: Brünnhilde moves forward on to the steps leading to the upper platform, where she looks anxiously towards the right upstage. 192/2: She ascends a further step. Ortlinde and Waltraute follow from afar; she turns back to speak to them, then descends again on to the *upper* platform, while Ortlinde and Waltraute run up, 193/2, to the summit. 193/3: Brünnhilde on the upper platform, the other Valkyrie ranked between her and Sieglinde. 194/1: Brünnhilde ascends a little, attempting despite her extreme agitation to scan the horizon. 194/1: The Valkyrie ascend, leaving Sieglinde alone. Brünnhilde, returning, 194/2, rushes into the group and arrives, 194/3, near Sieglinde whom she cradles in her arms, as the Valkyrie, having turned back, surround them again. 195: Brünnhilde remains close to Sieglinde. 195/4: The Valkyrie recoil in a *violent* movement. 196/1: Brünnhilde moves away bit by bit from Sieglinde, following the movement of the Valkyrie in such a way that at 196/3 they are all together on the middle of the lower platform and on the steps above; Sieglinde isolated on the left, Brünnhilde alone between her and the Valkyrie. 197/2: They recoil again, breaking up the group. 198/1: Rossweisse, Grimgerde and Schwertleite spring on to the ridge. 198/2: Helmwige, Gerhilde and Siegrune do the same, passing in front of the others, while singing, on to the overhang. Then all six descend again, running. 198/4: The Valkyrie gather around Brünnhilde who, in anguish, has ascended to the upper platform again, 199/1, to meet them; then mixes with them in great *animation*.

199/2: The Valkyrie detach themselves one by one from Brünnhilde, who speaks to them as they pass in front of her, so that, 200/1, she is left alone in the background at the right of the upper platform; the Valkyrie grouped to one side at the left and above. 200/3: 'rettet'; Brünnhilde darts once again on to the lower platform and covers Sieglinde with her body, her head still turned towards her sisters, who remain above in an agitated state. 201/5: Sieglinde, facing forward, presses against the rock behind her.

202: The Valkyrie reassemble one by one above Sieglinde, one or two remaining on the ridge, facing right. 202/1–2: Brünnhilde in her shining beauty, sings 'ein Wälsung wächste dir im Schoss', with a large, wild movement of her open hand in front of Sieglinde's body, and then draws back breathless as Sieglinde follows her. 203/1: Sieglinde at the centre of the lower platform violently grasps Brünnhilde, who, upright, turns upstage. The Valkyrie *in an unrestrained movement* ascend and descend, looking at the sky, and return at last, some coming down, the others remaining on the upper platform. Brünnhilde, still on the right, yields her arm to Sieglinde, but turns her head, motionless. 204/1: Sieglinde falls to her knees, clasping Brünnhilde's legs. All the Valkyrie approach. 204/2: Brünnhilde *suddenly* steps forward on to the path, raising and dragging Sieglinde. 205: The Valkyrie press around the two women. 205/4: They all set off, climbing hurriedly. Brünnhilde drags Sieglinde hastily into the foreground, and at 206/2, 'drängend', lets her go, remaining on Sieglinde's left, facing forward with Sieglinde in right profile.

'Fort denn, eile nach Osten gewandt!'

During 207/8–9, the Valkyrie circle around the ridge, sometimes together, sometimes separately, while the storm gathers force. The clouds have changed direction imperceptibly since Brünnhilde's entrance and are now being pushed from left to right in a whirlwind, ever darker but not yet completely hiding the rocks. The eye has grown accustomed to the lack of light so that the scene on the lower platform can be clearly followed, because of the white costumes. The foreground remains dark and Brünnhilde and Sieglinde indistinct; but the sky must be as bright as possible compared to the set, to ensure the silhouette effect above all. 208/3: Sieglinde recoils and at 208/4 sings in profile to Brünnhilde, who stands erect and gazes at her, hand raised as if to swear to the truth of her promise. Sieglinde departs by the right foreground.

The approach of Wotan

210: Clouds over the summit and the ridge (perhaps a gauze in front of the summit). Soft but *continuous* noise of wind to the right. Ceaseless lightning backstage suddenly making the Valkyrie visible and then plunging them into darkness. Prolonged rolls of thunder. A blood-red light grows in intensity to the right, completely distinct from the general lightning. All that can be done with projections must be used to make the sky look terrifying, emphasizing the right side as much as possible. 210: 'Stürmisch'; The Valkyrie are dispersed, some on the upper platform waiting anxiously

Figure 22 Appia's 1892 design for *The Valkyrie*, Act III. The Valkyrie gather in silhouette along the ridge of the mountain awaiting Wotan's entrance. Dimly visible in the foreground, Sieglinde kneels at the feet of Brünnhilde. Clouds swirl in the background, punctuated by bursts of lightning. Cf. Figure 6.

for Brünnhilde, the others circling around the ridge amidst the clouds. 210/3: Brünnhilde climbs among the others, and *stops dead at Wotan's call.* All the Valkyrie do the same. They fall stock still at once, *caught in mid-movement.* Ortlinde and Waltraute sing while descending. Brünnhilde, 211-1, arrives on the upper platform, welcomed by the 'Weh!' of the others. She climbs; Ortlinde and Waltraute come to meet her with 'Weh!' They all group around her.

The darkness obscures everything except the broad mass of their movement; these images run beneath it. The light increases without illuminating the Valkyrie. The wind and thunder *uninterrupted and without modulation,* grow as at the approach of a cataclysm. Lightning flashes blend ceaselessly with the light. The sky is a whirlwind from left to right; the summit is lost beneath clouds. 212: Helmwige alone attends Brünnhilde on the overhang; all the others follow them and stretch out into a compact mass above them. 213: The whole scene is like a dark whirlwind in which one can distinguish the Valkyrie only by their singing. 214/1: The wind and thunder are in full crescendo, having reached full volume. They *stop dead* on a great lightning flash without thunder. The blood-red light pierces the fir trees in a puff of smoke, lighting up the ridge and the clouds. The light increases until 214/2, when in a great burst of smoke, Wotan appears. The light dies out at once. The sky lightens bit by bit, just enough to make the figures distinct. The clouds desert the ridge but still obscure the summit. The foreground remains dark.

Entrance of Wotan

Wotan, in long strides, reaches the upper platform and crosses it in order to be at 214/3 in silhouette some distance in front of the Valkyrie for 'Wo ist Brünnhilde?' Several flickers of light in the sky. 215/1: The Valkyrie *assemble* during the music and at 215/2, 'Was thaten', become agitated without changing their place. Those singing 'Was thaten Vater' make their movement on 'Vater'; the others, on 'reizte'. 216: Wotan draws back a little, 217/1, 'Weichet von ihr', in a movement and manner which make them give way, letting him go, and thereby giving the ensemble that follows the quality of a picture in relief.

217/2: Complete stillness, Rossweisse in the middle of the group. 217/3, second bar: Grimgerde moves a step forward; fourth bar, Rossweisse does the same; 218/1, first bar: Waltraute, the same; third bar, Gerhilde the same; fourth bar, Helmwige the same; the others move very little.[12] 281/2, second bar: Helmwige ascends a step; Gerhilde crosses her; on the last three bars, the entire group in a single movement brandish their lances with arms outstretched. 219/1: A sudden drawing back of the group. All the movement of this ensemble is barely perceptible and enters into the unconscious harmony of the scene for the spectator. Wotan remains on the upper platform until 226/1. 220/5: Wotan has drawn back a moment earlier in order to underline the orchestral crescendo, returning now with an emphatic movement. 221/2: 'Hörst du mich Klage erheben'; he draws back again. 221/3: Wotan in three-quarter profile to the audience almost at the edge of the ridge to the right of the upper platform.

Brünnhilde has moved well away from the Valkyrie, who remain above the platform. 223/2: He turns back towards her, and she finds herself standing a little above him in complete silhouette. 224/1: 'Du noch bist'; He moves forward again up to the steps leading to the lower platform; she moves a step toward him. The Valkyrie agitated, but still huddled together, reach the left of the upper platform without advancing further: a moment of suspense. All remain like this until 226/1, when Wotan descends to the lower platform, during which the Valkyrie take over the upper platform and Brünnhilde stays on the steps above Wotan without, 227/1, looking at him. 227/2: He turns back towards her with an imposing stance. 227/4: He makes several steps to the left, still on the lower platform. 228/1: Brünnhilde follows, falling to her knees on the large step above her, against the rock (there are still two steps remaining down to the lower platform). The Valkyrie hurl themselves on to the steps in the greatest agitation.

'Halt ein, Vater' (Valkyrie)

Grimgerde and Schwertleite are the first, 228/1, to arrive on the lower platform. Rossweisse and Siegrune follow them; Gerhilde and Waltraute delay, looking towards Brünnhilde, and remain on the steps, followed by Helmwige and Ortlinde. 229/2: Helmwige descends, followed at once by Gerhilde and then Ortlinde. The first to have arrived return to Brünnhilde. 230/1: During the trumpet crescendo the Valkyrie group themselves one by one around Brünnhilde. 230/2: Gerhilde, Grimgerde and Siegrune go back towards Wotan. Helmwige remains above. 231/2: They all arrange themselves in front of Wotan as a compact group, in a savage and almost menacing way (not on their knees!). The music demands this position, or its expression is false and merely formulaic. 231/2: Wotan takes an angry step towards them; they draw back to Brünnhilde, whereupon she rises up again and waits in suspense. 233/2: Brünnhilde falls down from the height of two steps. The Valkyrie recoil, terrified, towards the right in a *tight* group, fearful and still. 234/2: 'Fort jetzt'; Wotan comes *very close* to Brünnhilde, where he remains until 246/3. 234/4: The second 'Weh' of the Valkyrie is from the wings.

The flight of the Valkyrie

The sky darkens again; up to now the clouds have noticeably diminished. The clear gaps in the clouds have become more numerous; little by little the sky has regained the appearance it had at the start of the act, except for the summit still lost in the clouds. 235/1–2: There are many faint lightning flashes behind the trees. 235/3: Lightning flashes reach the sky on the right, silhouetting a group of clouds that the wind is chasing towards the left background. 235/4: A projection like the earlier one shows the Valkyrie fleeing in the background, *their backs to the audience*. 235/5: A second projection showing them very indistinct and distant. The lightning dies down; the clouds diminish. The summit reappears; the sky brightens. At the start of the following scene there are still some wispy clouds, but the sky has become limpid and clear everywhere. 256–7 is the point at which the climax of a *restrained* sunset will occur, confined almost entirely to the background. From 260 night falls; a light bluish-green. At 266 a thin crescent moon rises behind the trees, dimly lighting the scene. 237: The foreground remains dark, but the twilight brightens it enough to make all that happens on the lower platform distinct.

Brünnhilde is on the left of Wotan (from the audience's viewpoint), in the middle of the set. Wotan is turned in three-quarter profile to the right. Brünnhilde has fallen to the ground, face down, her hair spread out. 239: She stands up. 240/3: 'zu gering'; Wotan turns a little towards her without making any other movement. She remains behind him *without coming forward* until 244 when she leaves her first position. 246/3: First movement of Wotan, who draws himself up and looks at her. 249/1: He moves forward a little on the path, without looking at her. 249/2: She steps towards him remaining some distance away. 249/3: He half turns towards her. 249/5: She approaches him; he moves forward again one or two steps towards the foreground.

In response to his movement she stops, close to him, but still behind. 250/4: 'dass sonst'; She takes a step on 'sonst'. 250/5: A step on 'Gott' that places her on the same level as Wotan. 251/2: 'dich selbst'; She finds herself in front of him, turning in profile to speak to him; 'zum Spiel', his movement is swift. 251/2–3: Wotan turns towards her sharply, and facing her, changes his position. 252/3: He steps left into the foreground, passing in front of Brünnhilde, who follows him without moving forward, speaking to him from behind. 253/1: He turns back to her, sharply, and then faces front. 253/2: At 'vernichten', she does not recoil, and continues. 253/4: 'in Schmerz und Leid'; She steps back again at the ferocity of what he says. 254/2: After an impatient gesture during which he does not look at her, 254/3, she climbs imperceptibly one step on to the path. Wotan closes the distance between them, and stops, 254/4, close enough to touch her.

'Und das ich ihm in Stücken schlug'

She recoils without moving from her position. On the 'rest' they remain *thus*. Wotan regains his composure but does not change position. 255/1: He takes a step along the path. 255/3: He goes a bit higher. 255/4: 'Was hast du erdacht, dass ich erdulde?'; Her back is to the audience, remaining behind Wotan who has reached the level of the lower platform. 255/4: He turns towards her. 256/2: She rushes forward, falling on to her knees before, *without touching him*. 257/1: She raises herself somewhat without standing up. 257/3–4: She falls down against him in an *unrestrained* movement, clasping his knees. Wotan stands with three-quarter profile away from the audience; she, in three-quarter profile towards it. 258: She will not rise until he lifts her during his farewell, and therefore it is not until 259/1 on 'Zagen' that she draws back, so that on 259/2, 'freisslichen Felsen', she finds herself on the first steps leading to the upper platform. 259/3: The beauty of his stance should lead naturally to the swelling orchestral sound.

'Leb wohl, du kühnes, herrliches Kind!'

Wotan advances holding out his arms so as to let his spear rest unnoticed against the rock. She falls to her knees against him. He lifts her up. Until 265/2 she remains there, supported only by him. The following section – completely lyrical – must be mimed as such but with great simplicity. They remain at the middle of the lower platform. 261/4: Crescendo while in this attitude. 262/1: He relaxes it somewhat. 262/5: They are one in *front* of the other; very solemn. 263/2: He is passive; it is she who gently, with respect and supreme love, fixes her eyes on his and sinks gently on to his chest. Only then, he clasps her, resting his head on hers – the great splendour of the music is *not pantomimic* and it is in the contrasting stillness of the scene that the effect is realized and its significance revealed in all its beauty.

The limpid night is bright enough to make the figures visible, as a vague, silvery light is spread in the sky. 264/1: As noted, she remains thus, well to the right, her raised head clasped by Wotan's hands, *completely still*. 264/2: *Is not to be emphasized by any movement*. 264/3–4: Wotan, still, *without moving*, in a low voice, slowly gathering momentum; returns on 'dieser Augen' to his initial tone. Brünnhilde remains still. 265/2: 'nach Weltenwonne'; She makes a vague gesture of tenderness, still gazing upon him. 265/3: 'zum letzen Mal'; He leans close to her eyes. 265/4: He leans over her again, as before, with the caress of his song, and then at 265/5, 'dem Unseligen', he slowly stands up. 266/1: She lets go of him – he holds her *facing him*, to kiss her eyes.

'So küsst er die Gottheit von dir'

She sinks back with no other movement. He remains still, holding her, until 266/3, when, clasping her in both arms before him, he walks slowly to the mound. Brünnhilde places her feet against the cleft in the earth, so that Wotan can lay her down. The cleft is *behind* the mound, invisible, and once she is reclining, he places her feet *on* the mound. He acts *very simply*, in the shadow, with a simple gesture. He finds the buckler, lance and shield placed against the rock on the right.

The thin crescent of the moon casts a silvery light. The branches stand out in fine relief; this is not a lighting *effect* – all is perfectly *calm* and clear. Brünnhilde sleeps, facing left, turned slightly upstage; in profile to the audience. 267/2: He turns away a little, then faces her once again as before. 267/3: He recovers his spear from the lower platform, gravely. 267/4: He grasps it powerfully, turns the point against the lower platform (in the direction of the foreground), and *leaves it thus*. 268/4: Whatever device is used for the blows on the rock, they must sound musically like stone on bronze. His gesture is violent, and at 269/1 he holds the lance against the rock until 270/3.

Magic fire

269/1: One flame then two, three, four, etc., emerging from the same point (the head of the spear), to form a beam of light *without steam*. 269/3: The beam of light, without diminishing, seems to divide itself into a dancing, shimmering multitude, remaining compact. 270/2: The central mass of flames spreads into a large semicircle, sparkling and dancing; a little steam. Everything is based on the projections that spread out, licking the rocks, intermingling, climbing rapidly. 270/3: Wotan traces at his feet with the point of his lance as if to mark a path which turns to his (the actor's) right. He climbs on to the rocks, and with a sweeping gesture encompasses the ridge, the lance held upright. The fire follows *precisely* his movement; the core of the light emanating from the point of his lance, followed by the sparkling and the wild dance of the flames. The steam, very light, and noiseless, in the wake of the light. The projections spreading over everything. 270/5: The flames reach the edge of the overhang and spread out mainly behind the ridge; descending and disappearing *quickly*. There remains nothing but a *glimmer*, which becomes still. The ridge and summit are encircled in steam, which rises slowly, lit from *below* with a red light. In the clear and limpid sky is a high crescent moon and several pale and scant stars.

Wotan has watched the trajectory of his spear and the fire. 271/1: He reaches the steps leading to the upper platform, his head held very high, facing Brünnhilde. 271/5: He ascends as far as the upper platform. 272/

1: On the platform above the steps, a hard silhouette against the light, his spear raised high at an angle in Brünnhilde's direction, his arm fully extended. 273/1: He lowers his spear, leaning against it, remaining still, his chest extended towards Brünnhilde. 273/5: He turns slowly to the left, crosses the upper platform, climbing. 274/3: He arrives on the overhang and turns back. 274/5: He disappears behind the rock into the light.

The final impression of great stillness

That Wotan should exit from the same place he entered would be an unfortunate effect, as if it matters to an all-powerful god.

The magic fire, being pantomimic, requires mathematical precision in relation to the music.

Notes

INTRODUCTION: ADOLPHE APPIA, 1862–1928

1 Adolphe Appia, 'Theatrical experiences and personal investigations', an essay of 1921: see pp. 22–8 of this volume.

2 Adolphe Appia, *Die Musik und die Inscenierung* (Munich, 1899), p. 48. Published in English (trans. Robert W. Corrigan and Mary Douglas Dirks, ed. Barnard Hewitt) as *Music and the Art of the Theatre* (Coral Gables, Fla., 1962).

3 Appia, 'Theatrical experiences'.

4 The phrase is used by Appia in 'Eurhythmics and the theatre'; see pp. 90–4 of this volume.

5 Appia, 'Theatrical experiences'.

6 Quoted in Beacham 1987: 93. A full account of the Milan production is given on pp. 86–96.

7 A fuller description of the Basle productions together with a review of the critical reception is given ibid.: 118–40. There is also an excellent account in Loeffler 1979: 57–83.

8 Appia's conclusion to *L'Oeuvre d'art vivant* (Geneva, 1921), excerpts from which are included on pp. 167–78 of this volume.

PART I THE REFORMATION OF THEATRICAL PRODUCTION

1 The date when a text was written by Appia appears in parentheses beneath it, followed by its publication history. Volbach refers to the book *Adolphe Appia, Essays, Scenarios, and Designs* (Appia 1989). Bablet refers to *Adolphe Appia: Oeuvres Complètes*, vols 1–6 (Appia 1983–) the first four volumes of which have now (1993) been published.

2 Appia is speaking of the period in the last decade of the nineteenth century when he first began to write out his ideas for scenic reform and prepared a number of scenarios and designs, based on applying his ideas to Wagnerian opera.

3 The history of production at the Festspielhaus after Wagner's death provides an example – charged with irony – of the gradual displacement of traditional staging by reforms conceived and initiated by Appia. Bayreuth's patrons, as well as its directors (and especially Wagner's widow, Cosima), were loath to change. Increasingly frequented by a conservative if not reactionary elite, it departed from Wagner's concept of a place for communal and classless celebration and as Wagner's son Siegfried himself admitted, 'threatened to become merely a rendezvous for snobs'. As, gradually, basic change did come, little credit was given to Appia. He suffered the double indignity of initially being a prophet so far ahead of his time that he was ridiculed and ignored; and then, when ultimately his ideas gained widespread acceptance, that few remembered or cared to know their source.

Not until 1951 did Wieland Wagner, when he became Bayreuth's director, offer belated recognition, admitting that 'it is part of the genuine tragedy of Wagner's work that Appia's ingenious conceptions were not realised on stage . . . Cosima Wagner's ban . . . rendered Bayreuth for decades the province of a long dead artistic style, and thus converted its once revolutionary role into the opposite'. For a fuller discussion of the process of reform at Bayreuth, see Beacham 1987: 150–6.

4 Although written in French, the book was first published in German in 1899 as *Die Musik und die Inscenierung* (F. Bruckmann, Munich). In 1962 it appeared in English, edited by Barnard Hewitt, and translated by Robert W. Corrigan and Mary D. Dirks, as *Music and the Art of the Theater* (University of Miami, Coral Gables, Fla.). The original French version was finally published in 1963, edited by Edmund Stadler, as *La Musique et la mise en scène* in vols 28–9 of the *Annuaire du théâtre suisse* 1962–3 (Theater Kultur-Verlag, Berne).

5 Appia's book was divided into three parts. The first section, in which his most innovatory ideas were laid out, was entitled 'The *mise en scène* as means of expression'. Part II explored these ideas through the specific example of Wagnerian opera, and was entitled, 'Richard Wagner and the *mise-en-scène*'. The third part, 'The word-tone drama *without* Richard Wagner', sketched out some of the implications of Appia's ideas for reform for future developments in theatrical art, subjects which were explored and detailed at far greater length in Appia's subsequent writings. The excerpts I include here are taken exclusively from Part I. As far as possible I have attempted to avoid including material which is repeated (often in a more comprehensive and accessible form) in some of the later essays included in the present volume. Appia himself provided an excellent succinct summary of the theory detailed in the first part of *Music and the Art of the Theatre* in the essay of 1902, 'Ideas on a reform of our *mise en scène*' which I have placed immediately following these excerpts, and the reader may wish to look at this first to obtain an overview before returning to the more detailed descriptions included in those passages excerpted from the earlier, lengthier work.

6 It is revealing to see how Appia modified in his later writings about 'living art' this notion of what the nature of the relationship of the artist and the public should be. In his essay 'Theatrical experiences and personal investigations' (1921) Appia himself draws attention to his change in attitude, noting that earlier, 'My most advanced ideas always were concerned exclusively with the *performance*.' This section of that essay is reprinted on pp. 161–6 of the present book.

7 At the apex of his hierarchy of production Appia placed the artist, the composer-dramatist, who creates the music and its dramatic libretto – what Appia terms the 'word-tone' drama. Such a work must consist of a total integration of drama and music – which in effect meant one of Wagner's operas. The term was suggested by Appia's friend, Houston Stewart Chamberlain: see Volbach 1968: 35–6. In the French version of his manuscript, Appia sometimes uses the term, 'poète-musicien'; in the German, 'Wort-Ton Dichter' for the author of what in both French and German he terms the 'Wort-Tondrama'.

8 Appia uses the term 'sign' to suggest an external indication representing a value, thing or condition, as opposed to 'expression' to convey an actual emotional quality. Anticipating later semiotic theory and analysis, he was the first to use the term in the context of theatrical art.

9 This is Appia's first reference to a system of musically based 'gymnastics' as vital to the training of the actor in his hierarchy of production. As he noted later in his essay, 'Theatrical experiences and personal investigations',

In the course of composing *Music und die Inscenierung* I felt the necessity for the actor to be trained in rhythmic gymnastics. The method . . . was revealed to me by Dalcroze in 1906. Without changing my basic orientation, eurhythmics freed me from too rigid a tradition, and in particular, from the decorative romanticism of Wagner . . . From that point on, I could clearly see the route my progress would follow. The discovery of the basic principle of the *mise en scène* was only a starting point; eurhythmics determined my further progress.

10 Appia seems to anticipate the sort of choreographic notation devised later by Rudolf Laban and others.

11 The ideas first tentatively put forward here about the expressive and aesthetic potential of the human body motivated by music were later, under the influence of eurhythmics, greatly expanded, and came to dominate Appia's later work and writings, including most notably, *The Work of Living Art*.

12 Appia echoes Wagner, who had called for the regeneration of music by emphasizing what he termed the basis 'of all pure human art, the plastic bodily movement expressed through musical rhythm'. See Wagner's description of 'The art form of the future' in *Gesammelte Schriften und Dichtungen*, Vol. 3 (Leipzig, 1907), p. 90.

13 Appia in a footnote here quotes H. A. Taine: 'The aim of the work of art is to reveal some essential, salient character, consequently some important idea, more clearly and more completely than can real objects. It achieves this through a group of parts whose *relationships it systematically modifies*' (*Philosophie de l'art*, Paris, 1881, 1: 41–2). Appia discusses it later at some length in his essay of 1908, 'Comments on the theatre', published as 'Notes sur le théâtre' in *La Vie musicale* I, no. 15, pp. 233–8, and no. 16, pp. 253–6. A translation is in Appia 1989: 173–82.

14 Appia's insistence on the depersonalization of the actor, and the necessity of integrating him with the other elements of production, anticipates Gordon Craig's call for actors without egos, the ultimate form of which was his famous concept of the 'Übermarionette' first put forward in 1908 in his article 'The actor and the über-marionette', *The Mask*, 1, no. 2, pp. 3–15. But it is important to note that Appia believed such subordination would allow the actor to practise a purified and ultimately more creative craft, once personal and subjective elements had been curtailed. As he pointed out in a passage occurring a little later, this approach, 'far from weakening the indispensable spontaneity of the actor, bestows that quality on him in the highest degree. Just as music allows only the purest expression of the dramatist's personal conception to emerge, so it allows only the noblest aspects of the actor's personality.'

15 Appia again anticipates Craig, who defined the art of production as the interplay of action, words, line, colour, objects, lighting effects, rhythm and so on, and called for these to be controlled and coordinated by a figure similar to Appia's director, whom Craig termed the 'Stage Manager'.

16 Appia anticipates here an account he gave later in the essay, 'Theatrical experiences and personal investigations' of his first experience of theatre (a production of Gounod's *Faust*) as an eighteen-year-old. 'Afterwards I toured the theatre alone, murmuring to myself, "is it for this that these thick walls were built, this massive construction?".' See Beacham 1987: 8–9.

17 Here and in the following passage Appia presents an idea – that of flexible theatre spaces – which he will develop at much greater length in later essays, for example 'Monumentality' (see pp. 135–43 of the present book), and will himself practise in his experiments at Hellerau.

18 In a footnote Appia points out that lighting and the shadows it produces can also be used when necessary to suggest certain objects required at various points in the action, such as a window or a ship's mast. His description of the evocation of a forest scene is nicely illustrated by the 'rhythmic design' of 1909 entitled 'The Forest Glade'. It may also be compared to the famous statement in the next essay in this section, which Appia wrote about 1902, 'Ideas on the reform of our *mise en scène*': 'we shall no longer attempt to give the illusion of a forest but instead the illusion of a *man* in the atmosphere of a forest . . . when the forest, stirred gently by a breeze, attracts Siegfried's attention, we, the spectators, *will observe Siegfried* bathed in lights and moving shadows, and no longer moving among bits of cut-up canvas operated by ropes.'

19 The phrase by Appia's friend and mentor is from his book, *Richard Wagner* (Munich, 1896), p. 196.

20 This is a reference by Appia to one of two mottoes which he placed at the beginning of his work, a slightly re-worked quotation from Schopenhauer: 'Music never expresses the phenomenon but only the inner essence of the phenomenon.' The complete quote and its context may be found in *Die Welt als Wille und Vorstellung*: 'die Welt als Vorstellung, zweite Betrachtung: "Die Vorstellung unabhängig vom Satze des Grundes" ' (Stuttgart, 1960), p. 364. The second motto is from Schiller: 'When music reaches its noblest power, it becomes form.' From 'Über die ästhetische Erziehung des Menschen in einer Reihe von Briefen', letter 22, *Sämtliche Werke* (Munich, 1960), p. 639. Appia cites both phrases frequently in his later writings.

21 Cf. Noel Coward's dictum: 'Just learn your lines, and don't bump into the furniture!'

22 Maurice Maeterlinck (1862–1949), Belgian poet and dramatist noted for his poetic dramas and use of symbolism. His *Pelléas et Mélisande* (1892) was an important example of symbolist drama and a challenge to contemporaneous staging technique.

PART II WRITINGS ON EURHYTHMICS

1 Isadora Duncan (1878–1927), the American dancer who revived a form of *orchesis*, ancient Greek dance, using flowing robes and bare feet. Her performances were an important and influential precursor of modern dance.

2 Appia here uses the word *eurythmie* literally (from the Greek), 'pleasing rhythm', to designate the type of bodily response to music which he more commonly refers to as *gymnastique rythmique*; 'rhythmic gymnastics'. In English the term most widely used is 'eurhythmics'.

3 Patriotic festivals were a venerable tradition in Switzerland, combining folk music, dance and drama to celebrate national occasions and commemorate historic events. Appia was later involved with Dalcroze in presenting a most elaborate example, the *Fête de Juin*, of 1914, celebrating the Geneva Republic's entry into the Swiss Confederation a century before (see Beacham 1987: 80–4). Dalcroze had participated in Swiss pageants earlier, including one held in 1903 at Lausanne, the *Fête de Vaudois*, which used over 1,500 performers. He later wrote a very interesting discussion of these festivals and the contribution to them of eurhythmics (Jaques-Dalcroze 1921: 166–73).

4 *Solfeggio* is the term for voice exercises using the sol-fa syllables to represent the tones of a melody or vocal part.

5 Cf. the letter written by Dalcroze to Appia a few weeks after the cornerstone was laid at Hellerau in the spring of 1911: 'We have made undeniable progress, following our path precisely, and with a single gesture have lifted the veil from

the Unknown, an Unknown which we love, and hope to overcome' (Stadler 1965: 439).

6 This is the occasion when Appia first encountered eurhythmics, which he describes in the excerpt from 'Theatrical experiences and personal investigations' on pp. 74–6.

7 Appia is mistaken about the invitation, which was given in November 1909 following a demonstration of eurhythmics at Dresden the previous month. The *Werkstätte* refers to the furniture factory which Wolf Dohrn (1878–1914) and Karl Schmidt (1873–1948) set up at Hellerau, under the auspices of the German *Werkbund*, an organization devoted to the development and promotion of the applied arts in German light industry. By 1910 the factory and first twenty-four homes had been built, with a population of over 2,000 projected for the summer of 1911, to rise ultimately to the maximum of 12,000. The construction and arrangement of Hellerau were scrupulously overseen by a commission which approved every building and generally safeguarded conditions, maintaining, for example, a ratio of one to five between developed and open land to ensure that Hellerau's inhabitants would be free from the squalid and cramped conditions prevalent in the industrial quarters of most cities, including neighbouring Dresden. Hellerau survived the Second World War and the destruction of Dresden relatively intact, and has emerged from the era of communist East Germany as an architectural gem. The *Werkstätte* continues to produce finely crafted furniture.

8 Wolf Dohrn, who had studied economics and been active for a time in liberal politics, was General Secretary of the *Werkbund*, which he had helped found in the summer of 1908. He was a tireless supporter of its projects, lecturing widely, serving on planning committees and acting generally as its spokesman and publicist. He was a man of very substantial gifts: he had an enormous capacity for enthusiasm and hard work, a talent for communicating his ideas and inspiring others with them and, most significantly, a deeply felt idealism and consequent espousal of the *Werkbund*'s goals. The establishment of eurhythmics as the defining and motivating spirit of the Hellerau experiment became Dohrn's primary goal, and 'from that moment on he devoted to this idea all his strength, extraordinary personality, confident will and great perseverance' (Wolkonski 1960: 49). The visit to Geneva took place in April 1910, and afterwards Dalcroze wrote an enthusiastic letter to Appia, reporting that Wolf Dohrn 'thinks of you as already being at Hellerau' (Stadler 1965: 430). On 24 April 1910 the scheme was formally approved by the Dresden city government which agreed to donate the necessary land and underwrite the costs of construction.

9 He moved with his family in June 1910, with the Institute opening in temporary quarters in Dresden on 17 October. During the first year thirteen courses were run, including two for student actors and one especially designed for members of the Dresden Royal Opera. In addition, a course was offered at Hellerau itself, both for adult inhabitants and for children. The normal course comprised eight subjects: *solfeggio*, improvisation, anatomy, choral music, *plastique animée*, dance, gymnastics and eurhythmics. In all, over 500 students participated.

10 Appia quotes Friedrich Schiller's *Hymn to Joy*, used by Beethoven in his Ninth Symphony. The translation is by Natalie MacFarren (London, 1902).

Participants from some fourteen nations attended Hellerau. Appia and Dalcroze ended their association with the Institute with the outbreak of the First World War. During the Nazi period the building was taken over by the state and used as a recreational facility for the SA. Following the destruction of

Dresden in the Second World War, its luminous drapes were torn down to make bandages, and from then until September 1992 it remained part of a garrison for Russian soldiers, entirely off-limits to the public.

The legacy of Hellerau was not, however, lost. It is hard to think of any comparable artistic movement over the last century or more which brought so many vital ideas together in productive synthesis, or created so much of lasting practical influence and significance in so brief a period. Nor was its utopian vision of a world transfigured through art wholly extinguished. A retrospective article fifty years later stressed that

> No land in all the world possessed a place of such grace, such charm, or such enthusiastic celebration of life, as Hellerau . . . Back in 1910, and until 1914, there was this extraordinary institution where not only dance, but eurhythmics, philosophy, aesthetics and love were taught. This Hellerau still survives – its spirit had no beginning and also no end; it was always looking into the future, so even today it must live still, this hidden god which concealed itself and feigned death before the laughter and derision of later times. It lives in fact, more than we think.
>
> ('Jugendstil', *Die Welt*, 16 April 1960)

Now there are active plans to renovate the Institute building (which has been badly neglected) and rededicate it as a place for meetings and exchange between artists: a workshop for European art and culture in the new conditions following the departure of Soviet forces and the reunification of Europe. Few places are more appropriate.

11 The phrase was used by Schopenhauer in the first volume of *Die Welt als Wille und Vorstellung*, chapter 63. It is taken from the *Upanishads*.

12 Critical accounts suggest that Appia's extravagant hopes for the festivals were substantially realized. Serge Wolkonski spoke for many in his assessment of the production of *Orpheus and Eurydice*:

> As Orpheus's song gradually transforms the angry roar of all Hell into benevolent compassion, one perceives perfectly that he sings not for us, the audience, but for those on stage – they hear him and react instead of, and differently from us: we hear only the music – whilst they, however, live in it. I can assure you that at that moment you forget that you are listening to music, and have been watching a performance. You have observed a portion of life which has become a holy act; the mystery of life and death, of hate and love, of asking and forgiveness . . . all this was ultimately achieved through the harmony between movement and music . . . the seen and the heard became an aural and visual unity which involved one's entire perception.
>
> (Wolkonski 1960: 25–6)

Another offered a similar assessment:

> it is thus a poignant and religious impression which envelops the spectators . . . one can affirm that – a rare thing – a drama was brought to life and not merely presented to titillate the eyes and ears of an indifferent and uncritical public . . . in the light of the perfection of the *Orpheus* interpretation, one is irresistibly drawn into believing that the only goal of the Institute is the staging of masterpieces of the lyric art from the past and present . . . but this is [the students'] daily activity, their own efforts towards an ideal of living human art; the sacred expression of their individual and

communal soul . . . and from this the representation of *Orpheus* itself acquires all its value and human significance.

(Bonifas 1913)

13 Quoted by Appia from the book of his friend, Houston Stewart Chamberlain, *Richard Wagner* (1896), p. 196.

14 This coordination of music and light (together with 'rhythmic space') to create an expressive atmosphere was used by Appia in creating the sets for *Orpheus and Eurydice*, and determining how they should be used. He wrote, for example, of his design for the 'Elysian Fields' sequence:

> If anyone recalls the music . . . he will understand that only inclined planes, without a vertical line of any kind to interrupt them, could in themselves express the perfect serenity of the place. Their arrangement is particularly difficult, but, happily, the score gives valuable clues in this respect. In such a space, physical movement is naturally calm and quiet and the soft light – with its uniformity and its gentle mobility – transforms the material reality of the actual construction into a kind of rocking movement that is wavelike in its effect. Thanks to the lighting, the characters share in this unreal atmosphere.

(Appia 1960: 110)

15 Appia seems here to anticipate the manner in which theatrical art would in the future strive to integrate sound and light into an expressive and unified medium, while foreseeing too, the 'decadent' possibility of virtuoso light shows and associated pyrotechnics, which in the absence of music, risk becoming mere sensationalism, devoid of meaning.

16 Serge Wolkonski relates an anecdote about a visitor to one of Dalcroze's classes at Hellerau:

> I remember during one practical session, the door up above was opened, and a man who didn't wish to disturb the lesson walked quickly across the gallery, opened the door opposite, exited, and shut the door. We, however, heard it in the music, which amusingly accompanied each step of the visitor up to the slamming of the door. It was delightful: without suspecting it, the man became the presenter of a eurhythmic pantomime.

(Wolkonski 1960: 11)

17 As indicated in his article, 'Eurhythmics and light', Appia did not approve of 'decadent' displays of lighting effects for their own sake, divorced from light's primary service to enhance the rhythmic combination of music and bodily movement. The hierarchy demands the centrality of the body, motivated by music; the light should serve, and not usurp, this hierarchy. It seems likely that – partly because of the temptation to exploit the novelty of the lighting installations at Hellerau – this balance may at times have been displaced, and Appia implicitly warns against this here.

18 In the light of the extraordinary achievements and influence of the only two festivals held at Hellerau (1912 and 1913) and the subsequent history of the place, Appia's prediction is both accurate and ironic. His arguably somewhat over-enthusiastic rhetoric on behalf of Hellerau and its ideals in this article and elsewhere may seem less extravagant perhaps, and certainly more poignant, when one notes that some eighty years later, in April 1990, an organization was formally established 'to promote a European Workshop for Art and Culture at Hellerau'. It has amongst its goals the rededication of Hellerau to utopian ideals, with the desire to promote 'eurhythmics and aesthetic innovation as

formerly the Dalcroze School did', and 'to restore to life the Festival House at Hellerau, and the ideas associated with it', including those of Appia which are specifically evoked. Here 'young people of Europe, artists and creative people of every kind will have the opportunity to meet, exchange ideas, and engage in collective work on innovative and ground-breaking projects'.

PART III ESSAYS ON THE ART OF THE THEATRE

1 The French title, 'Art vivant? ou nature morte?' is a play on words; the French expression for 'still life' is *nature morte*.

2 Shortly after he wrote this essay, Appia undertook to apply his ideas to the design and staging of a spoken drama, *Hamlet*. Together with the American writer Jessica Davis Van Wyck, he prepared a scenario and fourteen settings. Van Wyck published an engaging account of their work and its results (Van Wyck 1925). See also Beacham 1987: 97–104.

3 Appia's friend and collaborator Jean Mercier had recorded how, at their initial meeting, Gordon Craig identified the way in which Appia's theory of reform was dependent upon music:

> Craig wrote his name on the tablecloth and next to it that of Appia. He drew a circle around Appia on which he wrote the word 'music'. Admirable symbol of truth! The two pioneers of contemporary dramatic art rested their reform on the same base – the actor. But Craig was free in his reform; the reform of Appia was dominated and directed by a major force, music.
>
> (Mercier 1932: 628)

4 Dana Rufolo-Horhager has discussed the many ways in which the ideas put forward in 'Monumentality' have found expression in the Schaubühne am Lehniner Platz, in Berlin, the theatre that was used by the director Peter Stein (Rufolo-Horhager 1984).

5 As Richard Schechner expressed it (1973: 379):

> Putting everyone together in one space is the architectural version of sunlight. It makes people share in the event; it makes them *responsible* for the event . . . Performing in divided spaces leads to illusionism . . . Far from diminishing audience involvement, single space staging sharpens it by throwing each spectator on his own . . . You are free to move closer to something that calls you, further away from something that repulses you. All within the envelope of the single space which makes the experience more dangerous and more communal.

6 This is excerpted from an untitled manuscript Appia prepared for presentation on 3 April 1919 at the Olympic Institute in Lausanne, accompanied by slides illustrating his designs. The conference was entitled 'The future of drama and stage production'; the title 'Actor, space, light, painting' was given to an abbreviated version of Appia's essay after his death.

7 Appia's statement here may be compared with a letter of 30 November 1918 to Gordon Craig, referring to his 'vision of the *House*, a sort of cathedral of the future, which reunites in a vast open and *changeable* space, all the expressions of our social life, and in particular, dramatic art, *with or without spectators*' (Beacham 1988: 278). In the same letter Appia mentioned the conference at which this essay was to be read; 'Someone has asked me on behalf of the Olympic Institute (President Baron de Coubertin, a charming and serious Frenchman) for lectures with slides; one of my friends will read them. I will be pleased to see my designs (about 15) enlarged on the screen! The slides are

wonderful.' Appia concludes the essay with a few remarks on the subject of eurhythmics, linking it with the ideas informing the Olympic movement.

8 This article was written in the autumn of 1920 and may have been intended to serve as the introduction to a projected further volume of essays that Appia mentioned during this period, following the completion of *The Work of Living Art* in May 1919.

9 This essay was prepared for the International Exhibition of Theatre Design held at Amsterdam in January 1922, where both Appia's work and that of Gordon Craig were prominently displayed. It was republished the following year in Milan at the time of Appia's production of *Tristan and Isolde* at La Scala. Appia begins the essay by pointing out how difficult it is for an exhibition to give any valid impression of the essential elements of theatrical art, because of problems of scale and, above all, the inanimate nature of the materials employed.

10 Cf. the observation made by Dalcroze to Appia when confronted for the first time by the newly completed hall at Hellerau: 'I never go into it without shivering from pleasure, but also from apprehension, because I ask myself if we know how to profit as we must from this suggestive place . . . Do we know how to give life to these virgin spaces, animate these lines, and awaken these echoes?' (Stadler 1965: 440).

11 Appia's description here of both the spatial arrangement and costuming is closely based on actual practice at Hellerau, as described earlier, in the section on eurhythmics. The institute which he goes on to describe is also evocative of Hellerau and of Dalcroze's Geneva Institute opened in 1915, where, the year before this essay was written, Appia had participated in a production of *Echo and Narcissus*.

12 This lecture by Appia (who was intensely shy, and afflicted with a stutter) would have been given to the students of Dalcroze at the Geneva Institute by someone (possibly his friend Henry C. Bonifas) acting on his behalf.

13 Appia was on friendly terms with Georges Pitoëff (Russian and later prominent French director), Craig and Copeau, and had probably met Stanislavsky as well. See Beacham 1987: 105–17.

14 The Piazza della Signoria, the main square of Florence, dominated by a massive palace, and displaying numerous statues.

15 The remainder of the essay is presented by Appia as a dialogue between himself and a 'famed foreign architect', who outlines his ideas about a new type of architecture.

16 Cf. Appia's statement about the 'cathedral of the future' at the conclusion of his earlier article, 'Actor, space, light, painting'.

17 Appia's description of his theatre and its lighting corresponds closely to the practice actually followed at the Hellerau Institute, detailed elsewhere in this volume.

18 Cf. Rufulo-Horhager 1984: 37 on Peter Stein's Berlin Schaubühne:

> Certainly this stage space is strikingly reminiscent of Appia's words in 'Monumentality': a space which can be adapted to the needs of the presentation at hand; an auditorium which is contiguous with the stage; a floor which can be modulated by means of hydraulic levers; a diffused lighting source: all this is realized in the Schaubühne. Also in the use of decorative and construction materials; the Schaubühne recalls Appia's words . . . the interior of the building features basically the three non-decomposable materials of concrete, glass, and brass. The Theatre itself has walls of greyish concrete. There are no decorations or materials, as Appia recommended . . . The neu-

tral interior of the vast performance hall has been designed to accept whatever range of colors, motifs, and materials a scene-designer might choose to use.

19 This title is not Appia's but was written on the manuscript after his death. The lecture was for a conference held in Zurich early in 1925, shortly after the Basle débâcle which was to result in the cancellation of Appia's planned presentation of the complete *Ring*.

20 H. A. Taine, *Philosophie de l'art* (Paris, 1881), vol. 1, 41–2. Appia, who was particularly fond of the quote, discusses its implications and application at length in an earlier essay, 'Comments on the theatre'. See p. 234, n. 13.

21 The incident occurs in Homer's *Odyssey*, Book 8. The minstrel sang of the quarrel between Ulysses and Achilles.

PART IV AESTHETIC AND PROPHETIC WRITINGS

1 Appia deals at length with the term in *The Work of Living Art*, pp. 170–6 below. At the International Theatre Exhibition held in Amsterdam in 1922, Sarah Bernhardt, gazing at one of Appia's designs which included the term in its caption or commentary, was heard to remark: 'La grande Connue devant le grand Inconnu.'

2 Appia, 'Theatrical experiences', p. 162 of the present volume.

3 See amongst numerous examples, Plato's *Republic* 3.398 ff., or Aristotle, *Politics* 8.5–7.

4 Jacques Copeau, 'L'Art et l'oeuvre d'Adolphe Appia', *Comoedia*, 12 March 1928. Reprinted in Volbach 1968: 207–8.

5 The description Appia offers closely resembles actual practice at Hellerau; his remarks on the 'study site' are echoed in several of the essays included in the previous section, and those regarding costume are presented at length in 'Concerning the costume for eurhythmics', which was published at the time of the 1912 festival.

6 Appia touches on the same problem addressed later by Antonin Artaud in his call for a 'theatre of cruelty' to resensitize the audience to the sensual force of art and the need to shock and stimulate the spectator to experience its benefits.

7 The book was first published in French in 1921 (Atar, Geneva-Paris). It appeared in English in 1960, translated by H. D. Albright together with the essay 'Man is the measure of all things', edited by Barnard Hewitt (University of Miami, Coral Gables, Florida). In 1975 an Italian version appeared in the book *Attore musica e scena* (Feltrinelli, Milan), pp. 163–236. Thanks to the University of Miami edition and subsequent reprints, it is of all Appia's writings the one most readily available to English readers, and so I have included only a few excerpts here, from what I consider the most significant passages.

8 The reference to work with marionettes instead of living persons may be meant to bring to mind Edward Gordon Craig, who argued that a purified and integrated art of production could too easily be subverted or unbalanced by the ego and eccentricities of the actor. In its ultimate form Craig's theatre would abolish the actor altogether, replacing him with an obedient articulated simulacrum – the *Übermarionette*. From 1905 onwards Craig developed the concept not merely as an abstract ideal but (he hoped) as a practical alternative to conventional staging. For the relationship between Appia and Craig, see Beacham 1988.

9 Again Appia anticipates ideas that would inform Artaud's conception of the 'theatre of cruelty' which he wanted 'to swoop down upon a crowd of spectators with all the awesome horror of the plague, the Black Death of the Middle

Ages, with all its shattering impact, creating a complete upheaval, physical, mental and moral, among the population it struck' (quoted and translated in Esslin 1976: 76).

10 Appia refers to his essay, 'The gesture of art'.

11 Examples of Appia's observation abound, most famously perhaps, as far as theatrical practice is concerned, in the example of Max Reinhardt, who produced plays in many unconventional locales. His renowned 1910 production of *Oedipus*, for example, was first presented in a music hall in Munich, and later in a circus in Berlin. For details see my account in Walton 1987: 294–325.

12 Appia's essay was considerably shortened by his cousin, Edmund Appia, and it is this version that Volbach includes. Bablet restores the cuts in her edition. The text presented here is greatly abridged, but does include some passages from the complete version.

13 Appia used the term *dédoublement*, to mean, roughly, 'doubling' in the sense of giving the individual a dual attitude of being an observer of phenomena, but also one who sees beyond them to the inner essence of their symbolic meaning.

14 Appia in a footnote at this point cites the silent films of his day, noting how, 'at the cinema, the written explanations [interpersed within the scenes of action] are indispensable, whatever the talent the actors display'.

15 Appia makes a similar reference to this phrase from the *Upanishads* (used by Schopenhauer in *Die Welt als Wille und Vorstellung*, chapter 63), in his essay, 'Eurhythmics and the theatre', pp. 90–4 of the present book.

16 Cf. Appia's essay of 1920, 'Art is an attitude', pp. 116–18 of the present book.

17 Appia took up the subject of monumentality at length in an essay of that name, written during the same period in which he composed 'Picturesqueness'; see pp. 135–43.

18 Appia evidently has in mind what he considered to be the grotesqueness of certain contemporary portrait art, for example works by Kokoschka, Schiele and Dix; the movement, Neue Sachlichkeit ('New Objectivity'); and possibly the Expressionists generally. In calling for new forms of 'Living Art' based on the nobility and expressive potential of the human body, together with the personal and social benefits that such art would confer on its participants, Appia, as he notes, felt it necessary to clear away what he considered decadent expressions of a corrupted modern sensibility. This critical attitude, defensible in itself, is unfortunately tainted in retrospect for the reader of today by the manner in which we now know it was adapted and exploited by reactionary forces as part of a virulent political agenda. This reached its nadir in the case of the famous Nazi exhibition of so-called 'degenerate art' (*entartete Kunst*) organized by Hitler in July 1937, some fifteen years after Appia's essay.

19 Appia deals with a concept widely explored in contemporary dramatic and cinematic art, e.g. Georg Kaiser's *Gas Trilogy* (1917–20), Karel Čapek's *Rossum's Universal Robots* (1921), Fritz Lang's *Metropolis* (1926), or (a few years later), Chaplin's *Modern Times* (1936). Needless to say, it is an issue of ever-increasing and more urgent importance.

20 Sesostris, the name of three Egyptian pharaohs of the 12th dynasty (1970–1850 BC); Alcibiades (c. 450–404 BC) Athenian statesman, adventurer, general, and intimate of Socrates.

APPENDIX: APPIA'S COMMENTARY AND SCENARIO FOR *THE VALKYRIE*, ACT III

1 Appia in an unpublished letter to Karl Reyle, 4 March 1925.

2 Taken from the unpublished account in Gordon Craig's *Daybook III*, as

recounted by Appia. Entry for 13 February 1914. The copy of the *Daybook* is at the University of Texas at Austin, Humanities Research Center.

3 The term is that used by Appia himself to identify the solid scenic elements that he called for in place of the conventional painted flats and cut-outs normally used in the theatre of his day. They are, of course, essential for realizing Appia's innovative conception of stage setting as a three-dimensional *space* rather than a *picture* contrived from painted flats.

4 Appia always describes the setting as seen from the audience, and his practice has been followed here to avoid any possible confusion that might result from converting it to the modern convention of giving stage directions (i.e., stage right, stage left), as seen by the actor.

5 A short section of the scenario has been omitted, in which Appia refers to practical adaptations necessary for employing this setting elsewhere in the *Ring*.

6 Wagner's Bayreuth setting of 1876, which, with very minor alterations, remained unchanged through the first decades of this century, consisted of the standard cut-outs, executed with a good deal of superfluous pictorial embellishment. Painted rocks and tree trunks rose incongruously from the flat stage floor, and the summit itself was essentially a staircase masked by an arrangement of painted flats.

7 Once again, Appia probably intends an oblique reference to practice at Bayreuth, where the painted sets were characterized by overblown romanticism, and occasionally outlandish decoration and lurid *trompe-l'œil* effects.

8 Appia insisted that his designs were meaningful only when examined together with his complete descriptive scenarios. The essence of his scenic reform was that stage settings should *not* be thought of (evaluated) as primarily *pictures*, but rather as *spaces* in which a particular series of dramatic actions was to take place, and whose elements, arrangement and dimensions must emanate from within the drama itself.

9 The pagination refers to a standard edition of the libretto used by Appia that was published by Karl Klindworth. Pages 210–14 contain the climax of the storm, just prior to Wotan's entrance during which Appia stipulated that 'the summit is lost beneath clouds . . . The whole scene is like a dark whirlwind in which one can distinguish the Valkyrie only by their song.'

10 In production the 'Ride of the Valkyrie' had always been a major source of embarrassment. In 1876, at Bayreuth, a rather crudely executed static image of a Valkyrie on horseback was projected and moved across the backdrop. The effect was unsatisfactory and much criticized; it was replaced in the 1896 staging by children dressed as Valkyrie and flown in on wooden horses across the upstage area. Appia, writing several years before Edison's first perfected motion picture, was familiar with experiments that anticipated later developments, and foresaw that technology could provide a solution to the aesthetic problem of staging the scene.

11 The transcript of Appia's scenario is at places in a somewhat unfinished state, not in terms of its detail which is very great indeed, but in its punctuation and syntax. Here its punctuation has been regularized, the text divided up into additional paragraphs, and the broken phrases or sentences that occur from time to time have been completed. Even so, there are ambiguous passages where Appia's intended meaning is not altogether clear, and the text offered here has occasionally entailed a small amount of guesswork. The reader is reminded that unless specifically noted otherwise, Appia always gives his stage directions and descriptions from the spectator's viewpoint. Occasionally the

translation has had to resort to more modern terms in order to convey adequately the actual meaning.

Except for occasional direct quotation from the actual dialogue (which has been left in German), Appia bases his description on page and bar references drawn from the libretto as published by Klindworth. These have been retained (although occasionally simplified) for the general sense of the staging they convey (as well as a suggestion of the moment-by-moment progression) even to readers without ready access to that edition. If read together with any text of the libretto, a tolerably clear picture of the details of Appia's intended staging emerges.

12 Appia drew attention to this moment in his short published account of 1895, *Staging Wagnerian Drama* (Appia 1982: 45):

> The Valkyrie have hidden Brünnhilde among themselves and are busy soften-ing the temper of their father. The musical passage is very short, but the incomparable polyphony should here correspond to a spectacle that visualizes this polyphony; all the while the Valkyrie remain a unified group. We here have a light counterpoint, in which the successive entries reflect their timid supplication in a wholly individual way; thus each of the Valkyrie should underline her vocal entry by a step forward. The last bars have an irresistible glow of their own; the intertwining of the voices will have to make itself physically felt, always, of course, relying strictly on the musical notation. Thus the whole group, bent towards Wotan, will rise and step back right on cue with the hard chords of the god's crushing word.

Select Bibliography

Appia, A. (1960) *The Work of Living Art* (Geneva, 1921), trans. H. D. Albright, ed. B. Hewitt, Coral Gables, Fla.

—— (1962) *Music and the Art of the Theatre* (Munich, 1899), trans. R. W. Corrigan and M. D. Dirks, ed. B. Hewitt, Coral Gables, Fla.

—— (1982) *Staging Wagnerian Drama* (Paris, 1895), trans. P. Loeffler, Basle.

—— (1983–) *Oeuvres Complètes*, vols 1–4, ed. M. L. Bablet-Hahn, Lausanne.

—— (1989) *Adolphe Appia, Essays, Scenarios, and Designs*, trans. W. R. Volbach, ed. R. C. Beacham, Ann Arbor.

Bablet, D. (1962) *Edward Gordon Craig*, Paris.

—— (1971) 'Edward Gordon Craig and scenography', *Theatre Research* 11 (1): 7–22.

—— (1979) *Adolphe Appia, Darsteller, Raum, Licht*, Exhibition Catalogue, Zurich.

Bachmann, M. (1991) *Dalcroze Today*, trans. D. Parlett, Oxford.

Beacham, R. C. (1983a) 'Adolphe Appia and eurhythmics', *Maske und Kothurn* 29 (1–4): 141–52.

—— (1983b) 'Adolphe Appia, and the staging of Wagnerian opera', *Opera Quarterly* 1 (3): 114–39.

—— (1985a) 'Adolphe Appia, Emile Jaques-Dalcroze, and Hellerau, Part One: "Music made visible" ', *New Theatre Quarterly* 1 (2): 154–64.

—— (1985b) 'Adolphe Appia, Emile Jaques-Dalcroze, and Hellerau, Part Two: "Poetry in motion" ', *New Theatre Quarterly* 1 (3): 245–61.

—— (1987) *Adolphe Appia, Theatre Artist*, Cambridge.

—— (1988) ' "Brothers in suffering and joy": The Appia–Craig correspondence', *New Theatre Quarterly* 4 (15): 268–88.

Bonifas, H. C. (1913) 'A Propos des fêtes d'Hellerau', *Jeunesse littéraire*, 29 June.

Brunet-Lecomte, Hélène (1950) *Jaques-Dalcroze*, Geneva.

Carter, H. (1926) *The New Spirit in the European Theatre*, New York.

Chamberlain, H. S. (1896) *Richard Wagner*, Munich.

Cole, T. and Chinoy, H. K. (eds) (1953) *Directing the Play*, New York.

Craig, G. (1914) *On the Art of the Theatre*, London.

—— (1931) *Fourteen Notes*, Seattle.

Esslin, M. (1976) *Antonin Artaud*, New York.

Fuchs, G. (1904) *Die Schaubühne der Zukunft*, Berlin.

Giertz, G. (1975) *Kultus ohne Götter*, Munich.

Goethe, J. W. von (1950) *Sämtliche Gedichte*, ed. E. Beutler, Zurich.

—— (1961) *Gesamtausgabe der Werke und Schriften*, Stuttgart.

Hartmann, K. (1976) *Deutsche Gartenstadtbewegung*, Munich.

Hern, N. (1975) 'Expressionism', in R. Hayman (ed.) *The German Theatre*, London.

Hume, S. and Fuerst, W. (1928) *Twentieth Century Stage Decoration*, London.

Innes, C. (1986) *Edward Gordon Craig*, Cambridge.

Izenour, G. (1977) *Theater Design*, New York.

Jaques-Dalcroze, E. (1912) *The Eurhythmics of Jaques-Dalcroze*, ed. J. W. Harvey *et al.*, London.

—— (1921) *Rhythm, Music and Education*, trans. H. F. Rubenstein, London.

Keyserling, H. von (1948) *Reise durch die Zeit*, Vaduz.

Loeffler, M. P. (1979) *Oskar Wälterlin*, Basle.

Macgowan, K. (1921) *The Theatre of Tomorrow*, New York.

Mack, D. (1976) *Der Bayreuther Inszenierungsstil*, Munich.

Mercier, J. (1932) 'Adolphe Appia. The re-birth of dramatic art', *Theatre Arts Monthly* 16 (8): 616–30.

Moussinac, L. (1931) *The New Movement in the Theatre*, London.

Oenslager, D. (1936) *Scenery Then and Now*, New York.

Roth, M. (1980) 'Staging the master's works', *Theatre Research* 5 (2): 139–57.

Rufolo-Horhager, D. (1984) 'Adolphe Appia's "Monumentalité" and Peter Stein's Schaubühne', *Theatre Research* 9 (1): 29–38.

Salzmann, A. von (1913) 'Licht, Belichtung und Beleuchtung', in *Claudel-Progammbuch*, Hellerau.

Schechner, R. (1973) 'Towards the twenty-first century', in J. Schevill (ed.) *Break Out!*, Chicago.

Schiller, J. C. F. von (1967) *Sämtliche Werke*, ed. G. Fricke and H. Göpfert, Munich.

Schopenhauer, A. (1960) *Die Welt als Wille und Vorstellung*, Stuttgart.

Seidl, A. (1912) *Die Hellerauer Schulfeste*, Regensburg.

Shaw, B. (1967) *The Perfect Wagnerite*, repr., New York.

Simonson, L. (1932) *The Stage is Set*, New York.

—— (1950) *The Art of Scenic Design*, New York.

Sinclair, U. (1940) *World's End*, New York.

Skelton, G. (1965) *Wagner at Bayreuth*, London.

Stadler, E. (1964) 'Adolphe Appia und Emile Jaques-Dalcroze', *Maske und Kothurn* 10 (3–4): 660–72.

—— (1965) 'Adolphe Appia et Emile Jaques-Dalcroze', in F. Martin (ed.) *Emile Jaques-Dalcroze*, pp. 423–59, Neuchâtel.

Storck, K. (1912) *Emile Jaques-Dalcroze*, Stuttgart.

Styan, J. L. (1981) *Modern Drama in Theory and Practice*, vols 1–2, Cambridge.

Taine, H. (1881) *Philosophie de l'art*, vol. 1, Paris.

Van Wyck, J. D. (1924) 'Working with Appia', *Theatre Arts Monthly* 8 (12): 815–18.

—— (1925) 'Designing *Hamlet* with Appia', *Theatre Arts Monthly* 9 (1): 17–31.

Volbach, W. R. (1968) *Adolphe Appia, Prophet of the Modern Theatre: A Profile*, Middletown, Conn.

Wagner, C. (1934) *Cosima Wagner und Houston Stewart Chamberlain im Briefwechsel*, ed. P. Pretzsch, Leipzig.

Wagner, R. (1907) *Gesammelte Schriften und Dichtungen*, vol. 3, Leipzig.

Wälterlin, O. (1945) *Entzaubertes Theater*, Zurich.

—— (1955) *Bekenntnis zum Theater*, Zurich.

Walton, M. (1987) *Living Greek Theatre*, Westport, Conn.

Wolkonski, S. (1960) 'Meine Erinnerungen', in E. Feudel (ed.) *In Memoriam Hellerau*, Freiburg im Breisgau.

Index